Parker Company Macullar

King's how to see Boston

a trustworthy guide book

Parker Company Macullar

King's how to see Boston
a trustworthy guide book

ISBN/EAN: 9783337373917

Printed in Europe, USA, Canada, Australia, Japan

Cover: Foto ©Andreas Hilbeck / pixelio.de

More available books at **www.hansebooks.com**

MACULLAR, PARKER & COMPANY'S
SOUVENIR EDITION.

KING'S
HOW TO SEE
BOSTON

A·TRUSTWORTHY·
·GUIDE·BOOK·
250-ILLUSTRATIONS~MAPS-AND-PLANS~

EDITED AND PUBLISHED BY

MOSES KING
KING'S HANDBOOKS

Presented by
MACULLAR, PARKER & COMPANY.
BOSTON.

COPYRIGHT, 1895, BY MOSES KING.

BOSTON — THE MAIN PORTION, OR BOSTON PROPER.

KING'S "HOW TO SEE BOSTON."

A Practical Guide and an Artistic Souvenir.

COPYRIGHT, 1883, 1888, 1890 AND 1895, BY MOSES KING.

"*There are Boston and Concord and Lexington and Bunker Hill, and there they will remain forever.*"
—DANIEL WEBSTER.

THIS LITTLE BOOK presents a miniature vignette of the Puritan City, at once handy, trusty, compact, practical, and picturesque. There are more learned and compendious books about this interesting metropolis, but there is none so recent, none so useful, and none so popular in price. This edition is entirely a new book, with every line re-written, and a very extensive enlargement all around. The street maps and plans are also all new, and record the latest changes. The 250 illustrations are from original photographs, every illustration used in this book having been made especially for it in the most artistic manner; and will form an admirable memento.

The plan contemplates a dozen or more easy half-day routes, usually on foot or by street-cars, because the book is prepared for the masses of the people. However, persons of wealth who roll along in carriages will find it not less useful. By the help of this itinerary, visitors may gain a good idea of the Massachusetts metropolis, and there are myriads of Bostonians who could greatly enlarge their love of and interest in their dear home-city by taking this little companion along on their rambles.

The text was written chiefly by M. F. Sweetser, a lover of Boston, and a guide-writer of twenty-five years' experience.

The Index at the back of the book points out frequent double references to objects or places, when they are repeated on different routes.

BOSTON IN 1857.
REDUCED FROM A LARGE STEEL ENGRAVING IN POSSESSION OF STILLMAN F. KELLEY.

SUGGESTIONS TO VISITORS.

THE VISITOR who neglects the great retail and wholesale establishments, the extensive industries, the financial and other institutions, because they are places of business, misses the most edifying and interesting sights of a metropolis. In these may be seen so much of what makes up the world of to-day that they present an equal claim for observation with public institutions, parks, statues, landmarks, and other historical and descriptive matters.

To make clear this point, no visitor should fail to see Macullar, Parker & Company's establishment, where more than six hundred people are employed in workshops which are models for all the world; the enormous plant of the Waltham Watch Company, which contains an infinite variety of the most ingenious machinery, producing the most infinitesimally perfect particles of mechanism; the great storehouse of Jones, McDuffee & Stratton, which is a veritable museum of the fine arts of many countries; the huge manufactory of Chickering & Sons, the oldest and most famous of American piano-makers, whose instruments are found in palaces and homes throughout the wide world; the immense slaughtering and packing-houses of John P. Squire & Company, where in a single day six thousand hogs, cattle, and other animals can be humanely purified, divided, and put forth in many appetizing forms for human sustenance; and other noteworthy concerns.

With this in mind, many establishments have been mentioned and illustrated, but care has been taken to mention none that cannot be visited, or that are not well worth visiting.

Many of these extend a cordial welcome and have attendants to show visitors their establishments, as far as is reasonably practicable.

MACULLAR, PARKER & COMPANY IN 1872.
SHOWING THE BUILDING DESTROYED IN THE GREAT FIRE.

MACULLAR, PARKER & COMPANY'S STORE,
DECORATED FOR THE VISIT OF THE
KNIGHTS TEMPLARS TO BOSTON, AUGUST 27, 1895.

HISTORICAL.

OTHER cities may claim various distinctions, such as great populations, vast areas, extensive industries, enormous wealth, or grand situations, but the universally-conceded ideal city of the American Continent is Boston.

During its 265 years it has constantly developed in all of those commendable lines which naturally have given its citizens just cause for their great pride, and fully justify the whole world in the high esteem in which they hold the city, which has become known as "The Modern Athens," and the "Hub of the solar system."

Boston was called Shawmut, meaning "The Place Where Boats Go," by the Indians; TriMontaine, by the early English settlers at Charlestown, from the three bold peaks of Beacon Hill; and, finally, BOSTON,

WASHINGTON STREET IN HORSE-CAR DAYS OF 1885.

(in 1630), by the order of the Massachusetts Legislature, after a Lincolnshire sea-port from which some of its people came. That place was named Botolph's (or St. Boat-Help's) town, from a pious Saxon monk (whose prayers helped storm-tossed boats and sailors), dwelling thereby a thousand years before — (Botolph's Town=Bot's Town=Boston). Gov.

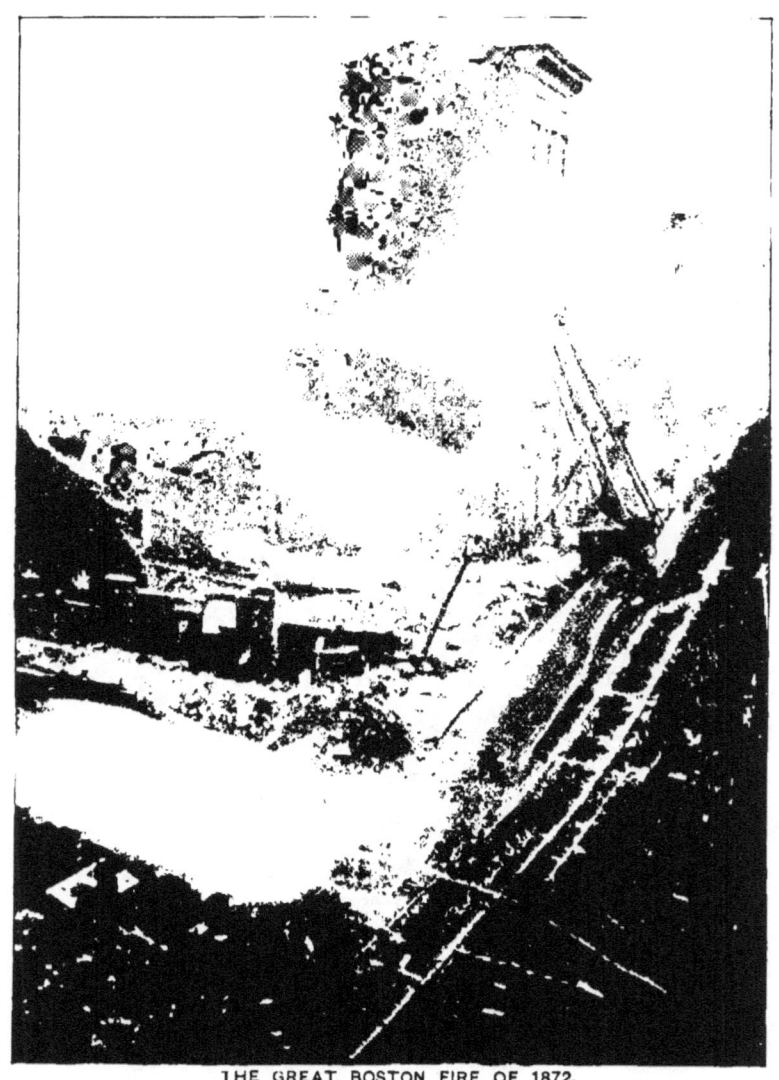

THE GREAT BOSTON FIRE OF 1872.
WASHINGTON STREET, AROUND THE RUINS OF MACULLAR, PARKER & COMPANY.

Winthrop's colony of English Puritans came hither by sea in the autumn of 1630, being dissatisfied with Salem and Charlestown, and founded here the capital of Massachusetts. Fortifications were quickly erected at Castle Island, Fort Hill and the Neck; ship-building became an active industry; a large foreign commerce began, and new tributary towns sprang up near by. The Puritans came here to found a place in the wilderness where their religion should be supreme; but many turbulent incoming sectaries of other beliefs disturbed the peace of the State. The Government disarmed the Antinomians, in 1637; hung or banished the Quakers, in 1648-77; nailed up the Baptist church; and persecuted the alleged witches; and the populace defiled and battered the Church-of-England chapel. Meantime, their train-bands annihilated the power of the Indians, in several sanguinary wars. For 30 years, only church-members could vote. In 1692, the Colonial Charter was abrogated by King William III., and Boston became the capital of a Royal Province, and the seat of a brilliant vice-regal court. It had 7,000 inhabitants, and was the wealthiest town in America. In 1709, there were 11,000 people; in 1742, 16,000; and in 1769, 20,000. In 1761 the resistance to British authority began, followed by the Stamp-Act riots of 1765, the non-importation league of 1767, the occupation by red-coat regiments in 1768, the Massacre in 1770, the Tea-party in 1773, the Royalist closing of the port in 1774, and the battles and siege in 1775-76. The town recovered slowly, after its ruin by the long British occupation and the American bombardment. It became a city in 1822, with 50,000 inhabitants, and a vast Asiatic and European commerce. The original area of 800 acres has been more than doubled by filling in the shoal parts of the harbor. Roxbury was annexed in 1868, Dorchester in 1870, and Charlestown, West Roxbury and Brighton in 1874. The city sent 26,175 men to the War for the Union. Nov. 9-10, 1872, a fire destroyed $75,000,000 worth of property. The decline of maritime commerce turned the people's energies to railroads, manufactures, and general trade, and this is now one of the world's great markets for wool, boots and shoes, and other commodities. In literature, art and religion the community holds great renown. Two-thirds of its people are of foreign parentage, but the dominant influence remains Puritan. The population reached 362,839 in 1880, and 448,477 in 1890. But within a radius of a dozen miles there are many towns and villages which are essentially part of the city, and including these the population can more correctly be called a million. The valuation exceeds $1,000,000,000. The net debt is $37,000,000; and the yearly city and county income, $14,000,000.

Boston possesses a grand harbor, unsurpassed in either hemisphere for the possibilities of Maritime commerce, and for charming situations for Summer homes and resorts. James Freeman Clarke, said: "*Every Sunrise in New England is more full of wonder than the Pyramids. Why go to see the Bay of Naples when we have not yet seen Boston Harbor?*"

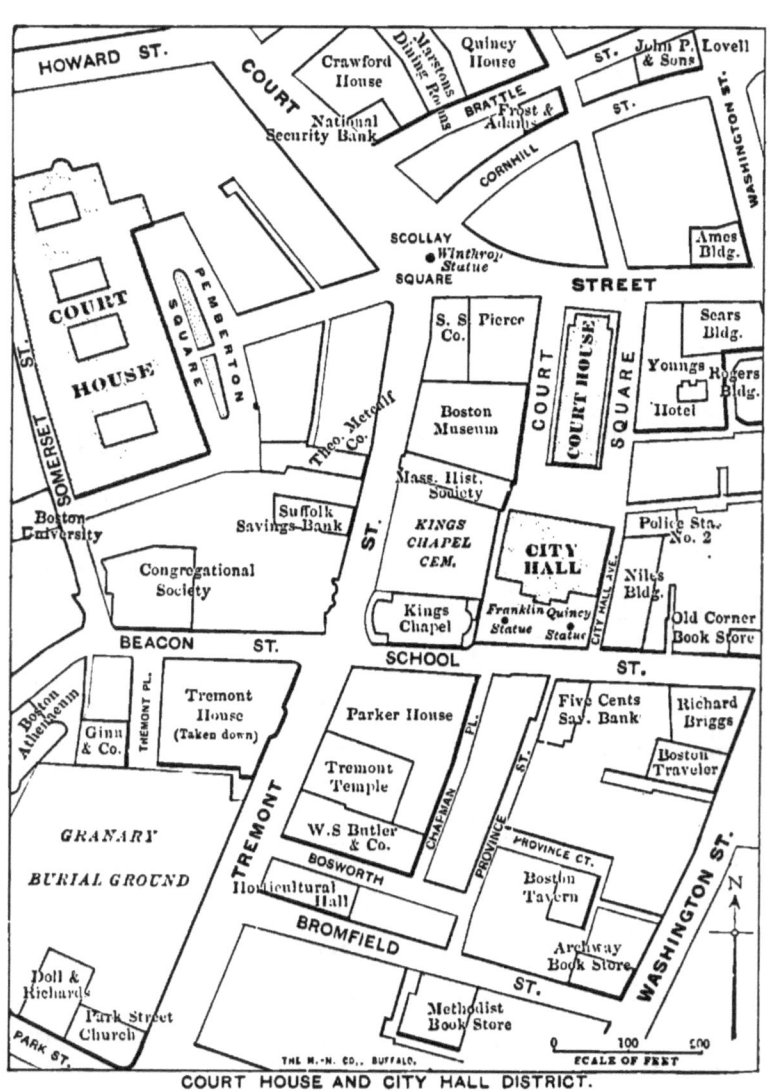

COURT HOUSE AND CITY HALL DISTRICT.

THE WHOLESALE BUSINESS DISTRICT.

THE wholesale business quarter may be bounded in a general way by Scollay and Bowdoin Squares and Washington St. on the west, the harbor on the east, Eliot and Kneeland Sts. on the south and Charles River on the north. This is the chief financial and commercial region, with the courts, banks, newspaper-offices, railway-stations and theatres; and here flow the deepest and most agitated currents of humanity.

Scollay Square has been chosen as our chief starting-point because it is a central plaza from which many street-car lines diverge. An English visitor said that the view south from Scollay Square was one of the most picturesque street-scenes in the world. In the driveways, a vast tangle of cars and wagons; on the sidewalks, animated currents of many phases of human life; and on the sides, the old pitch-roofed brick houses, the long triple-balconied front of the Boston Museum, the green trees of the burial-ground, the dark low tower of King's Chapel, and the lofty white marble pile of the Parker House. The view from the square down Court St. is not less impressive, with the quaint Old State House nestling low under the eaves of enormous new office-buildings, a true fragment of Tudor Boston, the English provincial seaport, overhung on all sides by the majestic commercial palaces of the Modern Athens.

GOV. WINTHROP'S STATUE IN SCOLLAY SQUARE.

The first owner of Scollay Square was Edward Bendall, whom the Puritans drove away, and then part of the land came to David Yale, brother of the founder of Yale College. A century ago, most of the square was covered by a wedge-shaped heap of ramshackle buildings, the chief of which belonged to Wm. Scollay, of a Scottish family from the lonely Orkney Islands. Scollay's Building was torn down in 1871, leaving the present great triangular open space, which is bordered by busy retail stores, hotels, restaurants and museums, and traversed by innumerable crowds and myriads of vehicles. Its presiding genius is the bronze statue of the founder of Massachusetts, Gov. Winthrop, in full Puritan costume, holding the Bible and the roll of the Colony Charter, and looking toward the sea. A rope tied around a tree-trunk indicates that he has just landed from a boat in the wilderness. This memorial, a duplicate of one in the U.-S. Capitol, was designed by R. S. Greenough, and erected in 1880, after a grand military and civic parade and orations. The lofty Hemenway Building at the south side of Scollay

SCOLLAY SQUARE, JUNCTION OF TREMONT, BRATTLE, CORNHILL AND COURT STREETS.

Square arose in 1884, on the site of the house where President Washington sojourned, in 1789 when Gov. John Hancock, from some dim idea of State sovereignty, declined to receive him, and where later were the offices of Harrison Gray Otis and Daniel Webster. Many lawyers of to-day hang up their green bags in the comfortable offices of the modern building. The lower floor is occupied by the ancient retail grocery-store of the S. S. Pierce Co. The land under the Hemenway Building is assessed at $350,000.

The Suffolk-County Court-House, in Pemberton Square, and plainly visible from Scollay Square, is an immense granite building, in German Renaissance architecture, completed in 1886, at a cost (including land) of $3,828,000. It encloses four open court-yards, and has several finely decorated halls. The grand rotunda, of white marble and polished granite, is richly adorned with frescoes, and with sculptures representing the

THE SUFFOLK COUNTY COURT HOUSE.
PEMBERTON SQUARE, EXTENDING THROUGH TO SOMERSET STREET.

human virtues. The Court-House also contains the Social Law Library, founded in 1804, and numbering 25,000 volumes. The building faces on Pemberton Square, where rose a harbor-viewing hill eighty feet high, until 1835, when it was removed, and replaced by a fashionable residence-square. Some of the old swell-front houses remain, used as public and law offices. Boston University's executive building, Jacob Sleeper Hall, is at the head of Pemberton Square.

On Howard St. is the Howard Athenæum, a spacious and popular variety-theatre of the cheaper sort, occupying the site of the Millerite Tabernacle of 1845, where the Adventists assembled in white ascension-robes, to be ready for the expected end of the world. Here was the estate of Capt. Cyprian Southack, of the Provincial navy, whose guest in 1711 was Admiral Sir Hovenden Walker, the leader of a mournfully disastrous expedition against Quebec. Theodore Lyman had a fine mansion at Howard St. and Tremont Row, where Lafayette was his guest in 1825.

ENTRANCE TO COURT HOUSE, PEMBERTON SQUARE.

Court St., leading past the Old Court House, to the Old State House, was anciently known as Prison Lane (here Capt. Kidd was confined); and then, from 1708 until after the Revolution, as Queen St. Here rises the gloomy Doric Quincy-granite colonnade of the old court-house, with columns weighing 28 tons each, built in 1833-36, and famous for the bloody Abolition riots in 1851 and 1854, when the place was surrounded by chains to keep off the patriot insurgents. Phillips, Parker and Higginson were indicted for their share in this attempted revolution. Here also occurred the dreadful Webster-Parkman trial. Behind is the City Hall; and just below towers the handsome seven-story sandstone front of Young's Hotel, containing on the ground-floor the beautiful and spacious ladies' dining-room, with its artistic decorations. This fine addition, built in 1882, adjoins the older part of the hotel, founded by George Young in 1845.

On the corner of Court and Washington Sts. is the white marble Sears Building, partly burned in 1890, and rebuilt, much taller than be-

OLD STATE HOUSE, AMES, SEARS AND OTHER BUILDINGS.
VIEW WESTWARD FROM THE BOSTON STOCK EXCHANGE.

AMES BUILDING AND COURT STREET TO SCOLLAY SQUARE.
VIEW FROM BALCONY OF OLD STATE HOUSE.

fore, in Italian Gothic architecture. It is full of banks, and offices of western railroads, New-England manufacturing corporations and lawyers. Here dwelt John Leverett, a soldier of Cromwell, knighted by Charles II., and Governor of Massachusetts during King Philip's War. Here, also, were the busy law offices of Choate, Andrew, Parsons, Chandler and Horace Mann. On the opposite corner rises the tremendous gray-granite sixteen-story pile of the Ames Building, designed by Shepley, Rutan & Coolidge, in a richly ornamental style, and devoted to offices, banks and trust companies. It is 190 feet high, and was finished in 1890, at a cost of $700,000. The land under it is assessed at $400,000. Just south of Court St., on Washington St., is the ever-busy Newspaper Row; and just north is Cornhill, a busy old-fashioned street, making a broad curve from Adams Square to Scollay Square. It is one of the street-car centers; and here a never-ceasing line of electrics make their starting point for various suburbs. It was formerly devoted to the book-trade, of which it retains some portion, mainly second-hand book stores. Here is the spacious and long-established store of Frost & Adams, founded before 1840, and occupying a five-story building with an immense and varied stock of artists' and architects' materials, mathematical instruments and articles for decorating. They import largely from Europe, and have an extensive trade all over America.

A short distance north of Cornhill is Brattle St., with the old Quincy House, founded in 1819, the first Quincy-granite building in Boston, and the oldest hotel now existing. It has been

SAM. ADAMS STATUE, ADAMS SQUARE.

often enlarged. Opposite is the site of the Brattle-square Church, built in 1772, and standing until 1871, with a cannon ball sticking in its side, fired by an American battery at Cambridge during the siege. Then it was a barrack for two regiments of British infantry. As Dr. Holmes wrote, it

"Wore on its bosom, as a bride might do,
 The iron breastpin which 'the rebels' threw."

FROST & ADAMS, ARTISTS' MATERIALS AND MATHEMATICAL INSTRUMENTS.
NO. 37 CORNHILL, BETWEEN WASHINGTON AND COURT STREETS.

Close by, at 23 to 29 Brattle St., is the great popular Marston restaurant, where thousands of people are served daily with good food at low prices. This famous restaurant had its beginning in 1847, when the present senior partner, Russell Marston, opened a small eating-place with a capacity for about 20 people. To-day the establishment, the largest in the city, can comfortably seat 800 people. The premises have been extended through to Hanover St., where an attractive building has been specially erected. Although the prices are quite moderate, the pleasant and well-conducted Marston restaurants are constantly patronized by the best people of Boston and all New England.

At the head of Brattle St. is the Crawford House, where the National Security Bank occupies the main corner.

Adams Square, just north of State St., is a broad paved open space, surrounded by tall buildings and shops, and traversed by great crowds of people. Here stands a spirited bronze statue of Samuel Adams, designed by Anne Whitney, and unveiled in 1880. It represents "The Chief of the Revolution" (as the British Ministry entitled him), just after his heroic act of demanding from Gov. Hutchinson that he should remove the redcoat regiments from the town, after the Massacre.

Dock Square is one of the anciently settled portions of the city and modern improvements have not yet made many inroads here. To the east it runs to Faneuil Hall and on the west it extends to Adams Square.

NEW WASHINGTON STREET, NORTH FROM ADAMS SQUARE.

Shops of various kinds are here, and at No. 20 is the hardware house of Burditt & Williams; the great sign over the top telling of this one building having been a hardware store for more than a hundred years. True

MARSTON'S DINING ROOMS — RUSSELL, MARSTON & CO.
NOS. 23 TO 29 BRATTLE STREET, EXTENDING THROUGH TO 19 AND 21 HANOVER STREET.

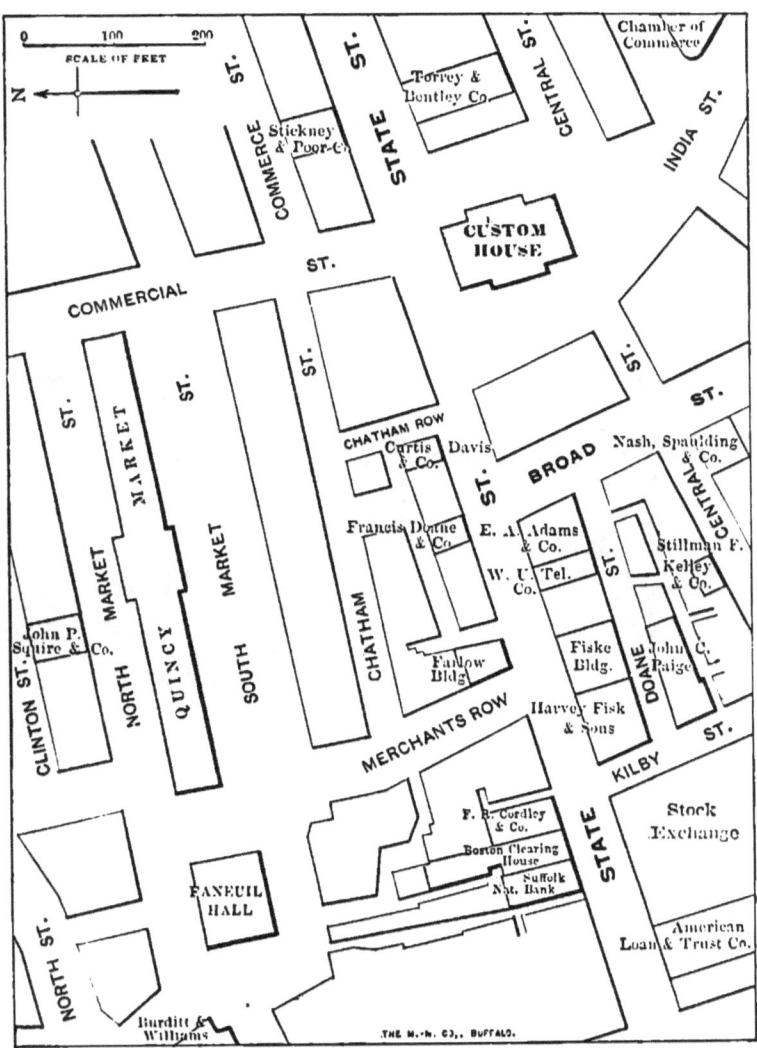

FANEUIL HALL, STOCK EXCHANGE AND CUSTOM HOUSE DISTRICT.

to its ripe age the firm which for two generations past has carried on the business under its present style keeps an exceptionally complete line of builders' and general hardware, cutlery and tools.

Faneuil Hall, "The Cradle of Liberty," was built in 1742, by Peter Faneuil, the Huguenot merchant, for a market and public hall, and presented to the town. Smibert, the pioneer painter, was the architect. It

DOCK SQUARE AND FANEUIL HALL, LOOKING EAST FROM ADAMS SQUARE.

was rebuilt after a fire, in 1763, and dedicated by James Otis ; and much enlarged in 1806, Bulfinch being the architect. This was the scene of many a famous patriotic town-meeting, illumination, feast or oration in the olden time ; and of the theatre of the British garrison ; the town offices until 1822 ; the State dinners to Count d'Estaing, Lafayette, the Prince de Joinville, Lords Ashburton and Elgin, and other dignitaries ; McClellan's reception, Burlingame's lying-in-state ; and countless meetings in behalf of various public movements, addressed by Otis, Webster, Everett, Sumner, Parker, Hillard, Channing, Garrison, Phillips, and other orators. The hall cannot be sold or leased, but may be occupied free for meetings whenever a stated number of persons apply for it under regulations. Then the interested ones assemble, and "rock the Cradle." Thus in 1895 the woes of Armenia and the demerits of the Subway and other

BURDITT & WILLIAMS, HARDWARE AND CUTLERY.
NO. 20 DOCK SQUARE, NEAR FANEUIL HALL.

themes have here been discussed; as in earlier times King George's tyranny, the Embargo, the tariff, slavery and the War for the Union had been. The hall is open all day free for visitors. It contains Healey's great painting of Webster in the U. S. Senate, answering Hayne, of South Carolina; and also fine portraits of Washington, Knox, Faneuil, Lincoln, Hancock, Sam.

FANEUIL HALL
FANEUIL-HALL SQUARE, BETWEEN NORTH AND SOUTH MARKET STREETS.

THE QUINCY, OR FANEUIL-HALL MARKET.
NORTH AND SOUTH MARKET STREETS, FROM FANEUIL-HALL SQUARE TO COMMERCIAL STREET.

Adams, Everett, Preble, John Adams, Gov. Andrew, Gen. Warren, and John Quincy Adams. The handsome old clock was presented by the school-children. The very quaint gilded grasshopper, with glass eyes, used as a vane on the cupola, was cunningly wrought by Deacon Shem Drowne, in the Provincial days, in imitation of a similar insect on the Royal Exchange of London. Faneuil Hall is in the dignified Provincial architecture, with broad galleries on Doric pillars, and a spacious rostrum from which many illustrious orators have spoken. There are no seats on the floor, which can thus accommodate a vast audience. Overhead is the armory of the Ancient and Honorable Artillery Company, founded in 1638, as the school of war for the colony, and the oldest military organization in America, with its ranks largely filled by officers of other organizations. Among its commanders have been Winthrop, Winslow, Heath, Dearborn, Martin, Cowdin and 14 other generals ; and Sir Charles Hobby and Sir John Leverett. Here is a valuable museum of military relics and curiosities. The lower floor of Faneuil Hall is still used for market stalls, and all the neighborhood abounds in tempting articles of food.

Immediately facing Faneuil Hall is Quincy Market, a two-story granite building 535 feet long, built in 1825-27, filled with large and well-kept stalls, abounding in all the vast variety of food sent to Boston by her tributary provinces, from Sicily to Alaska. It has a dome, over the rotunda occupied by the Boston Fruit and Produce Exchange, and two porticos of huge granite columns. Many visitors find delight in inspecting this wonderful market and its frequenters. The old Town Dock, with its wharves and shipping, formerly occupied this site, and reached up to opposite Elm Street, but was filled by Mayor Quincy in 1826, making six new streets and a large area of valuable land, upon part of which he erected the market-house.

On the north side of Quincy Market is the great incorporated meat and provision packing house of John P. Squire & Co., which has its unique office-building at 39 N. Market St. ; dates its origin from 1842 ; and has an entire block of works at East Cambridge. Its business amounts to over $15,000,000 a year. It is the largest concern of its kind in America excepting only those in Chicago.

The Old State House, at the head of State St., was built in 1748, in the walls of its predecessor erected in 1713, and on the site of the Town House of 1657 ; and for half a century the Honorable Provincial Council and the State Senate met in the eastern hall, and the House of Representatives in the western hall. Here, according to John Adams, "Independence was born ;" and for 14 years Sam. Adams and Hancock, Otis and Quincy and other patriots resisted British aggressions, with fiery eloquence. Here the Stamp-Act clearances were burned ; the British troops were quartered, in 1768 ; Gens. Howe and Clinton held their war-councils, surrounded by officers clad in scarlet and lace ; the State Constitution was planned ; Gov. Hancock received the Count d'Estaing and his

THE OLD STATE HOUSE.
WASHINGTON AND DEVONSHIRE STREETS, AT THE HEAD OR WEST END OF STATE STREET.

brilliant suite; and Washington, the man of the century, reviewed the citizenry. Within these walls the ancient courts convened; and the vice-regal governors held sway; and the sovereigns and governors were proclaimed. The sessions of the City Council took place here from 1830 to 1840. The Boston Massacre occurred in front of the Old State House, March 5, 1770, when the British main guard, provoked by missiles and epithets, opened fire upon a mob, and slew five persons. For many years the Old State House was given up to private business-offices, whose rentals went to the city. In 1882 the building was restored, and placed in the care of the patriotic Bostonian Society (of 500 members), which has here a vast and deeply interesting museum of antiquities and relics, open free from 9 to 5 daily. Large tablets are inscribed with the histories of the halls; and the lion and the unicorn (burned by the people in 1777, with every other royal emblem in Boston) have been replaced on the eastern gables. This very quaint old mid-street edifice makes a startling contrast with the immense modern buildings all about it. In the early days, the lower story was an open hall, with Doric columns, where the merchants used to meet and walk and arrange their business affairs. How vastly the local commerce has outgrown this primitive Exchange!

On the north side of State St., No. 28, is the handsome granite building of the Merchants' National Bank, a grand financial institution in which Bostonians take the utmost pride. It was founded in 1831, and has a capital of $3,000,000, a surplus of $1,500,000, making it the largest banking institution in New England. Franklin Haven and Franklin Haven, Jr., have been successively the presidents for nearly sixty years. The Merchants' Bank building was erected in 1824 by the United-States Bank at a cost of $120,000, but since then it has been very much altered and improved. It is now one of the most valuable buildings in the city, easily worth over a million dollars. It stands on the site of the old colonial Custom House.

The First Church in Boston, a thatched log structure, was erected in 1632 on State St., just south of the Old State House, on the site of Brazer's Building, a venerable office-structure which will probably be razed within a short time, for its dignified antiquity is maintained at too high a cost, since this is now one of the most valuable sites in Boston. It contains many offices of lawyers and real-estate agents, the most prominent of whom is Alexander S. Porter, who has already been prominently identified with various real-estate dealings of great magnitude, notably the Stock-Exchange Building mentioned later.

The conspicuous new structure of light brick on the south side of State St. occupying the little block formed by Congress Square and Congress St. is the Worthington Building, built by Roland Worthington, the former owner of *The Boston Traveller*, which was erstwhile located here. It is one of the most graceful office buildings in the city. It is peculiarly fortunate in its situation and with thoroughfares on all four sides it enjoys

MERCHANTS' NATIONAL BANK.
NO. 28 STATE STREET, NORTH SIDE, FROM DEVONSHIRE TO EXCHANGE STREETS

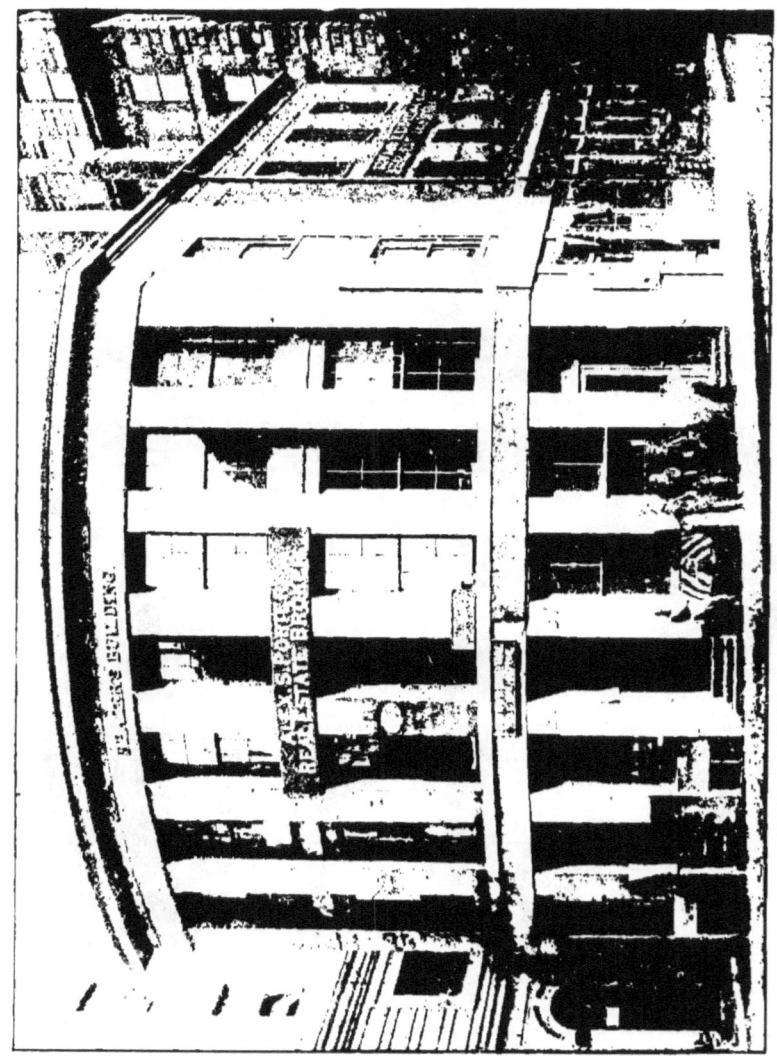

ALEX. S. PORTER, REAL ESTATE AGENT—BRAZER'S BUILDING.
NO. 27 STATE STREET, SOUTH SIDE, FROM DEVONSHIRE STREET TO CONGRESS SQUARE.

WORTHINGTON BUILDING, ERECTED BY ROLAND WORTHINGTON.
STATE STREET, SOUTH SIDE, BETWEEN CONGRESS SQUARE AND CONGRESS STREET.

advantages of light and views seldom found. It is ten stories in height and has been built in the modern fire-proof steel construction method. It was completed in 1895.

State St. leads east from the Old State House to the harbor. Change Avenue, north from State St. to Faneuil Hall is one of Boston's quaint and famous short cuts — a narrow alley between high buildings, traversed by myriads of hurrying footmen. A short tunnel leads thence to Corn Court, where Samuel Cole opened the first Boston tavern, in 1634, and

STOCK EXCHANGE.   TREMONT BANK,   CONGRESS STREET.   WORTHINGTON BUILDING.
CONGRESS STREET, LOOKING SOUTH FROM STATE STREET TO POST-OFFICE SQUARE.

entertained Miantonomah's painted Narragansett Indians, envoys to Gov. Sir Harry Vane. There Talleyrand, the great premier of France, boarded, in 1795, in the Braser Inn, whose quaint brick front still stands. Change Avenue (named for the Royal Exchange Tavern) enters State St. near the site of the pillory and whipping-post, on its left corner the site of the Custom House, where Gens Lincoln and Dearborn ruled as collectors; and on its right corner the stately brick office-building of the Massachusetts Hospital Life Insurance Company (founded in 1818).

HOWARD NATIONAL BANK OF BOSTON.
NO. 19 CONGRESS STREET, BETWEEN STATE STREET AND POST-OFFICE SQUARE.

A little south of State St., on the west side of Congress, at No. 19, is the handsome building of the Howard National Bank, an institution more than forty years old, having a capital of $1,000,000, with ramifications throughout the Union, and held in the highest esteem for conservative yet enterprising administration. At the corner of State and Congress Sts. is the Tremont Bank Building, which now pertains to the estate of the late William H. Hill.

The most notable modern feature of State St. is the twelve-story granite Stock Exchange (legally the State-Street Exchange Building), one of the largest office-buildings in America, with frontages of 170 feet on State St., 160 feet on Kilby St., and 53 feet on Exchange Place. This huge hive of banks, corporations, safe-deposit vaults, lawyers and business men, was built in 1889-1891, from designs by Peabody & Stearns, at a cost of $4,000,000. Alexander S. Porter, a prominent real-estate agent, conceived the plan, raised the money, and carried through the negotiations, which were strictly cash transactions, without mortgages. The magnificent Corinthian hall of the Stock Exchange (115 by 50 feet) affords very exciting scenes when the stock market is agitated. A gallery on the second floor is always open to visitors.

At the right side of the main entrance to the Stock Exchange, at 53 State St., is the great banking-room of the American Loan & Trust Company, which, besides carrying on a general banking business, is chartered as a legal depository for executors, guardians, trustees, and law courts, and as trustee and agent in financial matters, as trustee under mortgages, and as transfer agent and registrar of stocks and bonds. This notable corporation has gross assets exceeding $6,500,000, including its capital of $1,000,000 and its surplus of $500,000, and deposits exceeding $5,000,000.

On the left of the main entrance is the banking-room of the Massachusetts National Bank, with a single exception the oldest bank in the United States, a solid banking institution with a specialty of selling exchange on all countries of the world.

Just right of the entrance to the visitors' gallery, on the second floor, are the commodious banking-rooms of Pearmain & Brooks, very energetic members of the Stock Exchange, who have important connections with all the great stock exchanges of the country.

Immediately across from the Stock Exchange, at the southeast corner of State and Kilby Sts., is the banking-house of Harvey Fisk & Sons, whose dealings in United-States, state, county, city, and other high grade bonds have reached up into the hundreds of millions of dollars.

For nearly a century, State St. has been the financial nerve-center of New England, and one of the foremost monetary headquarters of the world. Here, and in the contiguous region as far as Milk St., are the most powerful banks and financial and brokerage houses, the various trust-companies, and many corporations of wide renown. The Clearing-House (established in 1856), at 66 State St., is second only to that of New York in the volume of its transactions.

BOSTON STOCK EXCHANGE — STATE STREET EXCHANGE BUILDING.
STATE, KILBY AND EXCHANGE STREETS.

AMERICAN LOAN & TRUST COMPANY OF BOSTON.
STOCK EXCHANGE BUILDING, NO. 53 STATE STREET, AT MAIN ENTRANCE TO THE EXCHANGE.

BOSTON STOCK EXCHANGE, MAIN FLOOR.
FROM PHOTO LOANED BY PEARMAIN & BROOKS, BANKERS, STOCK EXCHANGE, 53 STATE STREET.

HARVEY FISK & SONS, BANKERS AND BOND DEALERS.

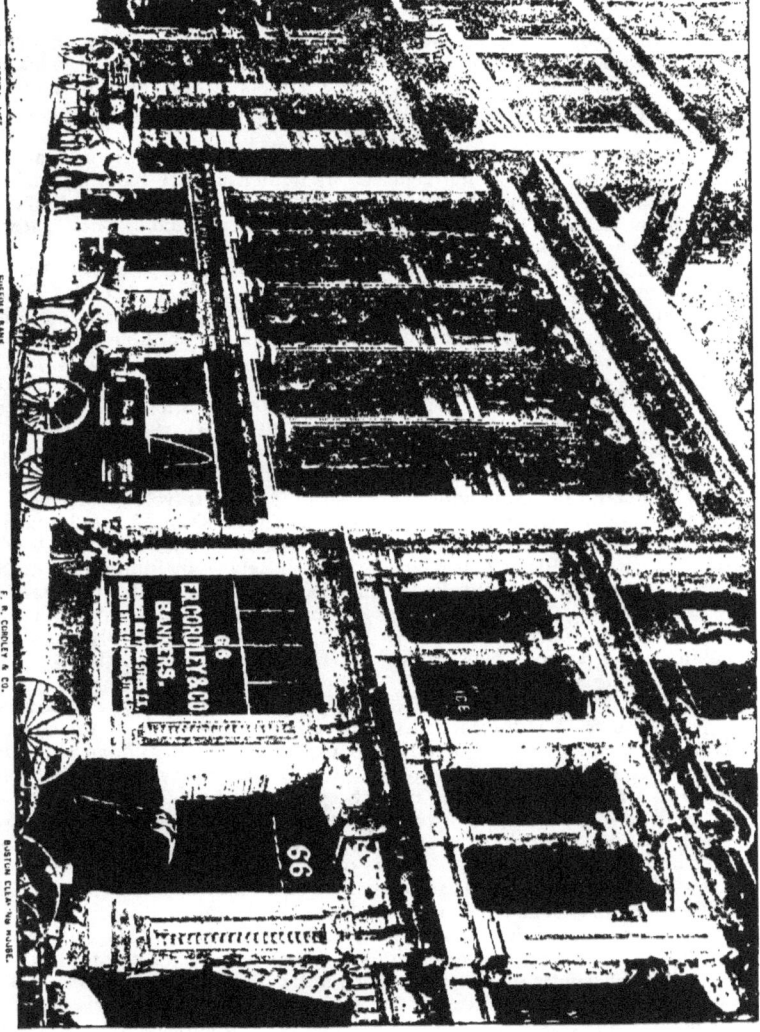

F. R. CORDLEY & CO., BANKERS AND BROKERS.
BOSTON CLEARING HOUSE BUILDING, NO. 66 STATE STREET, OPPOSITE STOCK EXCHANGE.

On the ground floor of the Clearing House building, which is immediately across the street from the Stock Exchange, are the banking-rooms of F. R. Cordley & Co., who are members of the Boston, New-York and Chicago exchanges, with influential connections at various important centres.

The sober and now sombre granite edifices erected along State St. half a century ago are being replaced by immense office-buildings, of the type made possible by elevators; and the oldtime monotony of the vista has been changed to a tumultuous diversity, which is not without picturesqueness.

All along on State St. are many prominent business-houses in various lines of industry. At 116 is the old house of Francis Doane & Co., established in 1825, manufacturers of blank books, stationers, and lithographers, supplying the great financial and commercial houses with their varied requisites. At 136 are the offices of Curtis Davis & Co., the oldest soap manufacturers in the State, whose "Welcome Soap" is sold throughout America. At 184 are the offices of the Stickney & Poor Co., the oldest mustard and spice house in the city. At 189 are the headquarters of the Torrey & Bentley Co., a corporation which exclusively represents large manufacturers, practically the only one of its character in New England, and employing a very large force of traveling salesmen.

State St. was until the Revolution known as King St., and reached only as far as Merchants' Row, which formed the harbor-strand, with wharves on one side. It has been trebled in length by filling out into the harbor. Beyond the lofty Fiske and Farlow buildings, it traverses the region of foreign consulates; passes the massive and sombre Custom House, dating from 1837-47, with sides, roof, dome and 32 huge fluted columns of granite; leads along the impressive State-St. Block; and reaches Long Wharf.

Among the many quaint streets adjacent to State St., is Central St. which leads from Kilby St., eastward past the south side of the Custom House to Central Wharf. At No. 18 are the offices of Stillman F. Kelley & Co., reputed to be the head of the molasses and syrups trades, with business transactions covering many States.

A little way southward from the Custom House, on India St., rises the handsome Romanesque and many-gabled structure of the Chamber of Commerce, built from designs of Shepley, Rutan & Coolidge in 1890-92, of pinkish-gray granite, with a fine domed, frescoed, and oak-wainscoted hall (visible from the visitors' gallery), reading-rooms, state parlors, and many offices. In this exchange are bulletined the telegraphic marine news, and current quotations of provisions, grain, cotton, etc.

Kilby St. (once eleven feet wide, and called Mackerel Lane) leads south from State St., between the site of the Bunch-of-Grapes tavern, founded in 1713, and a Patriot headquarters, where Washington and his officers were banqueted, in 1776, and the British Coffee House, frequented by the Tories and Royal officers. The first theatre-play in

STATE STREET, FROM BROAD TO WASHINGTON STREETS.
FROM THE CUSTOM HOUSE TO THE OLD STATE HOUSE.

FRANCIS DOANE & CO., STATIONERS AND BLANK BOOK MAN'F'RS.
NO. 116 STATE STREET, OPPOSITE BROAD STREET.

THE CUSTOM HOUSE.
STATE AND INDIA STREETS, OPPOSITE COMMERCIAL STREET.

CURTIS DAVIS & CO., SOAP MANUFACTURERS.
OFFICES: 136 STATE STREET, COR. COMMERCIAL STREET. WORKS: CAMBRIDGEPORT.

THE TORREY & BENTLEY COMPANY, MANUFACTURERS' AGENTS.
NOS. 189 AND 191 STATE STREET, JUST EAST OF THE CUSTOM HOUSE.

STILLMAN F. KELLEY & CO., CENTRAL STREET, CUSTOM HOUSE.

STILLMAN F. KELLEY & CO., MOLASSES AND SYRUPS.
NO. 18 CENTRAL STREET, BETWEEN BROAD AND KILBY STREETS.

CHAMBER OF COMMERCE.
INDIA AND CENTRAL STREETS, AT THE EAST END OF MILK STREET.

Boston (Otway's *The Orphan*) was given in the Coffee House, in 1750, and called out such harsh legislation that no more were performed for 42 years, except in the British garrison. On Kilby St. and in the immediate vicinity are the numerous insurance-offices, chief among which are those of John C. Paige, occupying an entire building, at 20 Kilby St., with 100 clerks. This is one of the largest underwriting agencies in existence, and its business is continental in scope. The first underwriter in America, Joseph Marion, in 1724, opened on the site of 22 State St. a thriving marine insurance office, and in 1728 started the Sun Fire Office, which latter was a forerunner of the modern insurance companies. Kilby St. leads to the great Mason Building and the Telephone Building, on Liberty Square, formerly a dock and shipyard. At the corner of Milk St. is the sumptuously equipped new building of the Exchange Club, a downtown lunch and dining club.

Congress St. (formerly Quaker Lane) runs from State St. through the banking and insurance quarter to the magnificent Post-Office Square, for which the easier names of Farragut Square and Federal Square have been suggested. At 19 Congress St. is the Howard National Bank, previously mentioned, and at the southeast corner of Exchange Place is the valuable building of the State Mutual Life Insurance Co., of Worcester, Massachusetts.

The Post-Office, an enormous pile of Cape-Ann granite, with an iron roof, was built in 1869-85, at a cost of nearly $6,000,000, and covers more than an acre. The front toward the Square is crowned by two heroic groups, sculptured in Vermont marble, by Daniel C. French. The one on the left shows Labor (a blacksmith with anvil) sustaining the Family (a mother and child) and the Fine Arts (a woman with a vase); that on the right, Science (in the centre) controlling the forces of Steam (a crouching slave) and Electricity. The U.-S. Sub-Treasury, on the second floor of this building, usually contains ten millions or more in money; and its Cash Room, 80 by 40 feet, in the Greek style, with Sicily and Siena marble, is one of the sights of the town. The U.-S. court-rooms are on the third floor; and the building contains also the Pension, Naval Pay, Internal Revenue, Lighthouse, and Treasury Special Agents' offices, occupying spacious quarters. The Signal Service is on the fifth floor, with its instruments and cautionary signals on the roof, and also the time-ball, dropping every noon by telegraphic signal from the Harvard Observatory. The Bar Association, founded in 1876, with 500 members, has its great library in this building. Bynner, the novelist, was its librarian.

The Hancock National Bank occupies one of the most conspicuous sites in Boston, at the northwest corner of Congress and Water Sts., opposite the Post-Office, at the beginning of Post-Office Square. The bank was originally established under a State charter, in 1831. In its long existence it has done a large business, which, with its reorganization, and a strong board of directors, it is rapidly increasing. With a single

JOHN C. PAIGE, INSURANCE AGENCY.
NO. 20 KILBY STREET, OPPOSITE STOCK EXCHANGE, BETWEEN DOANE AND CENTRAL STREETS.

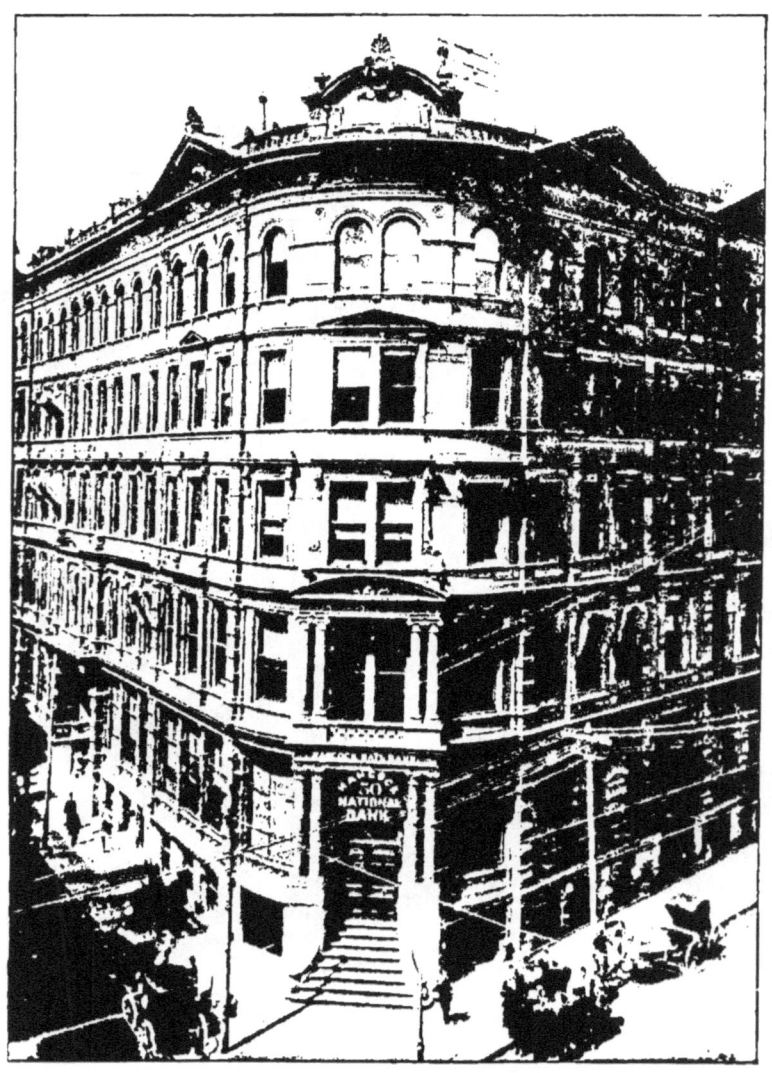

HANCOCK NATIONAL BANK OF BOSTON.
POST-OFFICE SQUARE, NO. 50 WATER STREET, NORTHWEST CORNER OF CONGRESS STREET.

UNITED STATES POST-OFFICE AND SUB-TREASURY.
POST-OFFICE SQUARE; MILK, DEVONSHIRE, WATER AND CONGRESS STREETS.

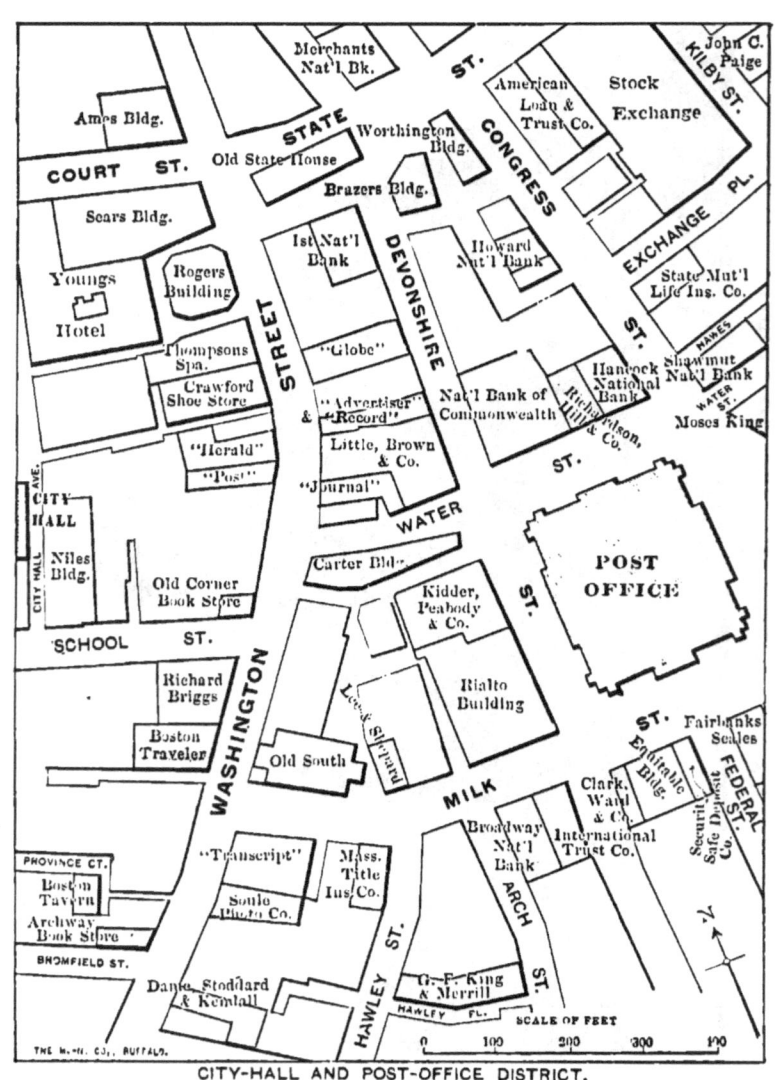

CITY-HALL AND POST-OFFICE DISTRICT.

RICHARDSON, HILL & CO., BANKERS.
NO. 40 WATER STREET, OPPOSITE THE POST-OFFICE, BETWEEN CONGRESS AND DEVONSHIRE STREETS.

exception this is the only United States bank named in honor of John Hancock, the illustrious signer of the Declaration of Independence.

Opposite the north side of the Post-Office, at 40 Water St., is the banking-house of Richardson, Hill & Co., one of Boston's prominent banking firms, transacting a general banking business, buying and selling securities, dealing in commercial paper, and members of the New-York, Boston and other stock exchanges.

Also at 40 Water St. are the offices of the Berkshire Life Insurance Co. (Col. W. H. Dyer, superintendent of agencies), a solid and enterprising corporation, chartered in 1851 under the salutary laws of Massachusetts.

The south side of Post-Office Square is occupied by the adjoining edifices of two great life-insurance corporations — the Mutual Life of New York and the New England Mutual of Boston, the two oldest regular life insurance companies in this country, both being purely mutual.

At Milk and Pearl Sts. is the $900,000 noble white-marble palace of the Mutual Life-Insurance Company of New York, one of the grandest office-buildings, with a lofty clock-tower 234 feet high to the top of the flag-staff, and 198 feet high to the sea-viewing balcony. Peabody & Stearns were the architects. This is the greatest fiduciary institution in the world, and has assets exceeding $200,000,000.

At Milk and Congress Sts. the New-England Mutual Life-Insurance Co., the largest in this State, has a million-dollar white granite office-building, uninflammable, with huge bronze emblematic statuary on top. It dates from 1874, and was planned by N. J. Bradlee. The company was chartered in 1835, and has been continuously prosperous, having now assets of $25,000,000. Benj. F. Stevens, the president, is a veritable veteran in the life-insurance profession, having been continuously connected with the New England Mutual for 48 years. The New England Mutual is esteemed the world over as one of the strongest and most conservative of all the life insurance corporations.

A little way farther up Milk St. rises the costly Equitable Life Building, made of granite, brick and iron, nine stories high, and erected mainly in 1873. Many persons go in the elevators up to the roof, which commands a singularly fine bird's-eye view of the island-studded harbor and the crowded town. The Equitable Life is one of the most colossal financial corporations in existence. Its ramifications are world-wide. Its assets approach $200,000,000. Its local force are an able body of life underwriters, including Nathan Warren (Resident Secretary), James B. Niver, James H. Lake, Fred'k B. K. Marter, Wm. A. Barton, F. A. Chesbro, E. R. Fowler, and Hodgman & Worth. The street-floor and the basements have been constructed with marvellous strength, especially for the Security Safe Deposit Co., whose enormous vaults are admirably arranged and ingeniously guarded to afford absolute security for valuables of every kind, and to provide all desirable conveniences and facilities for its patrons. Its reading-room is one of the most sumptuous apartments

MUTUAL LIFE INSURANCE COMPANY OF NEW YORK.
NO. 95 MILK, SOUTHWEST CORNER PEARL STREET, SOUTH SIDE POST-OFFICE SQUARE.

MUTUAL LIFE TOWER VIEW, LOOKING NORTHWARD.
MUTUAL LIFE INSURANCE BUILDING, POST-OFFICE SQUARE.

FEDERAL STREET. EQUITABLE BUILDING. MILK STREET. RIALTO. POST-OFFICE.

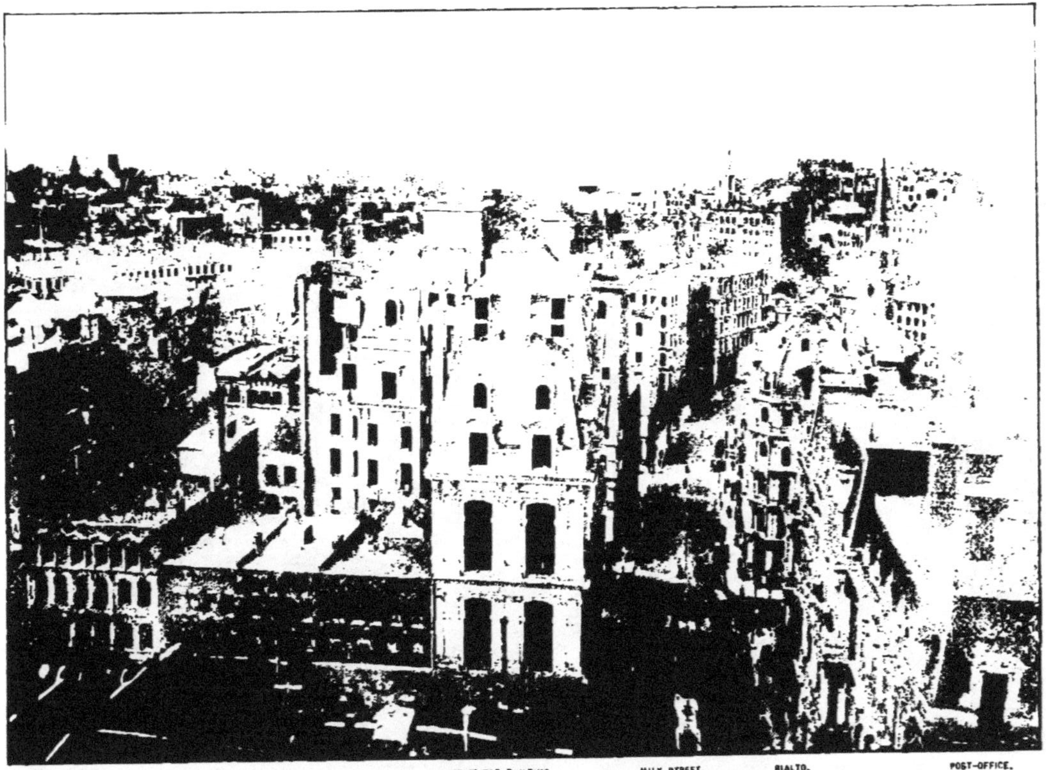

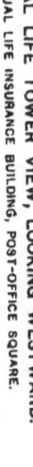

MUTUAL LIFE TOWER VIEW, LOOKING WESTWARD.

MUTUAL LIFE INSURANCE BUILDING, POST-OFFICE SQUARE.

MUTUAL LIFE TOWER VIEW, LOOKING SOUTHWARD.
MUTUAL LIFE INSURANCE BUILDING, POST-OFFICE SQUARE.

NEW-ENGLAND MUTUAL LIFE INSURANCE COMPANY.
COMPANY'S BUILDING, POST-OFFICE SQUARE, MILK AND CONGRESS STREETS.

in this country. On the street-floor of the Equitable Life Building, at the Devonshire and Milk St. corner, are the fine banking rooms of Clark, Ward & Co., bankers, members of the New York and Boston stock exchanges, transacting a very large business at all the exchanges.

At the southwest corner of Milk and Devonshire Sts., diagonally across from the Post Office, is the nine-story building of the International Trust Co. of Boston, one of the most elegant and graceful office buildings on the continent. It was completed in 1894. It is absolutely a fire-proof structure, and on its lower floors are public safety deposit vaults, protected by every desirable safeguard and furnished with all modern conveniences, where patrons can rent boxes of various sizes for the storage of valuables. The International Trust Co., which owns the building, is a general banking institution as well as a regular and special trust company, for individual and corporate trusts, with a capital of $1,000,000, surplus and undivided profits of almost $1,200,000, and gross assets of $9,000,000.

The Rialto, the John Hancock, and other adjacent structures contain banks and hundreds of corporation offices.

At 79 Milk St., at southeast corner of Federal St., is the head-quarters of the famous Fairbanks scales, whose business, founded in 1825, employs 1,000 men with branches all over the world. The Fairbanks Co. succeeded Fairbanks, Brown & Co. Besides scales, the products include Hancock inspirators, steam and water valves, store and warehouse trucks.

EXCHANGE CLUB, MILK AND BATTERYMARCH STREETS.

THE FAIRBANKS COMPANY,— THE FAIRBANKS' SCALES.
MILK STREET, SOUTHEAST CORNER OF FEDERAL STREET, POST-OFFICE SQUARE.

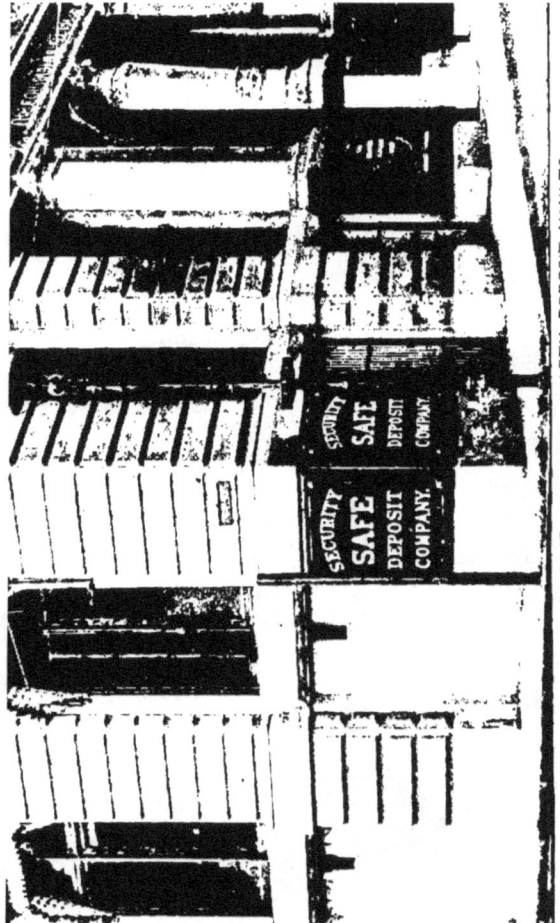

SECURITY SAFE DEPOSIT COMPANY, SAFETY DEPOSIT VAULTS.
EQUITABLE LIFE BUILDING, MILK, DEVONSHIRE AND FEDERAL STREETS, OPPOSITE SOUTH SIDE OF THE POST-OFFICE.

EQUITABLE LIFE ASSURANCE SOCIETY OF THE UNITED STATES.
EQUITABLE LIFE BUILDING, MILK, DEVONSHIRE AND FEDERAL STREETS.

CLARK, WARD & CO., BANKERS AND BROKERS.
EQUITABLE LIFE BUILDING, MILK STREET, SOUTHEAST CORNER OF DEVONSHIRE STREET, OPPOSITE THE POST-OFFICE.

INTERNATIONAL TRUST COMPANY OF BOSTON.
INTERNATIONAL TRUST BUILDING, MILK STREET, SOUTHWEST CORNER OF DEVONSHIRE STREET.

The Broadway National Bank, at 41 Milk, corner of Arch, was founded in 1853, in South Boston, and since its transfer to the financial district has become one of the most enterprising and successful of the city banks.

At the head of Milk St. is the Old South Meeting-house.

The district between Milk and Summer Sts., and farther south, is occupied by great business blocks, where a vast wholesale trade is carried on. The crockery houses are on Franklin St.; the paper firms, on and near Federal St.; the wholesale dry-goods stores, on and about Summer and Devonshire Sts.; the wool houses, about the intersection of Summer and

EXCHANGE CLUB. MASON BUILDING. TELEPHONE BUILDING.
LIBERTY SQUARE, JUNCTION KILBY, WATER AND BATTERYMARCH STREETS.

Federal Sts.; and the boot, shoe and leather trade, in High, Pearl, Purchase, Summer, Federal, and other streets. The Shoe and Leather Exchange is at 116-126 Bedford St. Most of this region was swept over in the appalling Great Fire of 1872, when $75,000,000 worth of property went up in flame and smoke. The region thus devastated lay between Summer St. and the Old South Meeting-House and the new Post Office and State St., and between Washington St. and the wharves. Afterwards, one could stand on Washington St. and see the harbor — the most conspicuous remains on the devastated Washington St. being the pure white marble front of Macullar, Parker & Co.'s building. The rebuilding

BROADWAY NATIONAL BANK OF BOSTON.
NO. 41 MILK STREET, SOUTHEAST CORNER OF ARCH STREET.

GEORGE F. KING & MERRILL, STATIONERY, PENS AND PENCILS.
NO. 38 HAWLEY STREET, EAST SIDE, BETWEEN MILK AND FRANKLIN STREETS.

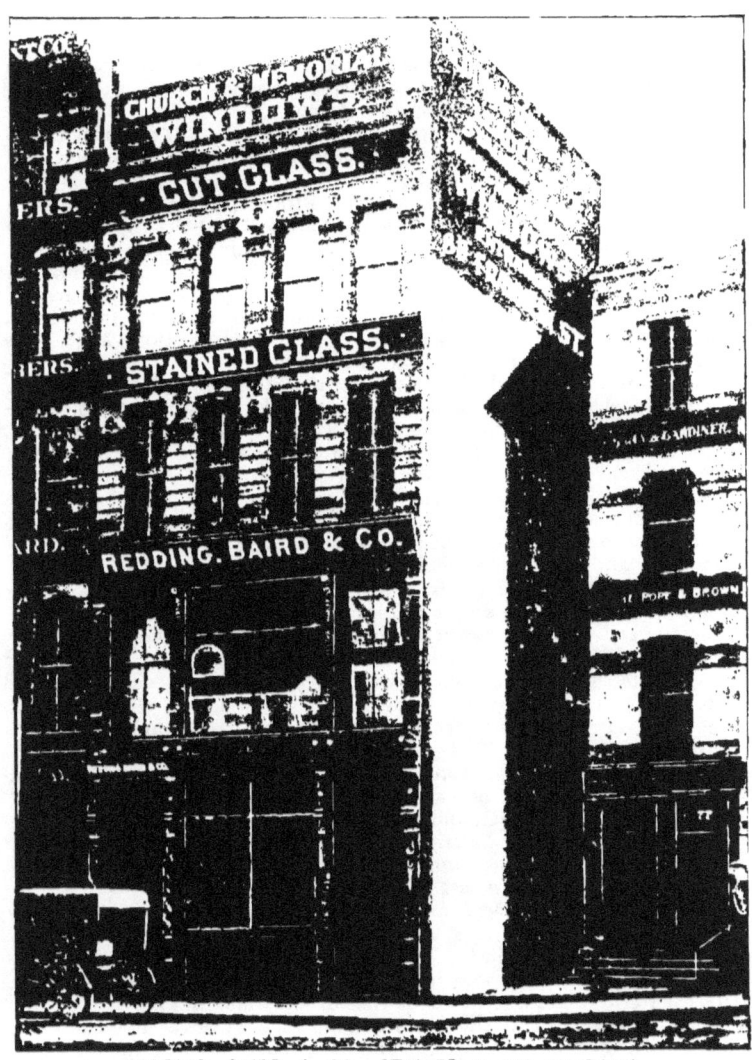

REDDING, BAIRD & CO., STAINED GLASS WINDOWS.
NO. 83 FRANKLIN STREET, SOUTHEAST CORNER OF ARCH STREET.

filled the district with handsome specimens of architecture, oftentimes very rich in design and material; and also gave opportunity for the widening and straightening of the queer old streets.

Hawley St. runs southward from Milk St., and at 38 is the busy establishment of Geo. F. King & Merrill, wholesale and retail stationers, and makers of King's pens and pencils.

Franklin St., quite bow-shaped still, although partially straightened after the Great Fire, runs from Washington to Broad St. It is a centre for Express Companies, and many notable wholesale and retail concerns.

At 83 Franklin St., corner of Arch St., are the offices and exhibition rooms of Redding, Baird & Co., whose productions of stained and leaded glass windows for homes, churches, and public buildings rival the highest grade of workmanship in this country. Their productions have been placed in notable edifices throughout the Union.

On Devonshire St., which meanders from State to Summer Sts., are many prominent business houses. At 181 are the executive offices of the Forbes Lithograph Manufacturing Co., whose works near Chelsea employ 600 men in fine illustrative and artistic work, with a large trade even in England and Germany. At the southwest corner of Devonshire and Franklin Sts. are the commodious banking rooms of the National Revere Bank, organized in 1859, and always one of Boston's most noted and conservative banking institutions. Its capital is $1,500,000 and its correspondents and connections cover the whole country. The whole upper floors of the building are occupied by the eastern headquarters of The Bradstreet Company, the oldest and strongest of the mercantile agencies, continually and vigilantly observing, rating and recording the history, prospects and progress of a million and a half business firms and corporations. At the southeast corner is the Cathedral Building, occupying the site of the Catholic Cathedral, constructed by Bulfinch in 1803, and sold in 1860 to Isaac Rich, who erected the present structure, and bequeathed it to Boston University. The great linen-thread importing and manufacturing house of J. R. Leeson & Co. occupies part of the Cathedral Building, 226 Devonshire St., as its headquarters for the "Real Scotch" and its other makes of linen and cotton thread for all uses.

Winthrop Square, the junction of Franklin, Devonshire and Otis Sts., has a group of prominent wholesale firms. At its centre is a fountain much used for watering horses.

At the corner of Franklin and Federal Sts. is the crockery establishment of Jones, McDuffee & Stratton, a veritable gallery of art china and glass, useful and ornamental. The several floors should be visited by all who come to Boston, for here are exhibited the choicest wares from the famous potteries and glass-works of the world. The site is notable from the fact that here stood the old Federal-street Theatre, in its day the greatest of Boston's play-houses. The firm, too, is notable from its age, having been established in 1810, and from its having been founded by the late Otis Norcross, a former mayor of Boston.

THE BRADSTREET COMPANY. THE BRADSTREET MERCANTILE AGENCY.
NO. 100 FRANKLIN STREET, NORTHWEST CORNER OF DEVONSHIRE STREET.

THE NATIONAL REVERE BANK OF BOSTON.
NO. 100 FRANKLIN STREET, NORTHWEST CORNER OF DEVONSHIRE STREET.

J. R. LEESON & CO., LINEN THREAD IMPORTERS AND MANUFACTURERS.
NO. 228 DEVONSHIRE STREET, CATHEDRAL BUILDING, SOUTHEAST CORNER OF FRANKLIN STREET.

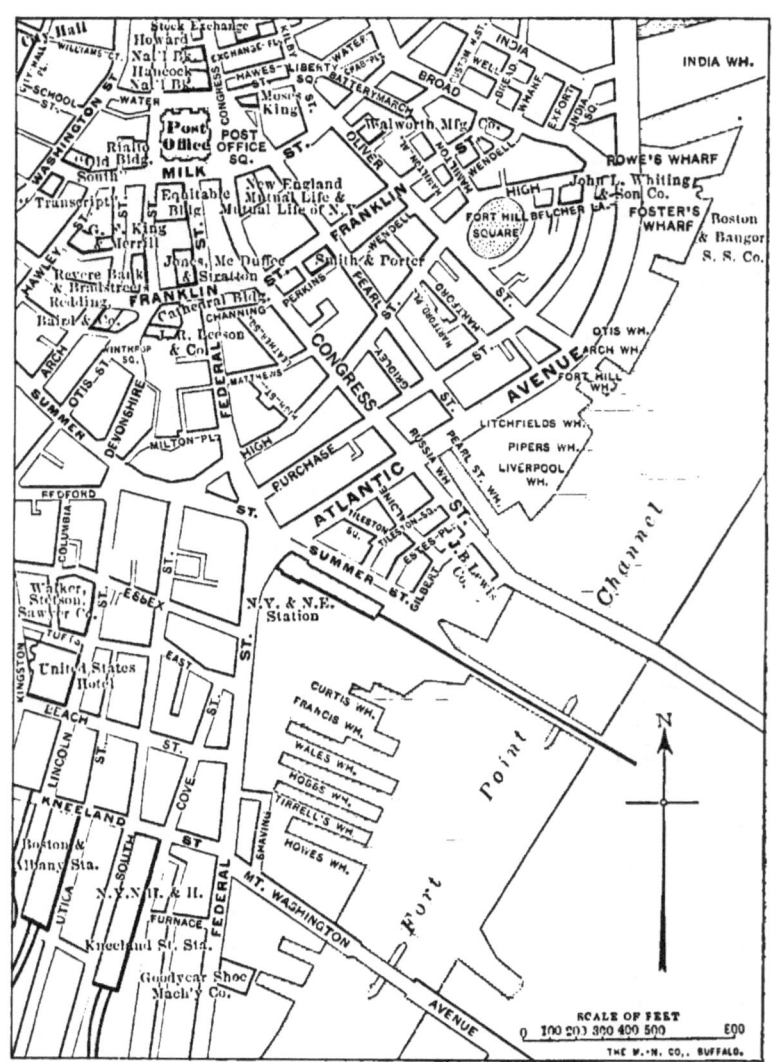

WHOLESALE DISTRICT.

JONES, McDUFFEE & STRATTON, FINE ART POTTERY, CHINA AND GLASSWARE.
FRANKLIN ST., NORTH SIDE, NORTHWEST CORNER OF FEDERAL ST., ONE BLOCK SOUTH OF POST OFFICE. (SEE PAGES 5 AND 70.)

At Franklin and Pearl Sts. is the extensive and finely equipped printing-house of Smith & Porter, the large building being owned by the firm. They are general commercial, job and book printers.

Fort-Hill Square, down towards the harbor, is the site of Fort Hill, 100 feet above, and crowned as early as 1632 by a harbor-commanding battery, from whose ramparts Sir Edmund Andros and his redcoats were dragged by the Boston train-bands in 1689. In 1774, this fortress had 35 guns; and was garrisoned by the Welsh Fusileers, the heroes of Minden. Early in this century, the hill was covered with patrician residences, ranged around Independence Park; but the Irish immigrants by degrees invaded it, and the scene became squalid. In 1866-73, the hill was cut down, and used in filling Atlantic Avenue; and its site is a level green park, surrounded by the buildings of iron and hardware and drug firms, and one of the model fire-engine houses of the city. At Nos. 16 to 24 Oliver St. are the offices and salesrooms of the Walworth Manufacturing Co., producers of steam apparatus and supplies, pipes and fittings, and whose extensive works are at South Boston. At 34 Oliver St. are the offices and salesrooms of the B. F. Sturtevant Co., whose blowers, engines and ventilating apparatus, made in their great works at Jamaica Plain, are in very general use. At Oliver and Purchase Sts. is the bindery and publishing warehouse of Thomas Y. Crowell & Co., who are famous as bookbinders and publishers, with a long list of books covering a wide range of strictly high-class literature and works of reference. At High and Purchase Sts. is the immense six-story factory of the John L. Whiting & Son Co., founded in 1864, and the largest manufacturers of brushes in America, with ingenious machinery and processes, and a large American and foreign trade. The ingenious mechanisms for making the universally approved "Goodyear Welts" and other products of the machines of the Goodyear Shoe-Machinery Co. are manufactured in their great factory on Federal St.; and their offices are at 158 Summer St.

All this section is hallowed by historical events which would require a volume to narrate. Emerson was born, in 1803, near the corner of Summer and Chauncey Sts.; the historian, Prescott, on Bedford St., close by; and Edgar A. Poe was born while his mother was playing at the Federal-Street Theatre, in 1809. His first book also appeared in Boston, in 1827. George Bancroft lived at the corner of Otis St. and Winthrop Square, near Nath'l Bowditch's, Gen. Heath's and Sir Wm. Pepperell's. Allston's studio, from 1818 to 1830, occupied the barn of the Prince house, in which Spurzheim, the Prussian phrenologist, died, on the northeast corner of Pearl and High Sts. Gilbert Stuart's studio was on Essex St., near Edinboro. An inscribed tablet at the junction of High and Summer Sts. shows where Webster long dwelt.

The district between State and Washington Sts. and the harbor was once sparsely occupied by humble village-farms, with pastures and orchards, diversified by a battery on Fort Hill, a windmill near the foot of Summer St., and a few rope-walks near the salt-marshes. In the

SMITH & PORTER, GENERAL PRINTERS.
SMITH & PORTER BUILDING, FRANKLIN STREET, SOUTHWEST CORNER OF PEARL STREET.

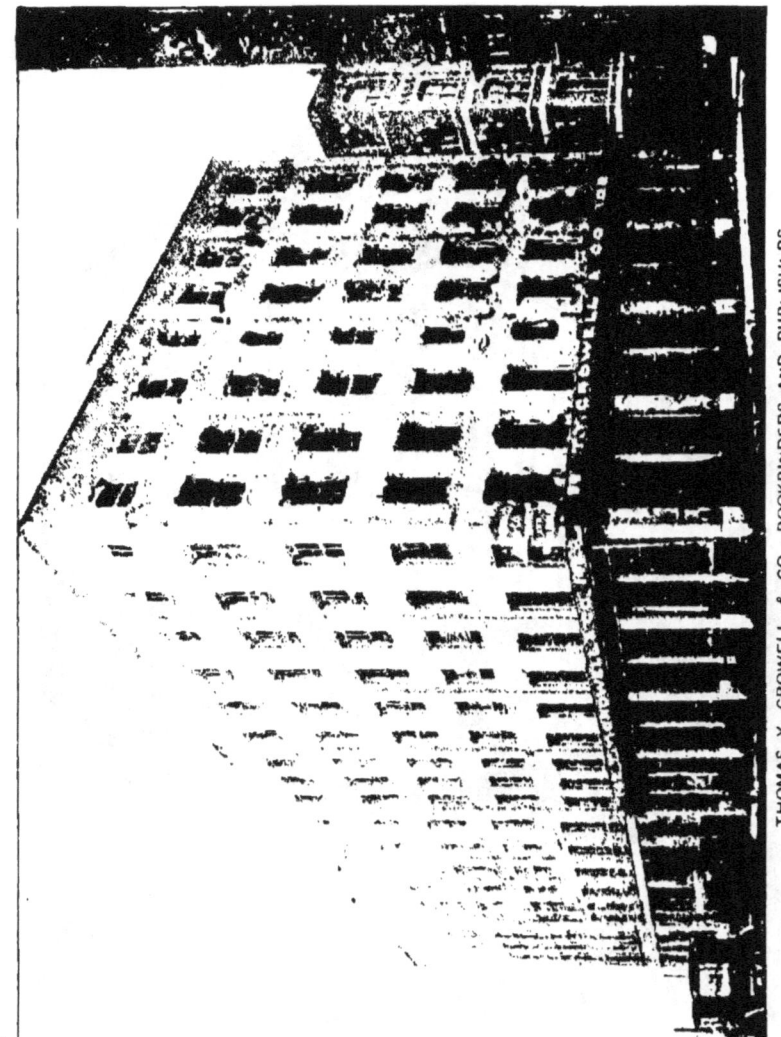

THOMAS Y. CROWELL & CO., BOOKBINDERS AND PUBLISHERS.
OLIVER STREET, SOUTHEAST CORNER OF PURCHASE STREET.

JOHN L. WHITING & SON CO., BRUSH MANUFACTURERS.
HIGH STREET, SOUTHWEST CORNER OF PURCHASE STREET, JUST EAST OF FORT HILL SQUARE.

Provincial time, the gentry had their country-seats here, with fish-ponds, rare fruits and rich gardens. About a century ago, Franklin St. was laid out across a marsh, for residences; and Summer St. became the handsomest rural thoroughfare in New England, with lines of noble old trees and parterres of brilliant flowers around its patrician mansions. Beach St. was on the beach; and Essex St. wound in its present odd curves along the water-side. Fort St. (leading from the governor's to the fort) became Milk St.; Pudding Lane, Devonshire St.; Bishop's Alley, Hawley St.; Blind Alley, Bedford St.; Cow Lane, High St. (because it ran *high* over Fort Hill); and Long Lane, Federal St. (because the Federal Constitution was ratified there). Over this tangle of lanes, and pastures and sea-marshes has arisen the present grand mercantile district, with its many scores of millions of value, and its influence over a continent.

FORT HILL SQUARE, FROM HIGH TO OLIVER STREETS.

Fires have done much toward the renovation of this locality, but the march of improvement did its full share. For some years hereabouts degenerated into poor tenement quarters, but the widening of streets and erection of fine buildings have entirely changed its appearance and uses.

The district near Bedford and Essex Sts., where the Thanksgiving-Day fire of 1889 destroyed $6,000,000, and the fire of March 10, 1893, swept off $4,000,000 more, is being occupied by long blocks of handsome commercial buildings, the homes of many famous wholesale shoe and dry-goods firms. At the junction of Bedford and Kingston Sts. stands the eminent wholesale notion, small wares, and fancy dry-goods establishment of the Walker-Stetson-Sawyer Co., one of the foremost houses in America in this trade, with customers extending from Maine to California. In 1896 this corporation will take possession of its grand new buildings, now being specially erected for it at Lincoln and Essex Sts.

At Beach, Lincoln and Kingston Sts. is an ancient hostelry, with a thoroughly modernized interior and a world-famous landlord, — the spacious and comfortable United States Hotel, kept by Tilly Haynes. This hotel is one of the largest and most popular in New England. A block or two farther south, on Kneeland St., are the simple, spacious and busy stations of the Boston & Albany and the Old Colony Railroads. Street-cars for almost everywhere pass there in unceasing processions.

WALKER-STETSON-SAWYER CO., WHOLESALE NOTIONS AND FANCY DRY GOODS.
BEDFORD STREET, SOUTHEAST CORNER OF KINGSTON STREET.

UNITED STATES HOTEL.—TILLY HAYNES, PROPRIETOR.
BEACH STREET, FROM KINGSTON TO LINCOLN STREETS.

THE RETAIL DISTRICT.

THE Retail District lies mainly between the Wholesale District, which has just been rambled through, and the Common, and includes the chief retail shops of all kinds, the theatres, newspaper-offices, municipal buildings, and some of the most important hotels. Its main arteries are Tremont St. and Washington St.; and the short thoroughfares connecting these two are also devoted to a lively retail trade. As Howells says :

"Nowhere in the world has shopping such an intensity of physiognomy as in Boston. It is unsparingly sincere. The lovely faces of the swarming crowd were almost fierce in their preoccupation."

Tremont St. passes out of Scollay Square, with the tall Hemenway Building on the left, just beyond which extends the long balconied and many-lanterned Renaissance front of the Boston Museum, built in 1846. This is the oldest local theatre (founded in 1841), and has a charming interior and a good stock company. Its quaint front hall contains a museum of curiosities and paintings; and the rural Puritans coming up to town used to wander in hither, ostensibly to see these instructive collections, but not without a purpose to observe the dramas and comedies on the stage. Wherefore it was called "the Ministers' Theatre." It was entirely remodelled not many years ago, with scientific heating and ventilation, nearly fireproof construction, and decorations by Gaugengigl. Edwin Booth made his *début* here, in 1849, and William Warren played in this company for over fifty years. Next comes the granite building occupied till 1894 by the Suffolk-County Probate Office (Robert Grant, the novelist, is Probate Judge); and also (since 1833) by the Massachusetts Historical Society, founded in 1791, and the oldest in America. This is a costly and aristocratic association of 100 scholarly gentlemen, largely Harvard graduates, and has published three or four score volumes of collections and proceedings. Visitors are welcomed to the rooms, with the library of 40,000 books and 100,000 pamphlets, and a rich museum containing the swords of Miles Standish, Sir Wm. Pepperrell, Col. Church, Gov. Carver, Col. Prescott of Bunker Hill, and Capt. Linzee, R. N.; King Philip's samp-bowl; ancient weapons and standards; and portraits of Govs. Endicott, Winslow, Pownall, Winthrop, Dummer, Hutchinson, Strong, and Gore.

King's-Chapel Burial-Ground, the oldest in Boston, dates from 1630, and contains the remains of the three Govs. Winthrop, Gov. Shirley, Gov. Leverett, Gov. Endicott, John Winslow, Lady Andros, and Cotton, Davenport, Oxenbridge, and other illustrious divines, with Brattle, Sheafe and other great Colonial merchants, and learned judges and several gallant officers. The bronze tablets on the wall are interestingly inscribed. The trees here have a vast population of birds, whose debates and bickerings often attract popular attention.

King's Chapel, quaint, dark and lowly, has a venerable Londonish interior, with many mural tablets, rich stained windows, rows of columns

WASHINGTON STREET, NORTH FROM MACULLAR, PARKER & CO.
EAST SIDE OF WASHINGTON STREET, BETWEEN FRANKLIN AND WATER STREETS.

WASHINGTON STREET, SOUTH FROM MACULLAR, PARKER & CO.
EAST SIDE OF WASHINGTON STREET, BETWEEN FRANKLIN AND SUMMER STREETS.

and an antique pulpit. Here was erected the first Episcopal church in Boston, in 1689, enlarged in 1710, and replaced in 1749-54 by the present house, built by Peter Harrison, one of the architects of Blenheim Palace, of granite boulders from the Braintree plains. Three British sovereigns enriched the chapel with plate, paintings, books, etc., and here the first organ in New England was set up. The Vice-regal court and army and navy officers attended service here, in state pews, and the walls and pillars bore royal and noble escutcheons. The rector fled to Halifax with the British army, in 1776, carrying away the valuable plate, and services were discontinued for some years. In 1785, the society expurgated Trinitarianism from the liturgy, and became the first Unitarian church in New England. Washington attended an oratorio here in 1789, clad in black velvet, and gave five guineas toward finishing the portico.

Across Tremont St. from the Museum and Chapel were the homes of John Cotton, "the spiritual father of Boston," Gov. Sir Harry Vane, Chief-Justice Sewall, Lord Percy, Gov. Bellingham, Peter Faneuil, Lieut.-Gov. Phillips, Davenport (founder of New Haven), and other magnates.

In the block opposite the Boston Museum and the Probate Office is the pharmacy and chemical laboratory of the Theodore Metcalf Co., at 39 Tremont St. It is one of the oldest and most trustworthy in the city, and was founded in 1837. Its toilet and pharmaceutic preparations are esteemed as of the highest grade by the medical professions, and its essences and extracts are standards everywhere.

School St. was so named because the Latin School stood here from 1634 to 1844, first on the back part of the King's-Chapel site, and after 1748 on the Parker-House site. Here studied Franklin, Hancock, Adams, Everett, Eliot, Bowdoin, Eustis, Winthrop, Dana, Bowditch, Otis, Hillard, Sumner, Everett, Emerson, Motley, Parkman, Evarts, Devens, Mather, Channing, H. W. Beecher, J. F. Clarke, E. E. Hale, Phillips Brooks, and many other notables. The immense and famous white-marble Parker House was founded in 1855, by Harvey D. Parker; and after frequent enlargements in 1886 dedicated its superb eight-story chateau-roofed extension, on the corner of Tremont St. The late T. O. H. P. Burnham, the owner of this corner (1,984 feet of land) had a bitter feud with Parker, and for many years refused to sell him the coveted ground. When peaceful death closed their warfare, the land was acquired for the hotel extension, at a cost of $200,000. Parker's, besides its travellers' trade, is a downtown rendezvous for politicians, business men, and club-dinners; and has several popular dining-rooms. It was the first European-plan hotel in America.

The City Hall, on the north side of School St., east of King's Chapel, is a substantial and fireproof Renaissance building, of white Concord granite, erected in 1862-65, at a cost of $500,000; and filled with commodious rooms for the many and costly municipal departments. Efforts are under way to erect a $4,000,000 municipal palace, alongside

THEODORE METCALF COMPANY, PHARMACISTS AND CHEMISTS.
NO. 39 TREMONT STREET, WEST SIDE, OPPOSITE BOSTON MUSEUM.

THE CITY HALL.
SCHOOL STREET, BETWEEN TREMONT AND WASHINGTON STREETS.

THE PARKER HOUSE, J. R. WHIPPLE & CO., PROPRIETORS.
TREMONT, SOUTHEAST CORNER SCHOOL STREET, OPPOSITE CITY HALL.

the State House. On the lawn in front stands Ball's bronze statue (erected in 1879) of Josiah Quincy, the great mayor (in 1823-28), also a Congressman (1805-13) and President of Harvard (1829-45). The drapery is heavy, but the portrait is good. Here, also, stands R. S. Greenough's fine bronze statue of Franklin, erected in 1856, from a popular contribution of $20,000, and dedicated by R. C. Winthrop. The verd-antique marble base has four interesting bronze reliefs: on the south, the boy Franklin learning to print; east, signing the Declaration of Independence; north, drawing electricity from the clouds; and west, signing the Treaty of Paris, in 1782, ensuring American independence. Farther down School St., No. 19 was the site of the Cromwell's-Head Tavern, where Lieut.-Col. George Washington dwelt, in 1756; and just beyond, on Washington St., is the Old Corner Book-Store. On the site of 28 School St. stood the French Huguenot church, from 1714 to 1748; the first Catholic church, from 1788 to 1802; and the Universalist church (built in 1817), where Ballou and Chapin were pastors.

Nearly opposite King's Chapel begins the sacred Beacon St.; and on its northern corner stands the lofty Albion building, partly occupied by Houghton & Dutton's Bazar. On the southern corner stood the famous Tremont House, from 1828 to 1894, entertaining as guests Presidents Jackson and Johnson, Henry Clay. Thackeray, Dickens, the Prince of Wales, Jenny Lind, and other notables. It had a long and sombre granite front, with a heavy Doric portico, and, as Dickens wrote, " more galleries, colonnades, piazzas and passages than I can remember." It was pulled down in 1894, to be replaced by a huge office-building.

Tremont Temple, on Tremont St., alongside the Parker House, has long been the headquarters of the Baptists of New England. It occupies the site of the Tremont Theatre, which ran from 1827 to 1843, and saw the triumphs of Murdoch, Vandenhoff, Sheridan Knowles, John Gilbert, Fanny Kemble, Charlotte Cushman (her *début*), Ellen Tree and Fanny Ellsler. The Baptists bought it in 1843, and remodelled it for free services. It was burnt in 1852, 1879, and 1893, and as often rebuilt. The present temple cost $500,000; and has a front largely of colored marble patterns in the Venetian manner, a superb basilica-like audience-hall, an unusually beautiful organ, and (on the upper floors) the headquarters of several Baptist societies. The Temple Church is known as "The Strangers' Sabbath Home," and has a very large and enthusiastic membership and a famous choir. Dr. Geo. C. Lorimer is the pastor. The elegant white-granite building beyond, with Milmore's statues of Flora (north), Ceres and Pomona, was built in 1864 by the Mass. Horticultural Society, founded in 1829; and contains its library of 16,000 volumes, many interesting portraits, and two halls, famous for their superb exhibitions of roses, rhododendrons, chrysanthemums, and other flowers, and fruits. Across Bromfield St. is the Studio Building, with the studios of Copeland, Gaugengigl, Griggs, Lansil, Ordway, Shapleigh, and other artists. At 36-38 Bromfield St. is the Wesleyan Building, erected in

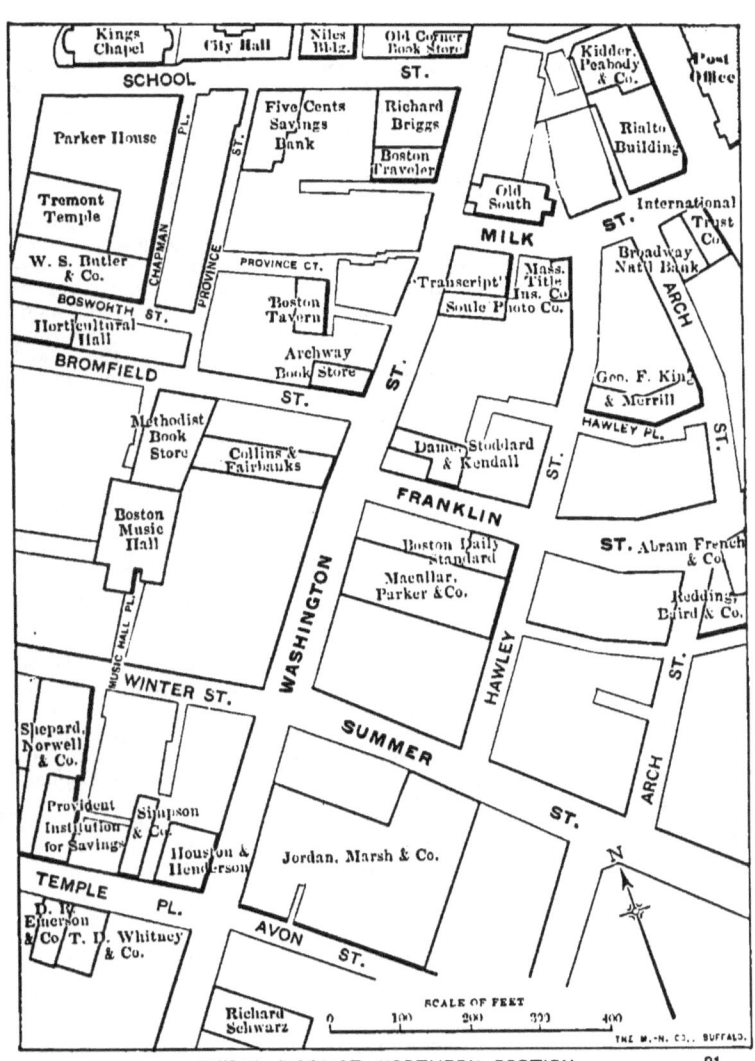

RETAIL DISTRICT, NORTHERN PORTION.

1870, and a notable Methodist headquarters, with the office of *Zion's Herald;* and next to it is the Bromfield-St. Methodist Church, founded in 1806. The rooms of the Boston Camera Club, including many famous amateurs, are at 50 Bromfield St.; and those of the Boston Press Club, at 12 Bosworth St.

The Granary Burial-Ground has more distinguished inmates than any other, including Govs. Bellingham, Dummer, Hancock, Sam. Adams, Bowdoin, Sullivan, Sumner and Gore; three signers of the Declaration of Independence, including Robert Treat Paine; Peter Faneuil, Paul Revere, Jeremy Belknap, Uriah Cotting, Chief-justice Sewall, Mintmaster Hull, Mayor Phillips, the Huguenot colony, and the victims of the Boston Massacre. Franklin's parents have the most conspicuous monument, erected in 1827 by citizens to replace one put up by the philosopher himself. This peaceful burial-ground was founded in 1660; and received its trees in 1830; the high iron fence and ivy-clad granite portal in 1840; and the memorial bronze tablets in 1882. A State monument to John Hancock is to be erected here soon. The glorious English elms set out in front of the burial-ground by Maj. Paddock, in 1762, were furtively cut down by our municipality in 1873.

The Granary, the largest building in Boston, was maintained by the town during most of the last century, holding 12,000 bushels of grain in reserve, to be sold at cost to the poor in time of famine. It stood on the place of the Park-St. Church, a plain old-fashioned meeting-house with a really fine spire, built by an English architect in 1809. The intense orthodoxy here preached won for the locality the name of Brimstone Corner; and the great choir had a wide renown.

Music Hall, built in 1852, at the end of Hamilton Place, opposite Park-St. Church (with main entrance from Winter St.), is the centre of musical culture, and the home of the world-renowned Boston Symphony Orchestra, the Handel and Hayden Society's oratorios, and the concerts of the Apollo, Cecilia, and other organizations. It is a large, lofty, simply adorned hall, admirable as to acoustics, and with 2,600 seats. The great organ of 5,474 pipes was in 1885 removed to the New-England Conservatory of Music; and near its place now stands Crawford's grand bronze statue of Beethoven. In this hall the churches ministered to by Theodore Parker, W. R. Alger, and W. H. H. Murray, held their services. In summer evenings popular promenade concerts, known as the "Pops," are held here.

Park Street leads up from the church alongside the Common to the State House. It formerly contained the Bridewell (built in 1712), the Workhouse for "rogues and vagabonds" (1738), and the Town Pound. Later, it was lined with patrician homes, now converted into stores, offices and club-rooms. At 2 Park St. Doll & Richards occupy a lofty and spacious building containing very interesting collections of engravings, etchings, photographs, sculpture and other art-works, and a multitude of fine paintings. This is in fact an art gallery which is of much

DOLL & RICHARDS, FINE PAINTINGS AND ENGRAVINGS.
NO. 2 PARK ST., BETWEEN TREMONT AND BEACON STREETS.

interest to all visitors. In the Quincy mansion (No. 4) are the offices of Houghton, Mifflin & Co., publishers of the works of the most remarkable group of eminent American authors, and of the Atlantic Monthly ; and next door are the rooms of the New-England Woman's Club and the Woman's Journal. At 8 Park St., the old Abbott-Lawrence mansion, is the Union Club, founded in 1863, to advance the cause of the imperilled American Republic, and presided over successively by Everett, Loring, Dana, Lee, Shaw, Russell, and Lowell ; Sumner, Andrew, Hoar, Rice, Gray and other patriots holding many councils here. It is now an aristocratic social club, with about 500 members, mostly professional men no longer young. Next above is the former home of Gov. Gore, artist Malbone, Secretary-of-War Dexter, and George Ticknor (from 1830 to 1871), the illustrious scholar. Here Lafayette dwelt for a week, in 1824. The Appalachian Mountain Club, with 1,000 members, has its rooms here.

Boston Common, the most famous of American parks, historically, is a noble expanse of 48 undulating acres of green turf and tall forest trees, in the very heart of the Puritan City. It was set apart in the very beginning, when a boulder-strewn and treeless expanse of huckleberry bushes, "for a trayning field and the feeding of cattell"; and penalties awaited all who spread stones, trash or carrion thereupon. The lowing kine were excluded in 1830, but the armed train-bands still march upon the parade-ground. Grand armies have been reviewed here ; Lord Amherst's brigades of Marlborough's British veterans, Baron de Vioménil's shining army of Rochambeau's French troops, Washington's columns of victorious American infantry, and countless regiments on the way to the War for the Union, and militia commands of later days. There were only three trees here in colonial times, but the great Mall on Tremont St. was planted in 1722-34, the Beacon-St. Mall in 1815-16, that on Charles St. in 1823, and that on Park St. in 1826. Most of the trees were cut down in 1775-76, for fuel by the British garrison, whose camps and redoubts covered the Common ; and on the day of their departure they set about to destroy those remaining, but were prevented by Gen. Howe. Military executions, duels, revivals by Whitefield and Lee, hangings of Quakers and insurgent Indians, marquee banquets, drum-head elections, and many other picturesque incidents have invested this venerable public domain with profound interest. The Ridge Path (so-called for a century), paved with asphalt blocks, and overarched by trees, leads from West St. to the Providence station, and is the busiest thoroughfare of the Common. The Long Path, a narrow track from Joy St. to Boylston St., is immortalized in Dr. Holmes's *Autocrat of the Breakfast Table*. It passes the Frog Pond, and the enrailed site of the Great Elm, older than Boston, which was blown down in 1876. In the burying-ground (opened in 1757), hundreds of British soldiers lie, in long trenches ; and also the remains of the artist Stuart and many others. Near Tremont St. is the Crispus Attucks Monument, erected in 1888, to the victims of the Boston Massacre of 1770, bearing an energetic bronze statue of Revolution breaking the

BOSTON COMMON.
TREMONT, PARK, BEACON, CHARLES AND BOYLSTON STREETS.

BOSTON COMMON.
TREMONT, PARK, BEACON, CHARLES AND BOYLSTON STREETS.

chains of tyranny. Above appear the names of the slain ; below, a bas-relief showing the scene of the affray. Near Park St. is the arid Brewer Fountain, whose statues of Neptune, Amphitrite, Acis and Galatea are popularly supposed to represent the Four Seasons ("of perpetual drought," Howells says). Near the State House is the monument (still in process of construction) designed by St. Gaudens to commemorate the valor of Col. Robert G. Shaw, slain in storming Fort Wagner, S. C., and "buried with his niggers." On Flagstaff Hill, over the parade, rises the Army and Navy Monument, erected in 1871-77, from Martin Milmore's design, at a cost of $75,000. It is a lofty white-granite Roman Doric column, bearing a colossal statue of the Genius of America, facing the south, the American flag in one hand, and in the other laurel wreaths and a drawn sword. At the base are high-relief statues of the North, South, East and West ; below these, on projecting pedestals, bronze statues of Peace, the Sailor (a capital work), the Muse of History and the Soldier. The great bronze reliefs are : The Departure for the War, showing Lowell, Shaw, Butler, Andrew, Phillips, Longfellow, Vinton, Phillips Brooks and others ; the Sanitary Commission, with E. E. Hale, J. R. Lowell, Rice, Ticknor, and Wilder ; The Return from the War, with Andrew, Bartlett, Banks, Devens, Claflin and Sumner ; and the Departure of the Sailors and a naval battle. The inscription, by President Eliot of Harvard, is :

TO THE MEN OF BOSTON WHO DIED FOR THEIR COUNTRY ON LAND AND SEA IN THE WAR WHICH KEPT THE UNION WHOLE, DESTROYED SLAVERY, AND MAINTAINED THE CONSTITUTION, THE GRATEFUL CITY HAS BUILT THIS MONUMENT THAT THEIR EXAMPLE MAY SPEAK TO COMING GENERATIONS.

In the old days, the tides of the Back Bay flowed along the western side of the Common, from which there was a charming sunset view across the water to "the country shore" of Brookline. The telescope man (Dr. Holmes's "Galileo of the Mall") and many itinerant musicians, peddlers and fakirs haunt the edges of the Common ; youths play ball on the Parade ; pensive poets and tramps and tired shoppers and rustics rest upon the benches ; nurse-maids and watery dogs haunt the Frog Pond ; and on summer evenings thousands of people assemble here at the fine band-concerts.

Returning from this divagation, to Tremont and Park Sts., let us recall that, in 1800, the east side of Tremont St., from Scollay Square to Boylston St., had only twenty scattered houses, mostly wooden dwellings, with trees and rambling outbuildings.

Winter St. is a short and narrow way, leading to Washington St., crowded with bright retail stores, — dry goods, trimmings, jewelry stores, etc., — hence also crowded with ladies anxiously shopping. The greatest attraction in Winter St. is the extensive establishment of Shepard, Norwell & Co., 26 to 42, one of the largest, best stocked and most satisfac-

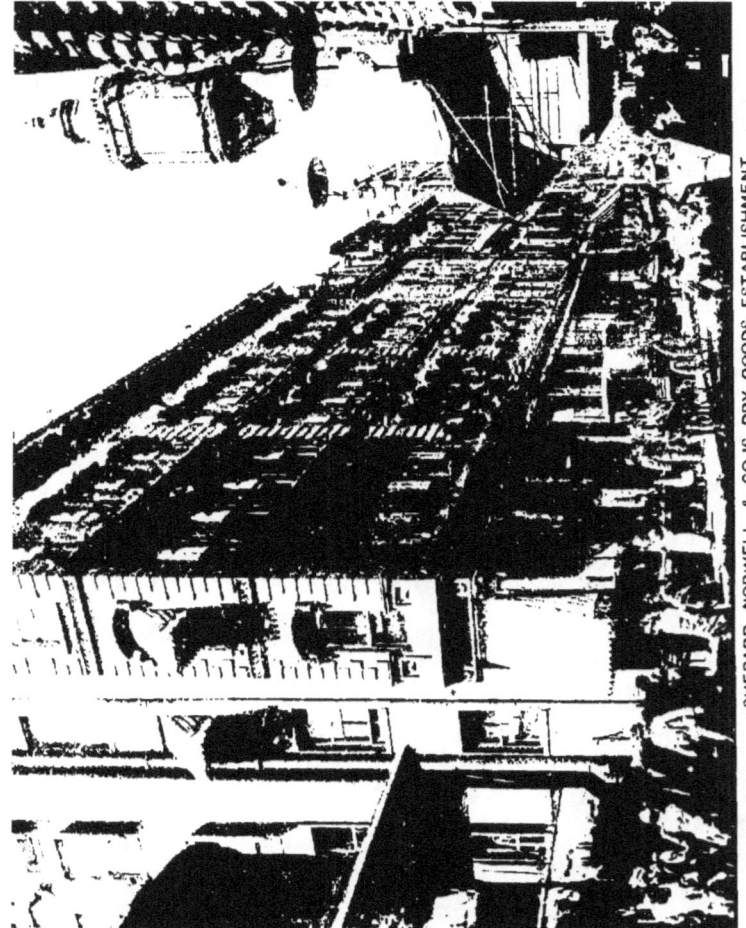

SHEPARD, NORWELL & CO.'S DRY GOODS ESTABLISHMENT.
WINTER STREET, SOUTH SIDE, EXTENDING THROUGH TO TEMPLE PLACE, BETWEEN WASHINGTON AND TREMONT STREETS.

tory of Boston's dry-goods houses, including many varied departments. It extends through the block to Temple Place. On the north side of Winter St. is the entrance to Music Hall. In Winter Place is the Winter-Place Hotel, which succeeded Ober's French Restaurant. It is an exceptionally attractive restaurant, saloon and café,—the most costly and showy in the city. At Winter St. and Winter Place is the site of Sam. Adams's home.

On Tremont St., between Winter St. and Temple Place, rises the gray Virginia sandstone portico of St. Paul's Church (Episcopal), built in 1820, to be a model of ancient classic art, and with the intent of having carvings representing St. Paul and Agrippa in the pediment. The simple and beautiful interior has a panelled cylindrical ceiling, a rich chancel window showing St. Paul at Athens, several mural tablets, the pew of Daniel Webster (No. 25), and, underneath, many tombs, now no longer in use.

At Tremont St. and Temple Place, next St. Paul's, is the dark granite building erected in 1830-32 for a Masonic Temple, and later the seat of the school kept by A. B. Alcott and Margaret Fuller, and of performances by Fanny Kemble and Ole Bull. From 1858 to 1885 it belonged to the United-States Government, and was the seat of the Federal courts. Skilful engineers then lifted it high into the air, and put under it two tall stories of iron pillars and glass windows; and the whole structure, very decidedly remodelled, has since been occupied by the fashionable and popular dry-goods establishment of R. H. Stearns & Co.

Temple Place, one block long, from Tremont to Washington St., abounding in street-cars, is made bright by the ladies shopping. Here stands the Provident Institution for Savings, the oldest savings-bank in America, founded in 1816, and holding nearly $30,000,000 on deposit. Emerson's, at 35 Temple Place, was founded in 1842 by D. R. Emerson, and has a very large retail trade in rich laces, trimmings, buttons, and other small wares, in amazing variety. T. D. Whitney & Co., at 39 Temple Place, have one of the finest linen stores in the United States, whence the households and wardrobes of thousands of well-to-do families are supplied. The Whitney linen store has a fame far beyond the limits of Boston, and from many miles around the city come its patrons.

Beyond Temple Place, Tremont St. affords a picturesquely brilliant scene, with handsome stores on one side, and the abundant foliage of the Common on the other. The sidewalk is broad, and pleasantly accommodates the crowds of promenaders, from Harrison-avenue Chinamen and North-End dagoes up to learned Puritan scholars or violet-bearing Symphony girls. This thoroughfare, with attractive shops on one side and umbrageous gardens on the other, leading up to a hill crowned by a famous public building, has been likened to the ever-charming Princes St. in Edinburgh. Dickens said: "My old likeness of Boston to Edinburgh has been constantly revived."

West St. once had the pillory and whipping-post at its head. At No. 30 is the Universalist Publishing House and headquarters, and the office

T. D. WHITNEY & CO., WHITNEY'S LINEN STORE.
NO. 39 TEMPLE PLACE, SOUTH SIDE, BETWEEN TREMONT AND WASHINGTON STREETS.

of *The Christian Leader.* Here are the main offices of the Boston and Bay-State Gas-Light Companies, and various candy and other retail stores.

Tremont St., towards Boylston, for some years has been called Piano Row, for a long row of piano agencies occupied a good portion of the block; but of late most of these have migrated to Boylston St. Chickering Hall, at 152 Tremont St., was for many years a favorite place for fashionable musicales, and the headquarters of the musical profession. Opposite the departing "Piano Row" stands the tumultuous Massacre (or Crispus Attucks) Monument, on the Common.

The Tremont Theatre, at 176 Tremont St., dates from 1889, and is one of the most beautiful and fashionable play-houses in Boston, celebrated for its Renaissance decorations, delicate colorings, and other charming details. It occupies the site of the Haymarket Theatre, opened in 1796.

The Masonic Temple, fronting on the Common, at Tremont and Boylston Sts., is a noble granite building, seven stories high, and 85 feet front, with a tower 121 feet high. The pillars of rare marble, Jachin and Boaz, adorn the sides of the entrance. All above the ground-floor is occupied by Masonic organizations; and the Corinthian, Egyptian and Gothic halls are very attractive. The Temple was founded in 1864, and dedicated on St. John's day, 1867, with an immense Masonic street parade, in which President Andrew Johnson appeared. Here meet the Grand Lodge of Massachusetts, the Grand Royal Arch Chapter, the Grand Council Royal and Select Masters, the Grand Commandery of Knights Templar, and about 30 lodges, besides the lodges of the Ancient and Accepted Scottish Rite. The first American Masonic lodge was organized in Boston, in 1733; St. Andrew's Lodge, for many decades the owner of the Green-Dragon Tavern, or Freemason's Arms, was chartered by the Grand Lodge of Scotland in 1756; and later this and certain lodges in the British regiments formed the first grand lodge, of which Gen. Warren and Paul Revere became Grand Masters. The temple is intended "to suggest the most effective poetical and historical associations connected with the Masonic institution."

Where Tremont St. leaves the Common, to meander away into the remote South End, Boylston St. turns to the right toward the sumptuous Back-Bay District, and to the left to the crowded Washington St. On one corner is the Hotel Pelham, a huge apartment and office house; and another, the Hotel Boylston, an office-building belonging to the Adams estate, on the site of the home of President J. Q. Adams and the birthplace of C. F. Adams, Sr.

The Young Men's Christian Union has a handsome and spacious Gothic building of Ohio sandstone (all paid for), with a clock-tower, at 48 Boylston St.; and welcomes strangers to its pleasant parlors, halls, reading and correspondence rooms, and other departments, open every day and evening. The Union dates from 1851, and is a great philanthropic agency, with 5,000 members, classes, games, baths, an immense

THE MASONIC TEMPLE.
102 TREMONT STREET, NORTHEAST CORNER OF BOYLSTON STREET, OPPOSITE THE COMMON.

YOUNG MEN'S CHRISTIAN UNION.
NO. 48 BOYLSTON STREET, BETWEEN TREMONT AND WASHINGTON STREETS.

gymnasium, employment agency, and library. Its great usefulness is mainly due to the eminently practical president, William H. Baldwin, who has energetically devoted the better part of a lifetime to its welfare. The Hotel Reynolds, at Boylston and Washington Sts., with 250 rooms, has in its public halls rich flower-paintings by Abbott Graves.

The light sandstone Continental Building, at Boylston and Washington Sts., covers the site of the Boylston Market, which stood from 1809 to 1888. It is an office-building, with a clothing-store on the ground floor, and the general offices and supply headquarters of Bouvé, Crawford & Co., the makers of the "Crawford Shoe," on the second story.

Opposite the foot of Boylston St., high up on 630 Washington St., is a tablet carved with a tree, showing where the Liberty Tree stood, and the Sons of Liberty held their fiery meetings before the Revolution, and hung effigies of British nobles. Close to the Liberty-Tree block, at 658 Washington St., is the huge and handsome Pray Building, built and owned by John H. Pray, Sons & Co., a business founded in 1817, and transacting one of the most extensive trades in the world, in all varieties of carpets, mattings, rugs, and upholsteries. On the upper floors of this building are the executive offices of the General Society of Christian Endeavor, whose hosts, numbering, it is said, upwards of 75,000, will convene in Boston in July, 1895. Here, too, are the offices of *The Golden Rule*, a family weekly, the Prang Educational Co. and L. Prang & Co., the world-famous art-publishers.

Essex St. curves away to the harbor, passing, a block east, the Chinese quarter, which extends along Harrison Avenue from Essex to Kneeland Sts. The Harrison-Avenue extension in 1882 destroyed the home of Wendell Phillips, on the north side of Essex St.; and that of Theodore Parker, at Exeter Place.

At Washington and Essex Sts. is the office of *The Pilot*, a strong Catholic newspaper, founded in 1838.

Washington St., narrow, winding and picturesque, has been called the most crowded thoroughfare in the world. Its sharp curves, terminated by quaint or handsome buildings, produce startling architectural effects; its narrow sidewalks are trod by jostling thousands; and its roadway is a close jam of vehicles. The block between Boylston and West Sts. is the Theatre District, affording a brilliant and inspiring scene at evening and matinée hours. The Park Theatre is a handsome house, built for H. E. Abbey in 1879, but now leased by John Stetson. Opposite stood until it was burned (in 1894) the Globe Theatre, founded in 1867, where Neilson, Bernhardt, Duse, and Salvini played. B. F. Keith's New Theatre, opened in 1882, on the site of the Lion Theatre of 1836, and quite recently rebuilt, is said to be the handsomest small theatre in the world. It gives genteel continuous vaudeville and varieties from 10 A. M. to 10 P. M., at low prices.

The Boston Theatre, built in 1854, is one of the largest and best in America, with seats for 3,000, an enormous stage, and handsome lobbies.

BOUVÉ, CRAWFORD & CO., CORPORATION. — "THE CRAWFORD SHOE."
BOYLSTON BUILDING, WASHINGTON STREET, SOUTHWEST CORNER OF BOYLSTON STREET.

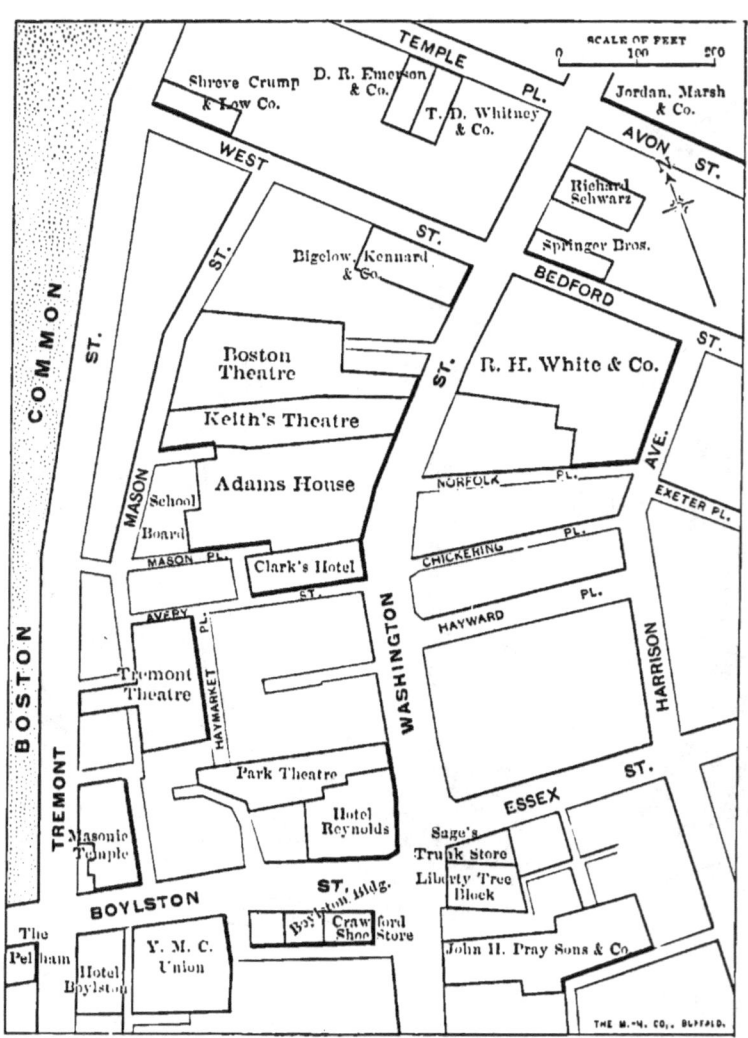

RETAIL DISTRICT, SOUTHERN PORTION.

JOHN H. PRAY, SONS & CO., CARPETS, RUGS AND UPHOLSTERY.
PRAY'S BUILDING, NO. 658 WASHINGTON STREET, OPPOSITE BOYLSTON STREET.

It is especially adapted to grand opera and spectacular pieces; and has witnessed the best work of Booth and Owens, Forrest and Fechter, Jefferson and McCullough, Ristori and Salvini, Janauschek and Sothern, Irving and Terry, besides the state balls given to the Prince of Wales and the Grand Duke Alexis. The Elks' building is at 24 Hayward Place.

In the midst of these theatres are the lofty, triple-towered marble walls of the Adams House, a European-plan hotel of 400 apartments, with a noble public dining-hall and singularly attractive dining and writing rooms. It occupies the site of the ancient Lamb Tavern, opened in 1745; and bears the name of a former proprietor, the father of "Oliver Optic." By its side is Clark's Hotel, a popular resort for men.

In every direction appear well-known firm-names, from whose shops myriads of shoppers from all New England replenish their worn-out clothing and jewelry, books and music, and a thousand other articles. It forms a lively and pleasing scene, extending over the short streets leading westward to the trees of the Common, and those toward the wholesale district, "stretching saltwards to the docks." Note the long-established jewelry-store of Bigelow, Kennard & Co., at Washington St., southwest corner of West St., with its extensive and varied artistic treasures of jewelry, silverware, plated ware, precious stones, watches, bronzes, etc. The house dates back many years, and is one of the oldest and most highly esteemed firms in Boston.

On Washington St., at the southeast corner of Bedford, is the enormous, flamboyant Gothic structure of R. H. White & Co., the largest and grandest retail establishment in New England.

Among the most fascinating of the stores on Washington St. is the great toy emporium of Richard Schwarz, at 484 and 486, by far the largest concern of its kind in the city. Everything desirable in imported or domestic toys, games and fancy goods, from the tiniest to the biggest, from the lowest-priced to the most costly, is shown here in endless variety. At Temple Place is the dry-goods house of Houston & Henderson.

At the corner of Washington and Avon Sts. is the immense Palladian building of Jordan, Marsh & Co., which easily ranks equal to the greatest bazaars of the world. At 451 and 453 Washington St. is the renowned music-publishing house of the Oliver Ditson Company.

On Summer St., east of Washington St., is the massive granite building, which is part of the group occupied by the substantial and esteemed dry-goods establishment of C. F. Hovey & Co.

At 398 and 400 are the Macullar, Parker & Company's buildings, where, in light and airy rooms, 600 liberally paid and generously treated employees make upon honor the finest clothing possible, all of which is sold at retail on the main floor. At 403 are the offices of the American Waltham Watch Company, whose vast works at Waltham employ 2,000 skilled artisans. At 81 Hawley St., is the wholesale piece goods department of Macullar, Parker & Co.

THEATRE DISTRICT: WASHINGTON STREET, BETWEEN WEST AND BOYLSTON STREETS.
VIEW LOOKING SOUTHWARD FROM WEST STREET.

BIGELOW, KENNARD & CO., JEWELERS AND SILVERSMITHS.
WASHINGTON STREET, SOUTHWEST CORNER OF WEST STREET.

RICHARD SCHWARZ, IMPORTER, JOBBER AND RETAILER OF TOYS.
NOS. 484 AND 486 WASHINGTON STREET, BETWEEN BEDFORD AND AVON STREETS.

On Franklin St., at the southwest corner of Hawley St., just one block east of Washington St., is the *Boston Daily Standard*, a paper started in 1895, with absolutely positive American ideas. It is a bright home newspaper, giving all the important news and eliminating the details of crimes and immoralities. It has quite a strong support through this section of the country, and bids fair to make a permanent success.

The first newspaper in America, *Publick Occurrences*, appeared in Boston in 1690, and was forthwith suppressed by the General Court. The next, and the first permanent paper in America, was *The Boston News-Letter*, published weekly from 1704 to 1776.

At 381, immediately opposite the head of Franklin St., is the aristocratic and extensive Collins & Fairbanks establishment, noted for its rich display of fashionable hats and caps, canes and umbrellas, a large portion of the stock being made or imported exclusively for this firm. At 365 is the Archway book-store of DeWolfe, Fiske & Co., with an extensive stock of popular books. At 374, just north of Franklin St.,

SUFFOLK SAVINGS BANK.   BOSTON MUSEUM.
TREMONT STREET, WEST SIDE, NORTH FROM SCHOOL STREET.

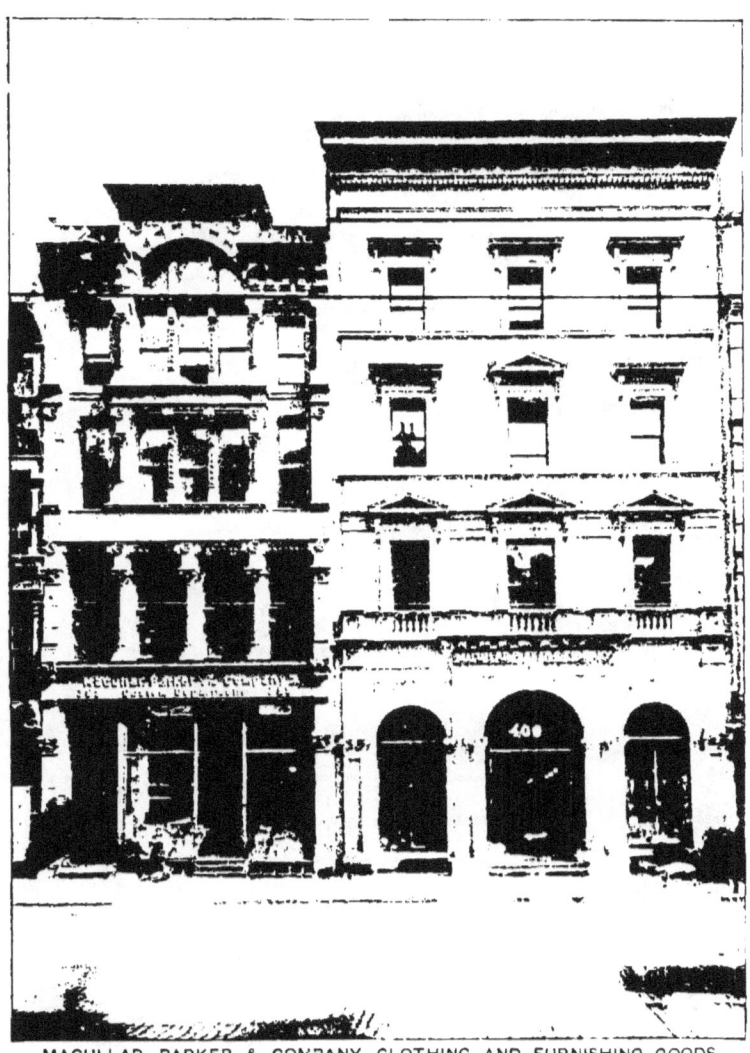

MACULLAR, PARKER & COMPANY, CLOTHING AND FURNISHING GOODS.
NOS. 398 AND 400 WASHINGTON STREET, BETWEEN FRANKLIN AND SUMMER STREETS.

MACULLAR, PARKER & COMPANY, WHOLESALE PIECE GOODS.
HAWLEY STREET FRONT, NO. 81 HAWLEY, EXTENDING TO 398 AND 400 WASHINGTON STREET.

THE BOSTON DAILY STANDARD.
FRANKLIN ST., SOUTHWEST CORNER OF HAWLEY ST., ONE BLOCK EAST OF WASHINGTON ST.

and directly opposite Bromfield St., is the old and trustworthy house of Dame, Stoddard & Kendall, founded in 1800, and importing very largely from Europe, carrying an unsurpassed stock of cutlery, fine hardware, fishing tackle, leather goods, athletic goods, and kindred wares, which

SCOLLAY SQUARE.   BOSTON MUSEUM.   MASS. HISTORICAL SOCIETY.
TREMONT STREET, EAST SIDE, NORTH FROM KING'S CHAPEL.

are retailed at this store, and which are also sold to wholesalers and jobbers throughout the whole country. At 338, midway between Franklin and Milk Sts., are the exhibition and sale rooms of the Soule Photograph Co., where may be obtained, mounted and unmounted photographs of many thousand subjects, this being probably the largest collection of its class to be found on the continent. Back of the rows of buildings on Washington St. may be seen the top of one of Boston's peculiar hotels, known as Clark's Boston Tavern, patronized solely by men. It is a ten-story building, of fire-proof construction, and has a first-class restaurant, and comfortable accommodations. It occupies a part of the site of the old Province House, which stood from 1667 to 1864, and which in 1715 became the State residence of the vice-regal governors. It was finally burned, but its walls remain in other structures on the same site.

At the corner of Washington and Milk Sts. is the granite building of the *Boston Transcript*, the favorite family tea-table paper, always refined and literary in tone. It is staunchly Republican, and was founded in 1830. At 17 Milk St., just below the Transcript Building, is the birth-

COLLINS & FAIRBANKS, HATTERS.
NO. 381 WASHINGTON STREET, IMMEDIATELY OPPOSITE FRANKLIN STREET.

DAME, STODDARD & KENDALL, CUTLERY, AQUATIC AND ATHLETIC GOODS.
NO. 374 WASHINGTON STREET, NEAR FRANKLIN STREET, AND OPPOSITE BROMFIELD STREET.

SOULE PHOTOGRAPH CO., PHOTOGRAPHERS AND PUBLISHERS.
NO. 333 WASHINGTON, BETWEEN FRANKLIN AND MILK STREETS.

THE OLD SOUTH.
WASHINGTON, NORTHEAST COR. MILK STREET.

place of Franklin; and immediately opposite, at No. 10, is the venerable house of Lee & Shepard, with its creditable list of publications.

The Old South Meeting-House lifts its ivy-clad tower and venerable steeple at Washington and Milk Sts. The newly-formed Third Church built here, in 1670, on the site of Gov. Winthrop's garden, a cedar meeting house, in which Franklin was baptized, and Judge Sewall confessed his error as to the witchcraft troubles. The present structure, dating from 1729, was the scene of the great patriotic town-meetings before the Revolution, the departing point of the Tea-Party Indians, the cavalry riding-school of the British garrison, the hall of the annual Election Sermons for 160 years, and many other stirring events. The advance of trade drove the parishioners to distant homes, wherefore the Third Society gave up this church, and built a new one, on the Back Bay, in 1872-74. The old site had an immense value for business purposes; and the society sold it (with the building) to the Old South Preservation Committee for $430,000, to be preserved as "The Nursery and Sanctuary of Freedom." It is occupied by a rich and varied museum of Colonial and Revolutionary relics, weapons, flags, furniture, pictures, etc., open daily,

HEAD OF MILK STREET, THE OLD SOUTH, AND BURNHAM ANTIQUE BOOKSTORE.
MILK STREET, NORTHEAST CORNER OF WASHINGTON STREET.

THE BOSTON TRAVELER. AN EVENING NEWSPAPER.
NO. 309 WASHINGTON STREET, OPPOSITE MILK STREET AND THE OLD SOUTH.

for 25 cents, the revenue going to the preservation fund. Series of free historical lectures are given here every year by famous scholars. The crypts contain Burnham's vast antiquarian book-store, with scores of thousands of volumes, old and new, amid which antiquaries and bibliophiles find many treasures. Just north of the Old South, Gov. Winthrop's house stood until 1775, when the half-frozen British garrison tore it down for fuel. At 307 Washington St., opposite the Old South, are the offices, editorial and printing rooms of the *Boston Traveler*, established in 1845, half a century ago, and now issuing every evening a twelve-page paper at one cent. It is clean, newsy and readable, and under its present energetic and experienced management it has gained a solid foothold among

FRANKLIN STATUE -- CITY HALL -- QUINCY STATUE.

the people, with a constantly increasing circulation and advertising patronage. At 301 is the publishing and bookselling house of Estes & Lauriat, with an extensive stock of imported books.

The Old Corner Bookstore, at School (leading to the City Hall) and Washington Sts., the oldest brick building in Boston, was erected in 1712, on the site of Anne Hutchinson's dwelling; and since 1828 has been a book-store, occupied for many years by Ticknor & Fields, and frequented by Longfellow and Lowell, Holmes and Whittier, Emerson and Thoreau, Dickens and Thackeray, and other illustrious authors. Here Oliver Ditson began his music business, at a small corner counter, in 1833. Besides

THE OLD CORNER BOOKSTORE, DAMRELL & UPHAM.
WASHINGTON STREET, NORTHWEST CORNER OF SCHOOL STREET.

general literature, the store, now pertaining to Damrell & Upham, has large Episcopal and guide-book and map departments. Spring Lane, almost opposite, contained the great spring of sweet water which attracted the colonists to Boston.

A tall, quaint office-structure called the Carter Building, with narrow front and peculiar shape, occupies the square between Spring Lane and Water St., both of which lead to the Post Office.

Newspaper Row covers both sides of a long bow-shaped block along Washington St., between Water and State Sts., and oftentimes is the most crowded part of the city. From this block are published the *Journal*, the *Post*, the *Herald*, the *Advertiser*, the *Record*, and the *Globe*, all of the daily papers excepting the *Traveler*, *Transcript*, and *Standard*.

GRANARY BURYING GROUND, TREMONT STREET, BETWEEN BEACON AND PARK STREETS.

The *Journal*, at Washington and Water Sts., is a thoroughly good morning and evening paper (founded in 1833) of great circulation, intensely devoted to Republicanism.

The *Post*, a bright Democratic one-cent morning paper, with a three-cent Sunday edition, dates from 1831, and has its home at 259 Washington St. The *Boston Herald*, at 255, the foremost of all the New-England papers, has one of the finest and best-equipped newspaper buildings in existence (erected in 1877-78), six stories high, in French Renaissance architecture. It is independent in politics. It was founded in 1846; and has several admirable daily editions, and a superb Sunday issue. The white-marble building at 248 was built for the *Advertiser*, "the Respect-

THE BOSTON HERALD.
NO. 255 WASHINGTON STREET, BETWEEN SCHOOL AND COURT STREETS.

LITTLE, BROWN & CO., IMPORTERS, BOOKSELLERS AND PUBLISHERS.
NO. 254 WASHINGTON STREET, EAST SIDE. NORTH OF WATER STREET.

able Daily," the oldest daily paper in Boston, founded in 1813, and from 1814 to 1864 directed by Nathan Hale, who married Edward Everett's sister, and whose son was E. E. Hale. The paper has always been calm, dignified and refined, Republican in politics, and paying special attention to maritime and commercial news. The *Evening Record* is a bright, spicy, and pungent penny paper, started in 1884, by the *Advertiser* corporation. At 236-238 the *Globe*, a strictly Democratic two-cent paper, with several editions each day, and with a monster Sunday paper, has a huge and handsome brown-stone building. It was started as a high-class literary journal, in 1872, by Maturin M. Ballou and others; and after several changes came under the present management, which has made it a marked success as a wide-awake newsgatherer for the masses, with an immense circulation.

In the midst of the newspapers, at 254, is the eminent publishing and importing house of Little, Brown & Co., with its own exceptionally strong list of standard books on law, history, and general literature, and the choicest stock of imported and American books of all publishers. The business was established over a century ago. The building belongs to Harvard University.

In and around Newspaper Row are many well-known periodicals; and likewise enterprising shops of all kinds, notably the Crawford Shoe-store, one of the scores of branches of Bouvé, Crawford & Co., whose signs cover the whole building at 225.

PARK STREET CHURCH AND GRANARY BURYING GROUND, TREMONT AND PARK STREETS.

Eating-places, too, abound, including the Silver Grill, 263, Dennett's, 243, Mrs. Atkinson's, 239, Hart's Imperial, 231, and Thompson's Spa, at 219.

Two quaint pedestrians' alleys lead to Court Square, back of the City Hall — Williams Court and Court Avenue, winding around by the hidden main entrance of Young's Hotel. It is only a few steps from Newspaper Row to the Old State House and State St., and to Court St., curving around to Scollay Square.

"THE CRAWFORD SHOE" STORE, BOUVE, CRAWFORD & CO.
NO. 225 WASHINGTON STREET, NORTH OF THE "HERALD" AND OPPOSITE THE "GLOBE."

THE BACK-BAY DISTRICT.

THIS grandly interesting part of Boston was made by filling up the immense salty bay of the Charles River back of Boston. It is now a very beautiful residence-quarter, with the fine churches, notable public buildings, and palatial hotels — in fact, the show district, the Court end, of the city. The Back-Bay cars, as well as other lines, taken at Scollay Square, or on Tremont St. along the Common, traverse this section. Turning from Tremont into Boylston St. (the ancient Frog Lane), at the south end of the Common, we pass the Hotel Pelham (studios and offices); the building occupied by the Public Library from 1858 to 1895; and the secluded Boylston Place, in which (at No. 4) stands the house of the Tavern Club, made up of 100 authors, artists and musicians. Howells and C. E. Norton have been its presidents; and receptions have been given to Holmes, Booth, Irving, Sala, and other great men. At 18 Boyl-

TREMONT STREET MALL, LOOKING NORTH TO PARK STREET CHURCH.

ston Place is the Boston Library, founded in 1794, with 28,000 volumes; and at No. 19, the Mass. Medical Society. One side of Boylston St. is the Common, where the excavating for the construction of the Subway has begun as this book goes to press.

The Subway is for the relief of the congestion in the heart of Boston by the opening of an underground street across the centre of the city. This substreet will extend from the Union Station to the junction of Tremont St. and Shawmut Avenue, and by a branch to the Boston & Providence Railroad station. It will be water-tight, brilliantly lighted and perfectly ventilated, warmer in winter and cooler in summer than the surface streets. All the street-car tracks over its line will be removed from the surface and run through it, thus affording a complete clearance of the surface streets, for the better accommodation of travel and avoidance of its existing dangers. By ingenious engineering there will be no grade crossing in the Subway, and passengers can take any car desired without crossing a track.

On the north side of Boylston St., about midway between Tremont St. and Park Square, at 156, is the very interesting establishment of the Murdock Parlor Grate Company, a title somewhat misleading from the fact that, besides parlor grates, this concern manufactures and puts up an infinite variety of high art metal, mosaic and woodwork, and supplies every necessity or ornament of the modern or ancient fireplace. A visit to this establishment will be well repaid.

ARMY AND NAVY MONUMENT, BOSTON COMMON.

Park Square is the diverging point of the broad and beautiful Columbus Avenue, to the South End, and Charles St., to the West End. It contains Ball's bronze Emancipation Group, showing Abraham Lincoln, and a slave kneeling at his feet, with fetters falling away. The pedestal is of polished red granite. This statuary was cast at Munich in 1879, at a cost of $17,000, and given by Moses Kimball. Here is the majestic Gothic terminal of the Providence Division of the N. Y., N. H. & H. R. R. to Providence (and New York), erected at a cost of $800,000, with a noble clock-tower, a beautiful Gothic hall (180 by 44 feet, and 80 feet high), and a very thorough equipment. It is 850 feet long, one of the largest in the world. This station is the terminal of the trains connecting with the glorious Sound steamers for New York, — the "Providence Line," and the "Fall-River Line." The Providence road was chartered in 1831, and finished in 1835. The station stands on the beach whence the British troops embarked on their mournful raid upon Lexington, in 1775. The tall building on the east corner of Boylston St. occupies the site of the gun-houses of the Sea Fencibles and New-England Guards, and Wm. M. Hunt's studio. On Carver St., back of it, Julian Hawthorne was born. Charles St. starts at Park Square, and runs between the Common and the Public Garden.

MURDOCK PARLOR GRATE CO., FIRE PLACES AND ART METAL AND MOSAIC WORK.
NO. 166 BOYLSTON STREET, SOUTH SIDE OF BOSTON COMMON, BETWEEN TREMONT STREET AND PARK SQUARE.

Boylston St. thence westward, facing the Public Garden, was until lately a favorite residence-quarter, but is fast being occupied by fashionable retail stores.

A prominent attraction for all visitors and residents is the famous Williams & Everett art-gallery, at 190, with its rich artistic interior and its collection of European and American paintings, etchings, carbons, statuary and photographs, many exhibited in ingenious, exquisite and appropriate frames from the firm's own shops. This historic firm began in 1810, and took its present style in 1855. The most prominent establishment on Boylston St. is the great and handsome brown-stone building of L. P. Hollander & Co., 202 to 210, which is filled with the finest and

TREMONT STREET, SOUTH OF PARK STREET. ENTRANCE TO BOSTON COMMON.

most exquisite fabrics and costumes for ladies and children, and a vast variety of dainty articles for personal adornment. It is the most aristocratic establishment of its kind in New England. On Boylston St., at 198, is Vercelli's, where Italian table d'hôte dinners are served and at Church St. is the Thorndike, a pleasant and well-situated European-plan hotel, built in 1885-86.

The Public Garden occupies a site which, with the parade ground on the Common, was formerly covered with marshes and salt water, flowing freely with the sea-tides. Rope-walks were erected here in 1794; but subsequently the area was filled in, and in 1862 the municipality fenced, graded and laid out the Garden. It is now a very beautiful park of 24 acres, with groups of choice trees and shrubbery, rich lawns, statuary, and a 4-acre lake abounding in quaint boats and crossed by "the Bridge of Size" (a ponderous affair, for footmen). The flower display is one of the most superb in the world, being drawn from millions of plants in the City hot-houses. In late spring come 100,000 crocuses, 500,000 or more vivid tulips and hyacinths, narcissi and lilies, and 100,000 golden lilies of Japan, followed by 700,000 pansy-plants, and daisies and forget-me-nots, and these by the June pomps of 16,000 rose-bushes and 10,000 hydrangeas, and many magnolias, tropical palms, ferns, and india-rubber trees. On a pleasant Sunday from 40,000 to 80,000 persons visit the garden. Thirty beds were given up in 1895 to rich carpet-bedding, or small foliage-plants, showing in their proper colors the emblems and badges of the Christian Endeavor Society and the Knights Templar.

The memorials include (on the south, or Boylston-St. side): Ball's bronze statue of Charles Sumner, erected in 1878, from a popular subscription of $15,000; and a stiff little granite statue of Col. Cass, of the 9th Mass.; (West side), Ball's noble equestrian Washington, the finest statue in New England, erected in 1869, 22 feet high, on a base 16 feet high, and designed, made and paid for in Massachusetts; a graceful fountain-veiled statue of Venus Rising from the Sea, popularly called "*The Maid of the Mist*"; and the Ether Monument, a stone shaft rising from a square basin, and crowned with statues of the Good Samaritan and his suffering *protégé*, dedicated in 1868, to commemorate the proving of the anæsthetic powers of ether, at the Mass. General Hospital in 1846. J. Q. A. Ward was the sculptor; T. Lee, the donor. On the Beacon-St. side is Story's dramatic bronze statue of Edward Everett, modelled at Rome, cast at Munich, and erected here by a popular subscription in 1867. The portrait is capital, and the gesture a favorite one of Everett's. As Mr. Howells says:

ST. PAUL'S EPISCOPAL CHURCH, TREMONT STREET, NEAR TEMPLE PLACE.

"Boston seemed to be a great place for images. An image of Washington on horseback, and some orator speaking, with his hand up, and on top of a monument a kind of Turk held up a man who looked sick. The man was almost naked, but he was not so bad as the image of a woman in a granite basin; it seemed to Barker that it ought not to be allowed there. . . . The marble Venus of the

WILLIAMS & EVERETT, PAINTINGS, STATUARY AND FRAMES.
NO. 190 BOYLSTON STREET, (EXTENDING THROUGH TO PARK SQUARE, OPPOSITE PUBLIC GARDEN.

BOSTON PUBLIC GARDEN.
BOYLSTON, CHARLES, BEACON AND ARLINGTON STREETS.

BOSTON PUBLIC GARDEN.
BOYLSTON, CHARLES, ARLINGTON AND BEACON STREETS.

fountain was surprised without her shower on ; and Mr. Ball's equestrian Washington drew his sword in solitude unbroken by a policeman upon Dr. Rimmer's Hamilton in Commonwealth Avenue."

Arlington Street, the west border of the Public Garden, has latterly seen trade invade its splendid mansions. At No. 16 is the Swedenborgian headquarters. The Arlington-St. Church (Unitarian), the first built on the Back Bay (in 1861), exemplifies Wren's London architecture, and has a sweet chime of 16 bells in its tall freestone spire, and a white Corinthian interior. It succeeds the Irish Church of the Presbyterian Strangers, founded in Long Lane (Federal St.) in 1727 ; and has had Channing and Gannett for pastors. The church lot is assessed at $360,000. Near by, at 2 Newbury St., is the pleasant house of the St. Botolph Club, of prominent professional men, artists and authors (like N. Y. Century Club), founded in 1880, and for some years presided over by Parkman. Nearly opposite is Emmanuel Episcopal Church, built in 1861-62, of Roxbury stone, and led by Huntington, Vinton and Parks. Dr. Vinton's bronze portrait tablet was made by St. Gaudens.

The Young Men's Christian Association has on Boylston St., at the southwest corner of Berkeley, a spacious and imposing Scottish-baronial building, erected in 1883, at a cost of $300,000. There are about 5,000 members, under easy entrance-conditions, though only members of evangelical churches may be voters and office-holders. It freely welcomes strangers to its parlors, library, reading-room, and game-room ; and provides lectures, concerts, receptions, classes, a spacious hall, and an elaborate and very large gymnasium. It was formed in 1851 and is the oldest Y. M. C. A. in the Republic.

On Berkeley St., just north of Boylston, is the Catholic nunnery-school and novitiate of Notre Dame.

The Museum of Natural History, on Boylston St., at the northwest corner of Berkeley, was built in 1864, for a society incorporated in 1831, on land given by the State ; and has a library of 20,000 volumes, and vast collections of birds, insects, fossils, skeletons, stuffed elephants and lions and other remarkable objects. It is open free Wednesdays and Saturdays (25 cents on other days). Burgess, the yacht-designer, was long the librarian here. The stately building is adorned with carved animals' heads on keystones, and eagle on roof, and has a fine Corinthian portico.

The Central Congregational Church, on Berkeley St., just north of the Museum, was built in 1867, of Roxbury stone, after designs by Upjohn, the famous Gothic architect ; and resembles a miniature cathedral in its ecclesiastical symmetry. The stone spire rises 236 feet, and is the tallest in the city, and, according to Dr. Holmes, by far the most beautiful. The interior was remodelled and superbly decorated in 1894-95, by the Tiffany Co., of New York, with favrile glass, a rich churchly chancel, and a famous sanctuary lamp. The society began in 1835, and built in Winter St. in 1841. It has been led by John E. Todd, J. T. Duryea and E. L. Clark.

BOYLSTON STREET, NORTH SIDE, FROM BERKELEY TO EXETER STREETS,
SHOWING NATURAL HISTORY MUSEUM, INSTITUTE OF TECHNOLOGY AND OLD SOUTH CHURCH.

The First Church (Unitarian), north of the Central, at Berkeley and Marlborough Sts., was built in 1868, at a cost of $325,000; and is a charming bit of English Gothic architecture, of Roxbury stone, with cloisters and a low steeple, and a rich dark interior, with London stained windows and a German organ. Winthrop and Dudley founded the society, in 1630; and for a century and a half it was Trinitarian Congregationalist. Its first church (in 1632-40) was at 27 State St.; the second (1640-1711) and third (1713-1808—"The Old Brick"), at 209 Washington St. (near Court); and the fourth (1808-68), in Chauncy Place, near Summer St.

The Mass. Institute of Technology, with two of its buildings and the Natural-History Museum charmingly filling the whole block on the north side of Boylston St., between Clarendon and Berkeley, is the leading technical and industrial-science college in America, if not in the world. It was incorporated in 1861; and teaches engineering, chemistry, metallurgy, architecture, physics, geology, etc., to more than 1,000 youths. Francis A. Walker is president. Several courses of free public lectures are given here yearly, by the foremost American and British scholars, from the income of $237,000 bequeathed therefor in 1839, by John Lowell, Jr., a Bostonian dying at Bombay. Among the Lowell lecturers have been Palfrey, Lowell, Howells, Agassiz, Lyell and Tyndall.

The Hotel Brunswick, one of the most delightful and most charmingly situated hotels of the world, is on the south side of Boylston St., at the corner of Clarendon, forming part of the east end of Copley Square. It is opposite the Technology Institute, and in the immediate vicinity of Trinity Church, the Art Museum, the Public Library, etc. It was built in 1874-76, at a cost of $1,000,000, with sumptuous furnishings, fine architecture, and an unrivalled situation. Among its guests have been Presidents Grant, Hayes and Arthur, and the Dukes of Argyll and Sutherland. The proprietors are Barnes & Dunklee.

Copley Square, with its superb churches, museums, library and colleges, is regarded by the Bostonians with a Florentine or Athenian civic pride, and bears the name of our greatest oldtime artist. The foremost architects have prepared competitive plans for its appropriate adornment, which will probably be in the form of a dainty sunken garden, with shrubbery, fountains and statuary. This work will have cost $75,000.

Trinity Church, on Copley Square, is the most artistic and impressive church in New England. Phillips Brooks was its rector from 1869 to 1891. The society dates from 1728; and the present church from 1877. It was designed by H. H. Richardson, in the Romanesque architecture of Southern France and Spain. The chief external features are the outlying chapel; the quaint cloisters, containing the ancient stone tracery from a window of St. Botolph's Church, in English Boston; the rich Galilee porch, built in 1894-95; and the vast and impressive central tower, suggested by one at Salamanca, and rising to a height of 211 feet, with a width of 46 feet. The ivy-clad walls are of yellowish Dedham granite and brown sandstone; and the huge tower-roof is of red Akron

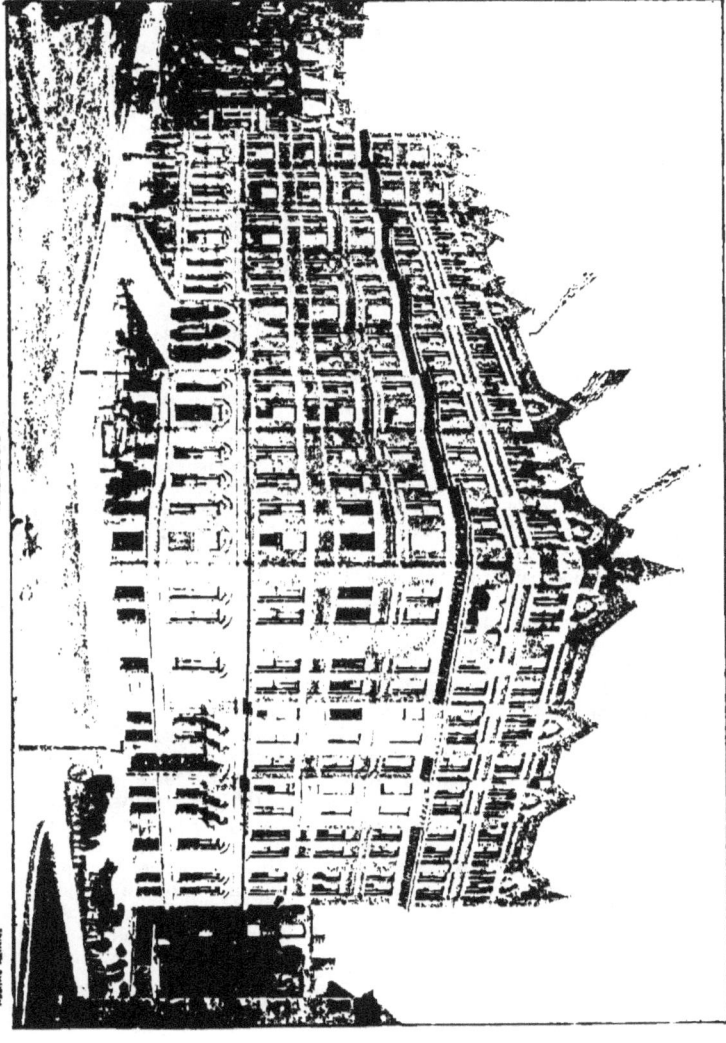

HOTEL BRUNSWICK, BARNES & DUNKLEE, PROPRIETORS.
BOYLSTON STREET, SOUTHEAST CORNER OF CLARENDON STREET, BEGINNING OF COPLEY SQUARE.

tiles. The interior is marvelously rich, with a chancel 57 x 53 feet in area; many English, Parisian and Tiffany stained-glass memorial windows; and the famous Biblical frescoes by John LaFarge, including Jesus and the Woman of Samaria. This majestic building cost over $800,000, and is all paid for. The services are "low." E. W. Donald is rector. The north cloister doors are open daily, from 8 to 4 (Saturdays, 8 to 12) to admit visitors. The attendant sells a booklet about the frescoes, windows, etc. Near by, at 233 Clarendon St., is the quaint rectory, where Phillips Brooks dwelt from 1869 until his death in 1893. South of Trinity is the Ludlow, an apartment house; and also the Technology Architectural, Engineering, and Laboratory buildings.

The Museum of Fine Arts fills the south side of Copley Square with its flamboyant Italian Gothic façade of brick, stone, and red and buff English terra cotta. It contains what is called the most symmetrically developed art-collection in America, inferior to New York in pictures, but with the finest set of sculptural casts in the world (except that at Berlin), and Japanese collections absolutely unapproachable elsewhere. Conspicuous terra-cotta reliefs on the outer walls represent the Triumph of Art, and the Union of Art and Industry. A large art-school is attached to the Museum. There were 265,000 visitors to the Museum in 1894. The building surrounds a broad quadrangle, and is to be doubled in size. The first floor is devoted to casts and antiquities, occupying 16 halls. The second floor has several rooms of paintings; the textile, coin, and metal-work collections; the tapestries and embroideries, porcelains and pottery; and the vast Japanese collections. There are 800 casts of famous classic and Renaissance statuary, large Egyptian and Cyprus collections, thousands of pieces of exquisite porcelain and glass ware, tapestries and embroideries, wood and ivory carvings, prints and drawings, coins and bronzes, weapons and armor; and many paintings by the old masters (Rubens, Holbein, Dürer Greuze, Reynolds, *et als.*), and by the best modern French and American artists (Corot, Millet, Bastien-Lepage, Allston, Copley, Hunt, Brown, Cole). Catalogues are sold at the door. The Museum is open from 9 to 5 daily (25 cents; free on Saturdays, and Sunday afternoons). It was founded in 1870, and subscriptions of $600,000 gave the means for the great quadrangular buildings, begun in 1876. The expenses are met by art-lovers' subscriptions. The Grundman, Harcourt and Pierce buildings, near by, have the studios of many artists. A few rods from the Museum, where Dartmouth St. crosses the Albany and Providence Railroads, is the South Armory, built in 1890, for the 1st Regiment, M. V. M., and the Naval Brigade. The 5th Regiment and the Cavalry Battalion have their headquarters here. The drill hall is of mammoth size, and the head-house, massive, battlemented and towered, has a fine military effect.

The Boston Public Library, occupying the west side of Copley Square, has the most costly and artistic library building in the world, and is by far the largest library in the world for free circulation. It was opened in

TRINITY PROTESTANT EPISCOPAL CHURCH.
COPLEY SQUARE, ST. JAMES AVENUE, CLARENDON AND BOYLSTON STREETS.

MUSEUM OF FINE ARTS.
COPLEY SQUARE; ST. JAMES AVENUE AND DARTMOUTH STREET.

BOSTON PUBLIC LIBRARY.
COPLEY SQUARE; DARTMOUTH STREET, FROM BOYLSTON STREET TO HUNTINGTON AVENUE.

1852, largely by the efforts of Everett and Ticknor ; and the building was finished in 1895, having cost over $2,500,000. C. F. McKim, of McKim, Mead & White, designed it, in the pure, stately and elegant style of the Italian Renaissance. It is of pinkish-gray Milford granite, and faces on three streets, with a conspicuous roof of brown Spanish tiles, and a cloistered courtyard inside containing a lawn and fountain. The building covers 1½ acres. The inscriptions, the outside granite terrace and seats, the Knoxville-marble vestibule, and the colored marble mosaics of the entrance hall, in floor and vaulting, are all noteworthy. The grand stairway, with colossal marble lions commemorating the dead of the 2d and 22d Mass. Regiments in 1861-65, leads to Bates Hall, an immense reading-room occupying all the Copley-Square front, with a barrel-vault ceiling and rich furnishings. Edwin A. Abbey's wonderful series of paintings of "The Search for the Holy Grail" and John S. Sargent's paintings of "The Growth of Religion" are in place here, Abbey's in the general delivery room, and Sargent's in the hall of the special libraries (third floor). Each artist receives $15,000, and they will require years to come to finish their series. The paintings are on canvas, fastened to the walls by white lead. LaFarge, Puvis de Chavannes (who will receive $50,000) and others are at work on other great mural decorations ; St. Gaudens is preparing two groups of three figures each, for the outer terrace ; and other statues are being made. Never before have architecture, sculpture and painting been so gloriously united in America. Here are kept many valuable MSS. and ancient books, the Cardinal-Tosti collection of engravings, Copley's great painting of Charles I. and Parliament, and the priceless Chamberlain autographs. The library has very rich special collections about costumes, Spanish literature, music, mathematics, patents, architecture, New-England history, Shakespeareana, etc., each in a special hall. It contains about 680,000 volumes ; and has many well-stocked branches in remote parts of the city. There are 150 employees ; and the expenses approach $200,000 a year. The magnificent newspaper-room contains current files of several hundred leading American, European and Asiatic papers, and has no rival anywhere. Parts of the library are open evenings and Sundays. The State gave most of the land for the site ; the city paid for the building and maintenance ; and private munificence gave most of the special libraries and art-treasures of this incomparable people's club-house, "The literary Common," as Robert C. Winthrop called it.

The Old South Church, opposite the Library, on the north side of Copley Square, is a superb North-Italian Gothic building, of Roxbury stone, erected in 1873-75, at a cost of $500,000, for a Congregational society founded in 1669. Quite noticeable outside are the gilded copper dome, the carved fruits and birds on the outer sandstone belts, and the inscriptions and Venetian mosaics in the arcade. The tower (which leans slightly) is one of the most beautiful in existence, with colored stone marquetry and noble Gothic windows ; and is 248 feet high. Inside, note the carved Caen-stone and Lisbon-marble screen, the open timber-

OLD SOUTH CONGREGATIONAL CHURCH.
COPLEY SQUARE; BOYLSTON STREET, NORTHWEST CORNER OF DARTMOUTH STREET.

roof, and the rich stained-glass windows, the shepherds of Bethlehem (east), the five parables (south), and the five miracles (north). The chapel and parsonage adjoin the church, on the west. Geo. A. Gordon has been pastor since 1884.

On Boylston St. in the block east of the Old South is the Chauncy-Hall School, the leading private school in Boston, founded in 1828, where Parkman, Ellis, Weiss and other famous men studied. Adjoining on the east is the Second Church, of brownstone, built in 1874 for a Congregational parish founded at the North End, and Unitarian for nearly a century past, and among whose pastors were the three Mathers, Ralph Waldo Emerson, R. L. Collier, and E. A. Horton.

The Boston Art Club, immediately north of the Old South, at Dartmouth and Newbury Sts., founded in 1854, in 1882 opened an artistic Romanesque house, with rich decorations, and a fine art-gallery wherein public exhibitions are frequent. Just opposite rises the battlemented front of the Hotel Victoria, a fashionable European-plan house, whose café is sometimes called "the Delmonico's of Boston."

Commonwealth Avenue, the handsomest thoroughfare in America, runs from the Public Garden to and across the Back-Bay Fens, and thence by Chestnut Hill across Brookline and Newton to Auburndale. It is 240 feet wide, from house to house, the middle being occupied by a continuous mall, with lawns and trees, paths and seats. The mall contains: near Arlington St., Dr. Rimmer's granite statue of Alexander Hamilton, given by T. Lee in 1865; near the First Baptist Church, Milmore's heroic bronze statue of Gen. Glover, of the Marblehead Continental Regiment, given by B. T. Reed in 1875; the seated Garrison statue; and, at the entrance to the Fens, Anne Whitney's heroic and ideal bronze statue of Leif Ericsson, the Norse Viking, who is by some supposed to have sailed from Iceland and landed in Massachusetts, A. D. 1000. The sturdy young sea-king wears a casque, a shirt of mail, and sandals. There is a galley-prow pedestal; and reliefs, showing Leif's landing, and his narrating his discoveries to friends in a Norse banquet-hall.

The First Baptist Church, a massive and fortress-like Roxbury-stone edifice, at Commonwealth Avenue and Clarendon St., was built in 1873, by H. H. Richardson, for the Brattle-square Unitarian Society (founded 1699; dissolved 1876), and in 1882 was acquired by the First Baptist society (founded in 1665). Its chief feature is the majestic bell-tower, 176 feet high, with an upper belt of colossal sculptures designed by Bartholdy, and representing Baptism, Communion, Marriage, and Death, with the angels of the judgment at the angles blowing golden trumpets. The interior has rose-windows and a basilica roof. The tower is so beautiful that a number of gentlemen bought the empty church in 1881, with the idea of tearing down the main building and replacing it with a little park, out of which the tower should rise alone, like an Italian campanile. Among the First Baptist pastors were Stillman, Neale (1847-77), Wayland and Moxom.

FIRST BAPTIST CHURCH.
COMMONWEALTH AVENUE, SOUTHWEST CORNER OF BERKELEY STREET.

The Vendome, Boston's palatial hotel, on Commonwealth Avenue and Dartmouth St., is but two short blocks north of Copley Square with its group of famous edifices. It is a vast eight-story million-dollar marble building, with 365 feet of street-frontage, in every way richly and comfortably furnished and equipped, with a fine rotunda and dining-halls. Many distinguished personages have of late years been guests here, among them Presidents Harrison and Cleveland, Blaine and McKinley, Sherman and Vanderbilt, Rockefeller and Carnegie, Booth and Barrett, Irving and Terry, Patti and Bernhardt. The Vendome, under the proprietorship of Charles H. Greenleaf & Co., has been notably successful. In front is Warner's heroic bronze statue of William Lloyd Garrison, the Abolitionist leader, erected in 1886, by the people. At 217 Commonwealth Avenue is the spacious and luxurious house of the Algonquin Club, organized in 1885, among prominent business men and bankers. The building (erected in 1888) cost $300,000; and is in the Renaissance style, of light-colored Indiana limestone, five stories high, and with 82 feet of frontage. The historic Algonquin nation included the chief New-England Indians. Not far away, at 270 Beacon St., is the home of the University Club, organized in 1892, of college-bred men. This palace (built as residences for the Higginson and Whittier families) has 40 rooms and halls, superbly decorated and furnished; and overlooks the broad Charles River. Near by, at 296 Beacon St., Oliver Wendell Holmes lived and died. This house is on the much-desired water-side of Beacon St., so brightly pictured in Howells's novels, and on which (at 304) the novelist once dwelt.

In the Back-Bay District the streets running parallel to the western border of the Public Garden are named in a simple alphabetical order, e. g., Arlington, Berkeley, Clarendon, Dartmouth, Exeter, Falmouth, Gloucester, Hereford, etc. On Exeter St., south of Commonwealth Avenue, are several notable places. At Newbury St. are four remarkable structures, one on each of the four corners, the South Congregational Church, the Spiritual Temple, the Normal Art School and the Prince School. The South Congregational (Unitarian) Church, with its lowly Byzantine tower, was built in 1883-84, for the Hollis-Street society, which was founded in 1730, and ministered to by Byles the Tory, Pierpont the reformer, Starr King the patriot, and H. B. Carpenter the poet. In 1887 this society united with the South Church (founded in 1827), of which Edward E. Hale has been pastor since 1856. There are beautiful memorial windows to Pierpont and Starr King. The First Spiritual Temple, the finest of that order in the world, was built by a wealthy Boston merchant, at a cost of $250,000, in 1885. It is a curious Romanesque stone edifice, with delicate carvings, several halls, organ, library, parlors, and frequent services. The Mass. Normal Art School is a three-story brick round-arched and high-roofed building, erected in 1886, for a State institution founded in 1873 to prepare drawing-teachers for the public schools. The Prince School, exemplifying German and Austrian school-construction, is one of the best of the public

THE HOTEL VENDOME, CHARLES H. GREENLEAF & CO., PROPRIETORS.
COMMONWEALTH AVENUE, SOUTHWEST CORNER OF DARTMOUTH STREET.

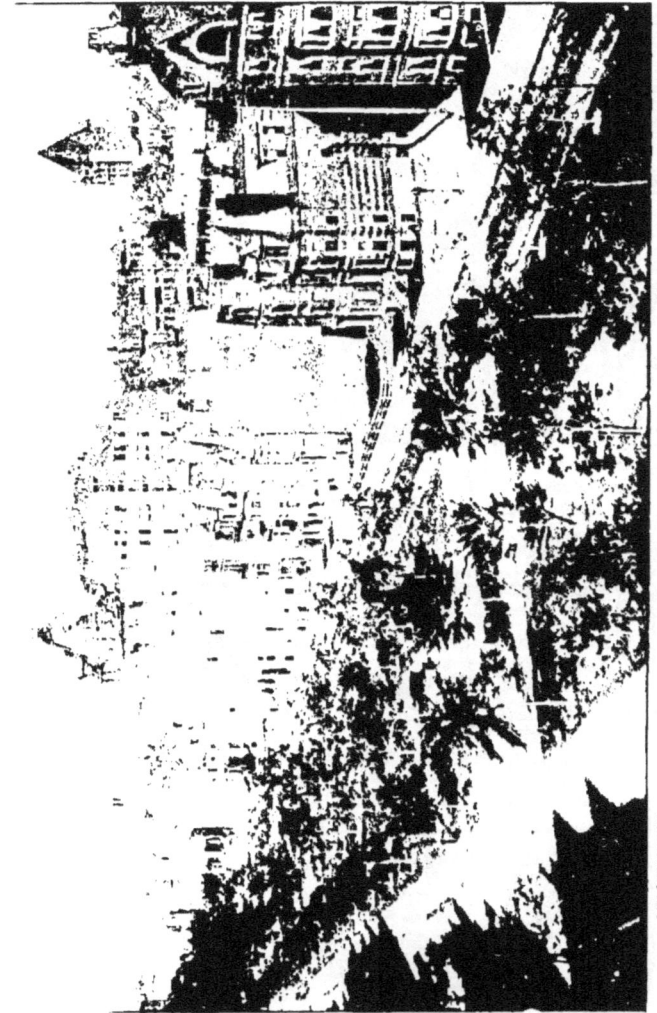

FIRST BAPTIST CHURCH.   VENDOME.   TRINITY TOWER.

COMMONWEALTH AVENUE AND THE HOTEL VENDOME.
SOUTH SIDE OF THE AVENUE FROM EXETER TO ARLINGTON STREETS

schools. East of the South Church, on Newbury St., is the Horace-Mann School for the Deaf, founded in 1869, and a part of the public-school system.

The Harvard Medical School, on Boylston and Exeter Sts., adjoining the Public Library, was founded in 1783, and in 1883 occupied this new $250,000 fireproof building. This noteworthy department of Harvard University, perfectly equipped, and with a wonderful museum, has 100 professors and 600 students. Alongside, on Exeter St., at Blagden, the Boston Athletic Association (founded in 1888; 2,000 members) has a very showy and spacious house, completely equipped for swimming, billiards, bowling, tennis, racquet, handball, fencing, boxing, running, and all gymnastic uses, and with large dining-rooms. It cost $300,000.

Huntington Avenue, running southwest from Copley Square, opens a fine vista to the Roxbury hills. Here are numerous hotels and apartment houses and residences, and several notable public institutions. At Huntington Avenue and Exeter St. is the elegant and highly modern Copley-Square Hotel, one of the best constructed and most comfortably furnished hotels in the city. It was opened in 1891 by F. S. Risteen & Co., its present proprietors, who conduct it in an admirable manner. It is in close proximity to the Back-Bay edifices. Only a block beyond, on Huntington Avenue, is the mammoth decorated Renaissance building, erected in 1881, at a cost of $500,000, for the exhibitions of the Mass. Charitable Mechanic Association (800 members), founded in 1795, to promote inventions, advance education, and help young or distressed mechanics. Mechanics Hall seats 8,000 persons, and is the home of grand opera in Boston. Garrison St. leads thence east to the Mass. College of Pharmacy, built in 1886, with library, laboratories and cabinets; and the Allen Gymnasium for ladies and children, with a variety of paraphernalia and baths. Farther out on the avenue is the Elysium Club (No. 218), an aristocratic Jewish social organization, founded in 1871 (house built in 1891). Beyond, one may see, at Westland Avenue, the picturesque but highly practical and useful Boston Storage Warehouse, whose huge elevators carry up loaded wagons, with any infinite variety of household and other goods which are placed in these fireproof and convenient warehouses for safe keeping; at Parker and Astor Sts., the Riding Academy, with an arena of 165x100 feet; at Gainsborough St., the Children's Hospital, a spacious and wisely-planned building, erected in 1882, and free to poor children of from 2 to 12 years; and on Gainsborough St., the Church of the Messiah, the home of an Episcopal society founded at the South End in 1843. It has daily prayers, a surpliced choir, and free seats.

The Christian Scientist Church, dedicated in 1895, pertains to the pioneer society of that faith, which was born in Boston in 1866. The church on Norway St. cost $200,000, and has some very curious and interesting traits.

COPLEY-SQUARE HOTEL, F. S. RISTEEN & CO., PROPRIETORS.
HUNTINGTON AVENUE, NORTHEAST CORNER OF EXETER STREET.

MECHANICS FAIR BUILDING,—MASSACHUSETTS CHARITABLE MECHANIC ASSOCIATION.
HUNTINGTON AVENUE AND WEST NEWTON STREET.

Beacon St., with almost interminable double lines of sombre brownstone residences, was built across the bay from the Common to Brookline, 1½ miles, in 1818-21, to serve as a mill-dam, to hold back at will the tidal waters for factory power, and also for a toll-road to the westward. The streets on either side of the ancient mill-dam waterway are known as Charlesgate East and Charlesgate West; and on the former is the lofty and luxurious Charlesgate, one of the finest of the grand apartment-houses for which the Back Bay is famous.

Massachusetts Avenue (partly old West Chester Park) is a fine thoroughfare several miles long, from near the harbor, in Dorchester, across the South End, to the Harvard Bridge, a very long structure (traversed by street-cars) across the Charles River from Beacon St. to Cambridge. Near the entrance to the bridge, at Beacon St. and Massachusetts Avenue, is the Mount-Vernon Congregational Church, dating from 1892, with triple-arched portal, rose-window, square tower, and open timbered roof. S. E. Herrick is pastor.

The Back-Bay District was gained from the salt-water tides by filling in, mainly between 1857 and 1887, the land-sales giving the State a profit of $3,500,000 above costs. The street-plan was designed by Arthur Gilman, the architect. It is one of the finest residence-quarters in the world, showing an edifying variety of architecture and materials, careful and delicate detail work, wrought iron, tiles, stained glass and fine carvings. The grand residences include the gray-brick house of John F. Andrew, the War-Governor's son, at Commonwealth Avenue and Fairfield St.; the Proctor house, at 273 Commonwealth Avenue; and the brown-stone Renaissance house of ex-Gov. Ames, at Commonwealth and Massachusetts Avenues. Hundreds of these beautiful homes on the spacious, sunny, airy and quiet street may well be observed with care. Many of these houses and churches (especially Emmanuel, Trinity, the First Baptist, the Art Club, and "doctors' row," on Boylston St.) are richly adorned with Boston ivy (*amphelopsis Veitchii*), a hardy Japanese climbing plant introduced here about 1870.

The Back-Bay Fens, formed at a cost of nearly $3,000,000, is a unique park of 100 acres, reproducing a sea-coast creek and shore, with sedgy banks, meadows, clumps of trees and shrubbery, fine bridges, and magnificent driveways, amid the highly artificial and finished surroundings of a splendid metropolis. Across this quaint plaisance appear the spires and towers of Longwood, Brookline and Cambridge, the house-crowned crest of Corey Hill, and the remote blue hills of Middlesex. The Fens is the beginning of an unbroken series of parks and parkways, extending south several miles to the great Franklin Park, and thence to be prolonged by the Strandway, etc., to the Marine Park on the seaward point of South Boston. These City Parks will no doubt be connected at various points by grand boulevards with the whole Metropolitan Park System. Street-cars from Charlesgate, or Harvard Bridge, soon lead back to the busy Tremont-St. side of the Common.

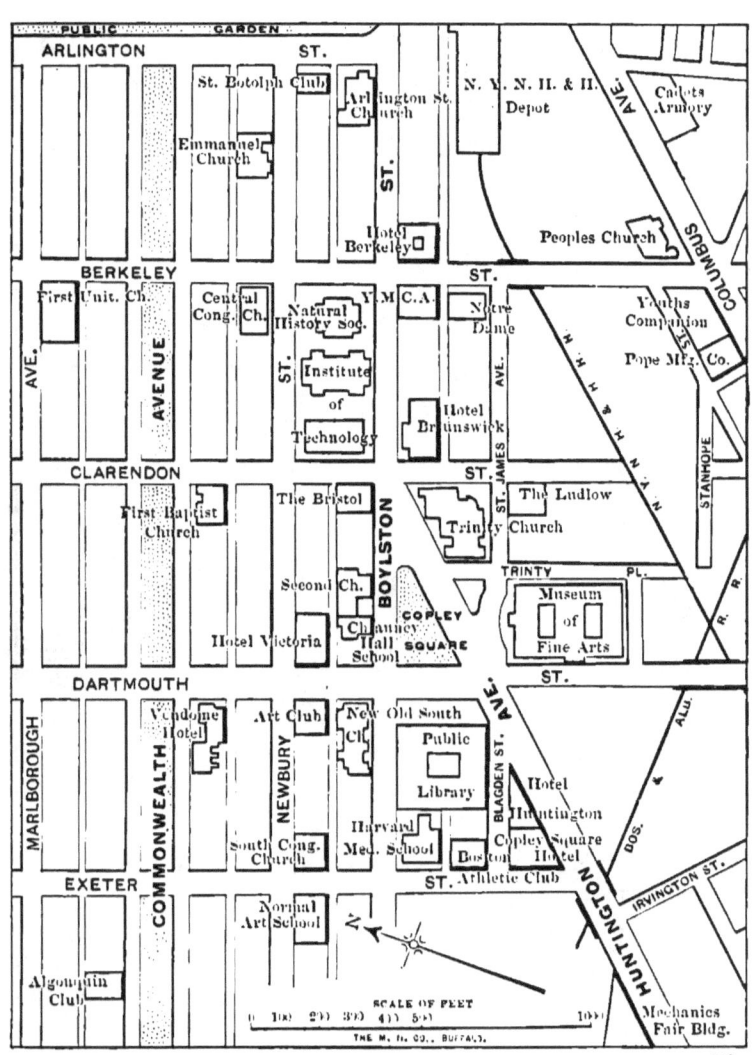

BACK-BAY DISTRICT.

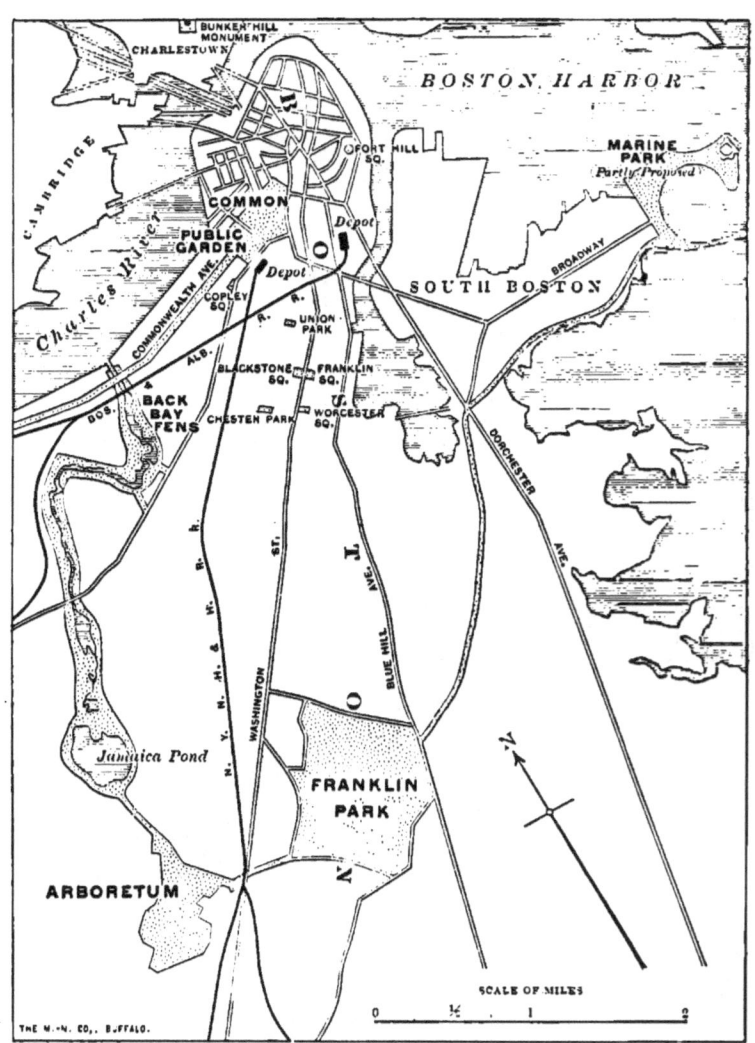

BOSTON'S PARK SYSTEM.

BEACON HILL AND THE WEST END.

BEACON HILL has no street-cars, and may comfortably be traversed on foot, ascending Beacon St. from Tremont, or Pemberton Square from Scollay Square. At Beacon and Somerset Sts. rises the faced-granite building erected about 1815 for a dwelling, afterwards occupied by the Somerset Club (1852-72), and since 1873 the Congregational House, "the Vatican of Congregationalism," the headquarters of various powerful Puritan societies. The A. B. C. F. M. museum is well worth seeing, with its obsolete gods; and the handsome library hall, with its 30,000 books, and 180,000 pamphlets. *The Congregationalist* and *The Literary World* are published here. The American Peace Society, founded in 1828, from this corner fights against wars. The American Board of Commissioners for Foreign Missions, with its main offices here, since 1812 has sent out 800 consecrated men to all parts of the earth, and established thousands of churches and schools, and powerful native ministries. Roberts Bros.' publishing house is at 3 Somerset St. The noted school-book publishers, Ginn & Co., have their headquarters at Nos. 7-13 Tremont Place, close to the Granary Burial-Ground.

Boston University, down Somerset St., is the headquarters of a coeducational Methodist institution, founded in 1869, with medical and musical schools at the South End, theological and liberal-arts schools,

EMANCIPATION STATUE.   PROVIDENCE STATION.
PARK SQUARE, COLUMBUS AVENUE AND PROVIDENCE STREET.

and a law-school (with 340 students) close by, at 10 Ashburton Place. The University has 1,300 students, and assets of $1,600,000. W. F. Warren is president. On the Somerset site stood Dr. Neale's First Baptist Church, whose sharp, slender and conspicuous spire won for it the popular name of "The Church of the Holy Toothpick." Just beyond, in Ashburton Place, stands the old Mount-Vernon Church (now abandoned), where Dr. E. N. Kirk preached from 1842 to 1874, and D. L. Moody was converted. Farther down, at No. 18 Somerset St. (the Court House is on the right) stands the building of the New-England Historic Genealogical Society, incorporated in 1845, whose library of 24,000 volumes is open daily from nine to five to persons interested in antiquarian studies.

The Boston Athenæum, at 10½ Beacon St., is a beautiful and spacious Palladian building, erected, of Paterson brownstone, in 1847-49, for a literary society incorporated in 1807, and now owning this costly place and its library of 180,000 books, and many precious paintings and sculptures. There are about 1,000 share-holders, whose families may draw out books; and although it is not a public library, scholars and strangers are courteously welcome to inspect the rooms, and sometimes to read and study here (except in the newspaper-room). The main hall, on the second floor, looking out on the trees of the Granary Burial-Ground, is a delightful place for reading and contemplation. The library of George Washington is preserved in this building. The librarian is Wm. C. Lane. Here, also, are the rooms and library of the American Academy of Arts and Sciences, a world-renowned society of scholars, founded in 1780, with members all over the country. Among them were Franklin, Bowdoin, Hancock and John Adams.

LINCOLN, OR EMANCIPATION STATUE, PARK SQUARE.

Opposite, a narrow alley leads behind the lofty Bellevue (formerly Dio Lewis's) hotel to the Freeman-Place Chapel, built half a century ago by James Freeman Clarke's church, and now the unique book-store of Charles C. Soule.

The Unitarian Building, at 25 Beacon St., corner of Bowdoin, dates from 1886, and is a fine specimen of massive Roman-palace architecture, in rusticated brownstone. It is the headquarters of the chief Unitarian societies in America. Here stood Gov. Bowdoin's mansion, and Burgoyne's headquarters. Bowdoin St. leads in a few steps from Beacon St. to Dr. Reed's New-Jerusalem Church, built in 1845, with a fine Gothic interior and memorial window; and then descends the hill to the Mission Church of St. John the Evangelist, a grim granite battlemented structure,

TRINITY CHURCH.

COMMONWEALTH AVENUE.

MARLBORO' STREET.

BEACON STREET.

HARVARD BRIDGE.

(HARVARD).

BEACON STREET, PUBLIC GARDEN AND BACK BAY DISTRICT.
VIEW LOOKING SOUTHWEST FROM THE STATE HOUSE.

161

built for Dr. Lyman Beecher's Congregationalists, and now for many years owned and occupied by the English Episcopal "Cowley Fathers," who go about the streets in long black robes, and do a vast amount of good among the poor—and the rich. Their frequent services are High Anglican. Father Hall, the Bishop of Vermont, was rector here. The General Theological Library, an unsectarian collection of 20,000 volumes, founded in 1860, is at 53 Mount-Vernon St., not far from the State House. It is largely used by country ministers, who may take books home.

The State House occupies the terraced crest of Beacon Hill, facing the Common. It was built in Sam. Adams's governorship, in 1795-98, on John Hancock's cow-pasture (bought for $4,000), with Bulfinch as architect. Crowning the highest point of Old Boston, it is a very noble landmark from distant points on sea and land. The high dome was covered in 1874 with sheets of pure gold-leaf (renewed since), and may thus be recognized, shining brightly, from leagues away in the coast and rural counties. Many people ascend to the top of the dome, which commands an incomparable view of the island-studded harbor and blue sea, the city and suburbs, and the far-away mountains, Wachusett, Monadnock, etc. Dr. Holmes has said: "Boston State House is the Hub of the solar system." The new State-House Extension, much larger than the original building, and of finer materials, but similar architecture, stretches northward. It was built in 1890-95, at a cost (with land) of $5,000,000, with fine marble colonnades, and a central courtyard. The chief feature is the Representatives' Hall, in Italian Renaissance architecture, elliptical, with mahogany finish, Corinthian columns, a domed ceiling of glass, frescoes by Frank Hill Smith, and the famous wooden codfish, five feet long, hung up in 1784, in the place of one placed in the Representatives' Hall before 1730. The fish is emblematic of one of the chief sources of the wealth of Massachusetts. The State Library, of 90,000 volumes, has a spacious reading-room, whose balcony overlooks the crowded northern suburbs. This was the first State library in America. It contains some interesting portraits. The book-shelves are of steel. The entrance-halls are noble in aspect; and the stair-rails show some fine work in wrought iron. Here may be seen nearly 300 flags of the State troops in the War for the Union, very sacredly guarded; Sir Francis Chantrey's esteemed statue of Washington, set up in 1828; Ball's excellent portrait-statue of John A. Andrew, the War Governor, erected in 1871, at a cost of $10,000; busts of Washington, Lincoln, Sumner, and Vice-President Wilson; the venerable portraits of dignitaries, in the handsome old-fashioned Senate Chamber; weapons and trophies from Lexington and Bennington; and other interesting pictures and antiquities. On the outside terrace stands Powers's statue of Webster, given by popular subscription in 1860, and Emma Stebbins's statue of Horace Mann, the educator, given by the school-children in 1869. In the grounds was the site of the Beacon (from 1634 to 1789), an iron cage filled with combustibles, whose firing would alarm the distant towns, and call out their

THE STATE HOUSE AND THE STATE HOUSE EXTENSION.
BEACON STREET, MOUNT VERNON AND TEMPLE STREETS.

train-bands. It stood just east of the middle of the Extension, on the old line of Temple St., where Sentry Hill rose then 80 feet above the present level. The same Beacon-Hill ridge had two other sharp peaks, Cotton Hill, 80 feet over Pemberton Square, and Mount Vernon, where Louisburg Square is. This three-spired ridge was the ancient *Trimontaine*, or *Tramount*.

On Beacon St., just west of the State House, a tablet on the fence before two pretentious brownstone dwellings marks the site of the gardens and the splendid and hospitable home of John Hancock, built in 1737 and torn down in 1863, in the face of a storm of popular dissent.

The Diocesan House, at Beacon and Joy Sts., the headquarters of Mass. Episcopalianism, was dedicated in 1892, and has the offices of several important societies and the archives of the diocese.

At Beacon and Walnut Sts., Wendell Phillips was born, in the then out-of-town house of his father, Boston's first mayor, afterwards occupied by Lieut.-Gov. T. L. Winthrop, father of R. C. Winthrop. Motley lived on Walnut St.

The Somerset Club, the most aristocratic and exclusive in Boston, has since 1872 occupied the ivy-clad, double swell-front, white stone house at 42 Beacon St., built by David Sears for his home. It is on the site of the far-viewing house of J. S. Copley, the famous portrait-painter, who owned 11 acres hereabouts, and sold the property for $18,550. Copley, though a patriot, moved to England in 1774 and died in 1813; and his son (born here) became Lord Lyndhurst, one of the noblest chancellors of Great Britain. Harrison Gray Otis lived in the double house next west of

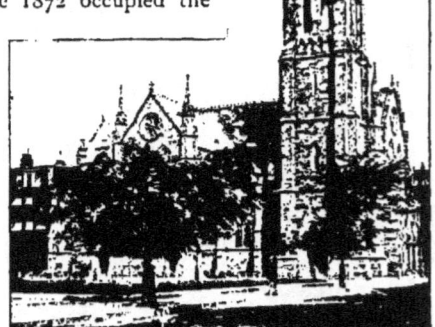

CENTRAL CONGREGATIONAL CHURCH, BERKELEY AND NEWBURY STREETS.

the Sears house; and Judge Cushing next east. The Puritan Club, founded in 1884, in 1889 occupied the old Amory mansion at Beacon and Spruce Sts.; and is made up of young professional men. At 55 Beacon St., not far from Charles St., a double swell-front, with balconies on pillars, William H. Prescott the historian dwelt in 1845-59, and wrote *The Conquest of Peru* and *Philip II*, while nearly blind. It was here that he died.

The six blocks of Beacon St. west of the State House face on the grand Beacon-St. Mall of Boston Common, planted from funds left over after fortifying the harbor in 1812.

Charles St. (with cars), running north from the foot of Beacon St. to the West End, was reclaimed from the water. Here stands James T. Fields's house (No. 148), inhabited by his widow, with whom Sarah Orne Jewett often dwells; and Aldrich long abode near by.

Chestnut St., crossing Charles St., is a venerable way, leading up the hill, by the R. H. Dana (No. 43), Parkman (No. 50), Bartol (No. 17), Edwin Booth, and Bishop-Paddock houses; and also along the riverward levels to the left (because of its many stables, there called Horse-Chestnut St.) to the commodious Swiss house and floats of the Union Boat Club, founded in 1851, and including 150 amateur oarsmen. The swell colored people's church of Boston began in 1836, and in 1877 bought from the white Baptists the venerable Charles-Street Church, which it now occupies, with 400 Methodist communicants. The Home for Aged Women, founded in 1849, is an excellent institution, at 108 Revere St.

Mount-Vernon St., from Charles St., climbs Beacon Hill to the State House, past scores of ancient mansions, embowered among gardens and trees. Here dwelt Channing, Aldrich, Webster, C. F. Adams, Gov. Claflin, Justice Gray, Margaret Deland, and Anne Whitney. At the

FIRST CHURCH (UNITARIAN) BERKELEY AND MARLBOROUGH STREETS.

corner of West Cedar St. is the home and unique library of the Harvard Musical Association, founded in 1837, and formerly famous for its symphony concerts, as well as for planning the erection of Music Hall. The Boston-University School of Theology occupies the fine building at 72 Mount-Vernon St. It is the oldest Methodist theological institution in America, having been founded in 1847.

Louisburg Square was laid out in 1834, where Blackstone's spring flowed two centuries before. In this quaint old enclosure stand little Italian marble statues of Aristides and Columbus, presented by Iasigi, the Turkish consul, in 1849-52. At the Pinckney-St. corner is the house and hospital of the Episcopal Sisterhood of St. Margaret, with a fine chapel. Whipple, the essayist, lived at 11 Pinckney St.

The Church of the Advent, at Mount Vernon and Brimmer Sts., near Charles River, was built in 1878-83, for an Episcopal parish founded in 1844, in accord with the Puseyite doctrines of the Anglo-Catholic revival, and mainly for active free-church work among the poor. It is the foremost High church in the city, with many ceremonial services, and superb music by a large surpliced male choir (aided by Symphony-

MASS. INSTITUTE OF TECHNOLOGY, BOYLSTON STREET, EAST OF CLARENDON STREET.

Orchestra artists at festivals, in Gounod's and other mass-music). The church and chapel walls inside are of brick and stone; the lofty roodscreen of wrought iron; and the storied windows of imported stained glass. The reredos is a very beautiful work, presented in 1890. Father Grafton, now Bishop of Fond du Lac, held the rectorate for many years.

The Mass. Charitable Eye and Ear Infirmary, at 176 Charles St., was founded in 1824, and has done a world of good, with State aid and private munificence.

Cambridge St. is a long and heterogeneous thoroughfare, from the bridge leading to Cambridge (traversed by street-cars) back east to Bowdoin Square. Charlesbank includes the shore from this bridge to Craigie's Bridge, and is a charming water-side park for the crowded poor region adjacent, with trees and shrubberies, walks and lawns, seats and landings, and admirable public gymnasiums for men and women, and children's playgrounds and sandcourts. Back of Charles St. rise the cold gray walls of the Suffolk-County Jail, built in 1851, at a cost of $450,000. Each cell-floor is a single block of stone, and so is each roof. It is a place of detention, of short-term confinements, and (rarely) of executions. Northeast, at the foot of North Grove St., is the Harvard Dental School, where Prof. Webster murdered Dr. Parkman, in 1849.

Just north, with entrance on Blossom St., are the spacious tree-shaded grounds and dignified classic buildings and modern pavilions of the Mass. General Hospital, founded in 1799, for the treatment (free, if needful) of American or Canadian sick persons, without infectious or chronic diseases. This institution is very wealthy, and employs the most eminent doctors. It has nurse-schools; and (at Waverly) a Convalescents' Home and the McLean Asylum for the Insane.

TRINITY CHURCH CHANCEL, COPLEY SQUARE.

It is well to take the street-cars from the Cambridge bridge eastward, because Cambridge St. is unattractive. As Howells says: "Gentility fled it long ago, and middle-class houses have fallen to the grade of mechanics' lodgings." On the south, steep streets climb through the negro quarter up Beacon Hill. St. Augustine's, at 71 Phillips St., is one of the Cowley Fathers' missions, with an open timber roof, a chime of bells, and a surpliced choir of negro men and boys. The Grand Lodge of colored Masons meets at 20 Blossom St. On Chambers St., north of Cambridge St., is the pretty St. Andrew's Church, maintained by Trinity Church, and doing very useful work.

The West Church, a quaint edifice at Cambridge and Lynde Sts., built in 1806, witnessed the Unitarian pastorate of Charles Lowell (father of the poet) from 1806 to 1861, and that of Cyrus A. Bartol from 1837 to 1889. The society dissolved in 1889, and the building was bought by the city in 1894, for a branch library. A church tower on this site in 1737 was used as a signal-station, whence the patriots in town communicated with the Americans at Cambridge during the siege. The British tore it down. Near by, at 20 Hancock St., dwelt Charles Sumner.

Bowdoin Square, once embowered in trees, and the centre of rich gardens and estates of grand families, is now the crowded and noisy meeting-point of the Cambridge and other street-cars, and the Rialto of an overcrowded cosmopolitan district. The Revere House, built in 1847, and opened by Paran Stevens, in its early period, had among its guests Presidents Fillmore, Pierce, Johnson and Grant, Gens. Sherman and Sheridan, Dom Pedro, Alexis, Wales, Kalakaua, Webster, Parepa, Patti, Jenny Lind and Nilsson. Back of it is the armory of the National Lancers, a famous and brilliantly equipped old cavalry corps (organized in

BOSTON ART CLUB, DARTMOUTH AND NEWBURY STREETS.

1836) of the M. V. M., whose pennon-bearing lances make a brave show when they escort the Governor to the Harvard Commencement every June. William Warren and Walt Whitman dwelt on Bulfinch Place. The Central Charity Bureau, on Chardon St., just north of Bowdoin Square, has three large brick buildings, the headquarters of the municipal, Associated, and many private charities. Opposite the Revere is the Baptist Tabernacle, a gloomy and heavy-towered granite building, erected in 1840, before whose doors occurred the Elder-Knapp riots, when the Lancers in mounted squadrons had to clear the streets. At No. 1 is the Bowdoin-Square Theatre, opened in 1892, with a large stage and an ivory-and-gold auditorium. It is but a short walk to Scollay Square.

THE SOUTH END.

STREET-CARS from Scollay Square and other points are continually flitting away to the vast residence-district of the South End, and across it to Roxbury and Dorchester. The chief objects accessible from each of the three main arteries, Columbus Avenue, Tremont St. and Washington St., will be narrated so as to suit any trip. Nearly all the South End is made land. The South Bay, making in from the harbor, and the Back Bay, an expansion of Charles River, nearly islanded the Boston hills, which were connected with the main land only by a narrow neck a mile long, as Nahant is. At full tides, the salt water overflowed the highway, up to the knees of the passing horses. If vessels laid up to the shore on either side, their bowsprits nearly closed the country road. The Neck began at Beach St., and reached its narrowest point at Dover St. In 1631 a detachment of Puritan men-at-arms was placed here on guard, to keep the Indians away; and the barrier-gates were closed at evening, so that no one could go in or out. In 1710, a heavier defence was erected, with powerful guns, just south of Dover St. In 1774, the British garrison strengthened and augmented these works with redans, bastions, abattis, ponderous gates, drawbridges, a deep tide-water moat, and the 59th Regiment on guard. The Green-Store Battery, on the site of the Grand Museum, at Dover St., mounted 23 cannon; and the advanced works near Canton St. had 26 guns and several mortars, with floating batteries covering the water-approaches. Showers of shot poured for

COMMONWEALTH AVENUE, EASTWARD FROM THE VENDOME.

months from these ramparts upon Roxbury; and many daring deeds of war were done between the Royal fortress, where Lord Percy commanded, and the American intrenchments, the famous Roxbury Lines, near Lenox St. The American advanced post was at the George Tavern, on the site of Washington Market; the British at Brown's farm, just south of Blackstone Square. Afterwards, the Neck was a favorite place for sportsmen,

COMMONWEALTH AVENUE, WESTWARD FROM THE VENDOME.

in search of sea-birds; and Puritan guards were placed on duty to prevent their shooting on Sunday. In 1794, there were fewer than a score of buildings between Dover St. and Roxbury; and in 1800, only two between the Cathedral and Roxbury. After 1850 the flats were filled up, and the convenient street-railways soon made this the favorite residence-district. Later, Fashion led the way to the newly filled Back Bay, where (and in Brookline and Milton) most of the swells and many rich persons now dwell. The South End is a broad and quiet region of pleasant homes, including miles of ivy-clad swell-fronts, and dotted with pleasant little parks, important churches and hotels, and many neighborhood retail stores.

Columbus Avenue (with street-cars) runs from Park Square and Boston Common nearly to Roxbury, and is being prolonged to Franklin Park. It is a noble straight street, 80 feet wide, paved with asphalt, and lined with blocks of handsome houses, diversified in material and architecture, and tall apartment-hotels. Many boarding-houses are found here. Going up, the Providence freight-houses occupy the right; and on

EMANCIPATION STATUE.   PARK SQUARE.

PROVIDENCE STATION; NEW YORK, NEW HAVEN & HARTFORD RAILROAD.
PARK SQUARE, AT THE BEGINNING OF COLUMBUS AVENUE.

the other side rises the long castellated granite armory of the First Corps of Cadets, M. V. M., an aristocratic four-company battalion of first-families young men, organized in 1741, and once commanded by John Hancock. It fought in the Rhode-Island campaign of 1778; and furnished hundreds of officers in the War for the Union.

Berkeley St., from the South End to the Back Bay, has its four Columbus-Avenue corners well occupied : one by the Hoffman House (apartments); another by the People's Church, a Methodist institution,

JOHN GLOVER. -- COMMONWEALTH AVENUE. -- ALEXANDER HAMILTON.

built in 1879-84, and giving free seats to over 3,000 persons; a third by the First Presbyterian Church, with its spire; and the fourth by *The Youth's Companion*, an immense and impressive brownstone building, erected in 1892 exclusively for its own use. This journal was founded in 1827, by the father of N. P. Willis and Fanny Fern; and has had among its contributors Whittier and Parkman, Howells and Trowbridge, Lords Lorne and Lytton, Froude and Müller, Lubbock and Black, and virtually the whole list of noted authors of our time. It is the foremost family literary paper in the world, with a circulation exceeding 540,000 copies. The adjacent beautiful white marble building was erected for the Pope Manufacturing Co.'s immense bicycle trade, which extends all over the world. Bicycling was first practically brought into America by Col. Albert A. Pope, of Boston, as recently as 1877, and the enormous

THE POPE BUILDING, POPE MANUFACTURING CO., "COLUMBIA CYCLES."
COLUMBUS AVENUE, WEST SIDE, BETWEEN BERKELEY AND CLARENDON STREETS.

development of this ubiquitous and indispensable means of locomotion is due to the able and energetic methods which he inaugurated.

The Second Universalist Church, on Columbus Avenue and Clarendon St., just beyond the Albany-Railroad bridge and station, is a high-spired stone building, with rich stained-glass windows. Hosea Ballou (from 1817 to 1852) and E. H. Chapin were pastors of this church; and A. A. Miner has held the office since 1848.

At Columbus Avenue and Dartmouth St. is Wm. J. Conklin's apothecary store, a widely known pharmacy which supplies drugs, medicines and toilet articles to the thousands of neighboring families. The furnishings and fittings are said to be the most elaborate and costly of any drug store in this city.

Dartmouth St. leads on the left to the Normal and Rice Training School, where the Boston school-teachers are educated; and on the right past the Reformed Episcopal Church (built in 1882-83) to Copley Square.

West Canton St. leads left to the Warren-Avenue Baptist Church, built in 1865, for a society founded in Baldwin Place, at the North End, in 1743. Baron Stow and G. F. Pentecost were

LEIF ERICSSON STATUE, BACK-BAY PARK.

pastors here. The Church of the Disciples, just off Columbus Avenue, on Warren Avenue, was founded in 1841, as a free and social Unitarian society, in which the members should take active part. This brick building, eccentric in shape, dates from 1869. James Freeman Clarke held the pastorate in 1841-88 ; C. G. Ames, since.

The Union Church, at Columbus Avenue and West Newton St., is a very picturesque ivy-clad building, of Roxbury stone, well-set amid lawns. It was founded in 1822, in Essex St.; and the present building arose in 1869. Nehemiah Adams was pastor from 1834 to 1878. N. Boynton is pastor now. East of the church, on West Newton St., is the Home for Little Wanderers (formerly in Baldwin Place), an unsectarian institution for sheltering and educating homeless children. Farther out, we cross the

CONKLIN'S CORNER; WILLIAM. J. CONKLIN & CO'S PHARMACY.
COLUMBUS AVENUE, NORTHWEST CORNER OF DARTMOUTH STREET.

grand Massachusetts Avenue. Just beyond is the Temple Adath Israel, a Jewish shrine founded in 1885. Across Northampton St. is the piano-factory erected by the man who was once toasted as "Jonas Chickering, like his pianos, Grand, Square, and Upright." This mammoth factory occupies the whole square from Columbus Avenue to Tremont St., and from Northampton to Camden Sts. The making of pianos in this country was begun by Jonas Chickering, who was not only the pioneer, but by nature constituted to found and develop the world-famous industry which has been continued so creditably and successfully for almost three score and ten years. The principle of producing only the finest possible instruments has made the Chickering name a household word in all civilized lands.

Tremont St. traverses the South End, about midway between Columbus Avenue and Washington St. After leaving the Common it passes near Van Rensselaer Place, with its French restaurants, the Hollis-St. Theatre, the Children's Mission to the Children of the Destitute (277 Tremont St.), and the Y. W. C. A. (66 Warrenton St.). Just beyond the crossing of the Albany Railroad is the splendid new Castle-Square Theatre, between Appleton and Chandler Sts., opened in 1894. A short distance east on Middlesex St. is the Turner headquarters and German theatre; beyond which rises the tall spire of the German Catholic Church of the Holy Trinity, on Shawmut Avenue. The School of Veterinary Medicine of Harvard University, at Village and Lucas Sts., has an interesting hospital for sick horses, dogs and cattle.

ALGONQUIN CLUB, 217 COMMONWEALTH AVENUE.

Odd-Fellows' Hall, at Tremont and Berkeley Sts., is a handsome and spacious four-story white-granite structure, erected in 1871-72, and occupied by encampment, banquet and lodge halls. Near by stood the immense brick Moody-and-Sankey Tabernacle, in 1877.

Berkeley Temple lifts its tall telescopic spire at Berkeley St. and Warren Avenue. It is a Congregational institutional church, busy in religion

CHICKERING & SONS, MANUFACTORY OF THE CHICKERING PIANOS,
TREMONT STREET, SOUTHWEST CORNER OF NORTHAMPTON STREET.

and benevolence every day of the week, with trusty bands of trained volunteer helpers. The society was founded in Pine St. in 1827, and has had H. M. Dexter and W. B. Wright for pastors. C. A. Dickinson now leads it.

The Young Women's Christian Association has at 40 Berkeley St. its large and handsome main house (with a boarding-house for 250 on Warrenton St.), with hall, gymnasium and library, and many classes for industrial and literary instruction. This powerful society protects young working-women, and furnishes them low-priced board, and many comforts and entertainments.

OLIVER WENDELL HOLMES HOUSE, 296 BEACON.

Paine Memorial Hall, on Appleton St., near Tremont, commemorates Thomas Paine, patriot and infidel. James Lick of California gave $18,000 towards it. Parker Memorial Hall, alongside, at Berkeley St., honors Theodore Parker, radical reformer and scholarly divine, and belongs to the Benevolent Fraternity of Churches.

The Clarendon-St. Baptist Church, with its brick spire, is close at hand, where Tremont crosses Clarendon St. It was founded in Federal St., in 1827; and the late A. J. Gordon was its pastor for many years.

The English High and Latin School, next to the church, on Warren Avenue, extending through to Montgomery St., is the largest and costliest public-school building in the world. It was built in 1877–81, in modern Renaissance architecture, at a cost of $750,000; with 48 class-rooms, several assembly-halls, laboratories, libraries, memorial statuary, a spacious gymnasium, and an immense and handsome drill-hall, with calked thick plank floors laid on concrete. The Latin School, founded in 1634, has the Warren-Avenue front; and the English High School, founded in 1821, has the Montgomery-St. front. Each street-front of the great quadrangle includes three pavilions, with decorations in terra cotta.

The pleasant Union Park leads thence to the Catholic Cathedral on Washington St., passing the fashionable Synagogue Ohabei Shalom (founded in 1843), occupying the building which formerly was E. E. Hale's South Church.

ENGLISH HIGH AND LATIN SCHOOL FOR BOYS.
WARREN AVENUE AND MONTGOMERY STREET, BETWEEN CLARENDON AND DARTMOUTH STREETS.

The Shawmut Congregational Church, at Tremont and Brookline Sts. has a lofty Lombardic clock-tower, and rich interior. The society dates from 1849; the building from 1864. E. B. Webb was pastor in 1860-85; and W. E. Griffis in 1886-93. Brookline St. leads right to the Church of the Disciples and near the Warren-Avenue Baptist Church; and left to the Every-Day Church, a noble Universalist religious, benevolent and educational institutional society, near Blackstone Square. West Newton St. leads right to the Union Church and the Mechanics' Fair Building and the Back Bay; and left to the radical Unitarian Church of the Unity, a gray classic temple, built in 1861, where M. J. Savage has been pastor since 1874. On West Newton St. is the Girls' High School and Girls' Latin School, a large brick building with 66 rooms, and a hall adorned with many statues. At 59 West Newton St., in the old St. Mark's Church, is the armory of Battery A, Light Artillery, M. V. M.

SOUTH CONGREGATIONAL CHURCH, EXETER AND NEWBURY STREETS.

The Tremont-St. Methodist Church, at West Concord St., is a handsome Gothic building of Roxbury stone, designed by Hammatt Billings, and erected in 1862. It has two spires, and spacious and pleasant grounds. On Camden St. is the home of the Scots' Charitable Society, founded in 1657.

The Boston Base-ball Grounds are entered by Walpole St., from Tremont, and attract enormous crowds to the match-games, when the local club (founded in 1871) is in town. Many ladies watch these exciting games from the grand stand.

Washington St. continues to be, as it has been for centuries, the main route through the South End. Soon after leaving Boylston St. it crosses Eliot St., up which the Providence station appears on the right; and Kneeland St., on the left, leading to the Albany and Old-Colony stations, and near the great Catholic church of St. James, on Harrison Avenue, with its Aberdeen-granite colonnaded basilica interior. Next, Hollis St. leads on the right to the Hollis-St. Theatre; and Bennet St. diverges left to the central Boston Dispensary. At 37 Common St. Wendell

Phillips spent his last years; and on Warrenton St. is the Y. W. C. A. Pleasant St. leads on the right to the Providence station, and left to South Boston. At Washington and Motte Sts. is the first-class Columbia Theatre, opened in 1891, in the walls of the old Catholic Pro-Cathedral, and adorned with a Moorish front of yellow brick and terra cotta. To the right is the tall-spired Church of the Holy Trinity; and down Florence St. appears the Episcopal Mission Church of St. Stephen. At 987 Washington St. is the building erected in 1883 for the Wells Memorial Working Men's Club and Institute, with a casino, English coffeehouse, gymnasium, rooms for reading, billiards, games, talking, classes and entertainments, a savings-bank, and classes for drawing, debating, singing and dramatic art. Each member pays $1 a year. It was founded

MASSACHUSETTS NORMAL ART SCHOOL, EXETER AND NEWBURY STREETS.

by wealthy men, as a memorial to Father E. M. P. Wells, for 30 years Episcopal city missionary. The site of the ancient ramparts is at Dover St., which runs to South Boston, across Fort-Point Channel. A little way beyond is the Grand Opera House, a spacious and inexpensive popular theatre, built in 1888.

The Cathedral of the Holy Cross, at Washington and Malden Sts., looms over the small houses about it with sombre and grandiose effect. It is the largest Catholic church in New England; and in size surpasses most of the European cathedrals. It is 364 feet long, and 170 feet wide at the transepts, covering over an acre, with a nave 120 feet high. The material is Roxbury stone; and the style a severe Early English Gothic.

The main spire is to be 300 feet high. The Cathedral was built in 1867-75. The impressive character of the vast interior, where lines of bronzed metal columns uphold a clerestory and a rich roof of wood mosaics, is heightened by many brilliant stained-glass windows. Those in the transepts cover 800 sq. ft. each, and represent the Finding of the True Cross, and the Exaltation of the Cross by the Emperor Heraclius; and the chancel windows, over the exquisite marble altar, show forth the Nativity, Crucifixion and Ascension. The western rose-window is near the great organ, with its 5,292 pipes. The beautiful Chapel of the

FIRST SPIRITUAL TEMPLE, EXETER AND NEWBURY STREETS.

Blessed Sacrament contains the altar from the old Cathedral on Franklin St. Beneath the nave are burial-vaults for the hierarchy. The Archbishop's (Williams) mansion and offices adjoin the Cathedral on Union-Park St. In front stands Buyens's bronze statue of Columbus, dedicated in 1892, a duplicate of one in San Domingo.

Franklin Square and Blackstone Square, crossed by Washington St. beyond the Cathedral, cover 5 acres, with lawns and trees, fountains, paths and benches, the delight of the dense surrounding populations. The New-England Conservatory of Music occupies the former St.-James Hotel, on Franklin Square, with concert, practice, and reading rooms, library, parlors, and boarding accommodations for hundreds of girl-students. It has 16 separate schools, or departments, forming a general college of culture, with 100 instructors and nearly 1,700 pupils, from many countries. Dr. Eben Tourjée founded the Conservatory in 1867. South of the building is the South Burying-Ground, established in 1810.

The Church of the Immaculate Conception, close by, on Harrison Ave., near Newton St., is a fine classic granite structure, erected by the Jesuits in 1857-61, with a brilliant white interior, long Ionic colonnades, and many statues and paintings. The music is famed for high excellence.

PUBLIC LIBRARY.   MEDICAL SCHOOL.   ATHLETIC CLUB.   COPLEY-SQUARE HOTEL.
HARVARD MEDICAL SCHOOL, BOYLSTON AND EXETER STREETS.

Adjoining on the north, on Harrison Avenue, is the plain brick Boston College, a Jesuit school for 400 boys, dedicated in 1860; and opposite rises the Home for Destitute Catholic Children, conducted by the Sisters of Charity. At Concord and Thorn Sts. are the Mass. Homœopathic Hospital (built in 1876-92, the largest in America) and the Medical School of Boston University (founded in 1873; 170 students), a group of commodious modern brick buildings, amid pleasant grounds. Across Stoughton St. rises the spacious East Armory, built in 1891, and the headquarters of the Ninth Regiment, M. V. M., made up of Irishmen. It lost 258 men by death in the War for the Union.

The Boston City Hospital, on Harrison Avenue, at the foot of Worcester Square, has a handsome Administration Building, with colonnaded front and high dome, connected by corridors with several spacious pavilions, amid pleasant grounds. It is for sick or injured Bostonians, needing temporary relief; with free treatment for the poor. One of the large detached buildings is for infectious diseases. This institution cost nearly $1,000,000, and was opened in 1864. It employs 70 physicians. Its superintendent is Dr. Geo. H. M. Rowe.

The Langham Hotel, at Washington and Worcester Sts., is a very spacious marble house, used mainly by families, for long sojourns.

A short distance beyond, Washington St. crosses Massachusetts Avenue (late Chester Park), the grand route from Dorchester across the Back Bay over the Harvard Bridge via Cambridge, past Harvard University, and through Arlington to Lexington. This Avenue, recently made by renaming various old streets is twenty miles or more in length, with many right-angled turns, forming one of the longest and most interesting thoroughfares in New England.

BOSTON ATHLETIC ASSOCIATION, EXETER AND BLAGDEN STREETS.

Shawmut Avenue, almost parallel to Washington St. and to the eastward of Tremont St., from which it branches in the vicinity of Hollis and Warrenton Sts., runs to the Highlands.

This is a good point at which to turn backward into the city, walking through the pleasant old Chester Square (the Nankeen Square of Howells's novels) to Shawmut Ave. or Tremont St. or Columbus Ave., and returning thereon by street-cars.

Walt Whitman says that: "The New-England metropolis of to-day may be described as sunny, joyous, receptive, full of ardor, sparkling, a certain element of yearning, magnificently tolerant, yet not to be fooled, fond of good eating and drinking — costly in costume as its purse can buy; and all through its best average of houses, streets, people, that subtle something which effuses behind the whirl of animation, study, business, a happy and joyous public spirit — makes one think of the glints we get of the jolly old Greek cities."

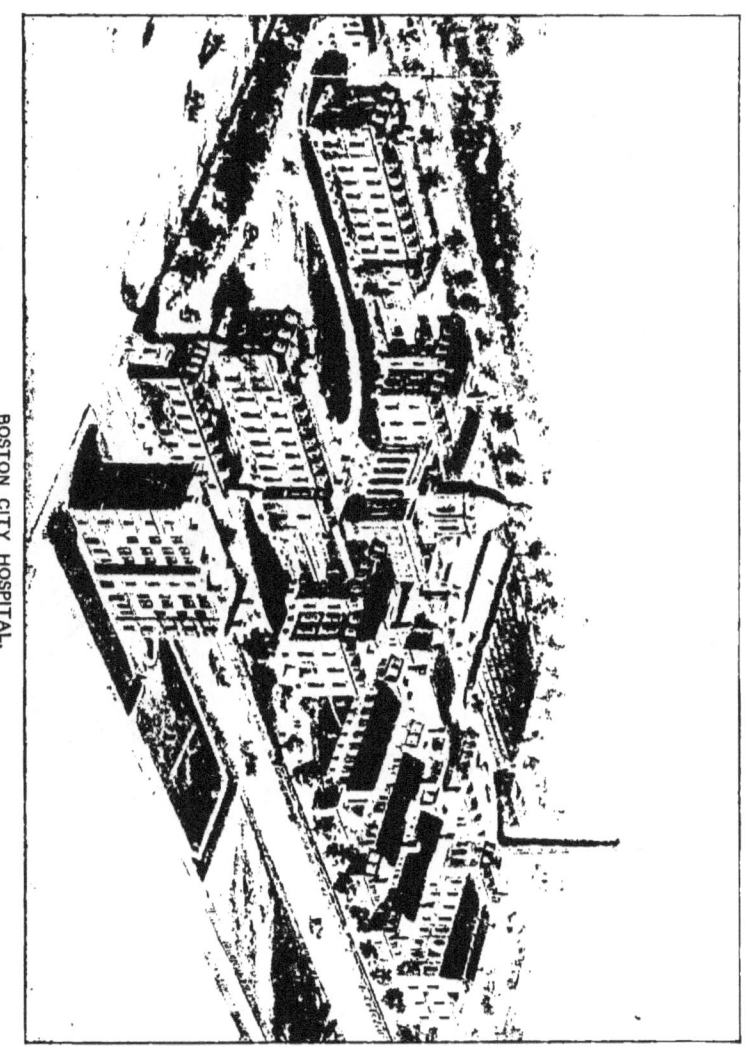

BOSTON CITY HOSPITAL.
HARRISON AVENUE, BETWEEN CONCORD AND SPRINGFIELD STREETS, OPPOSITE WORCESTER SQUARE.

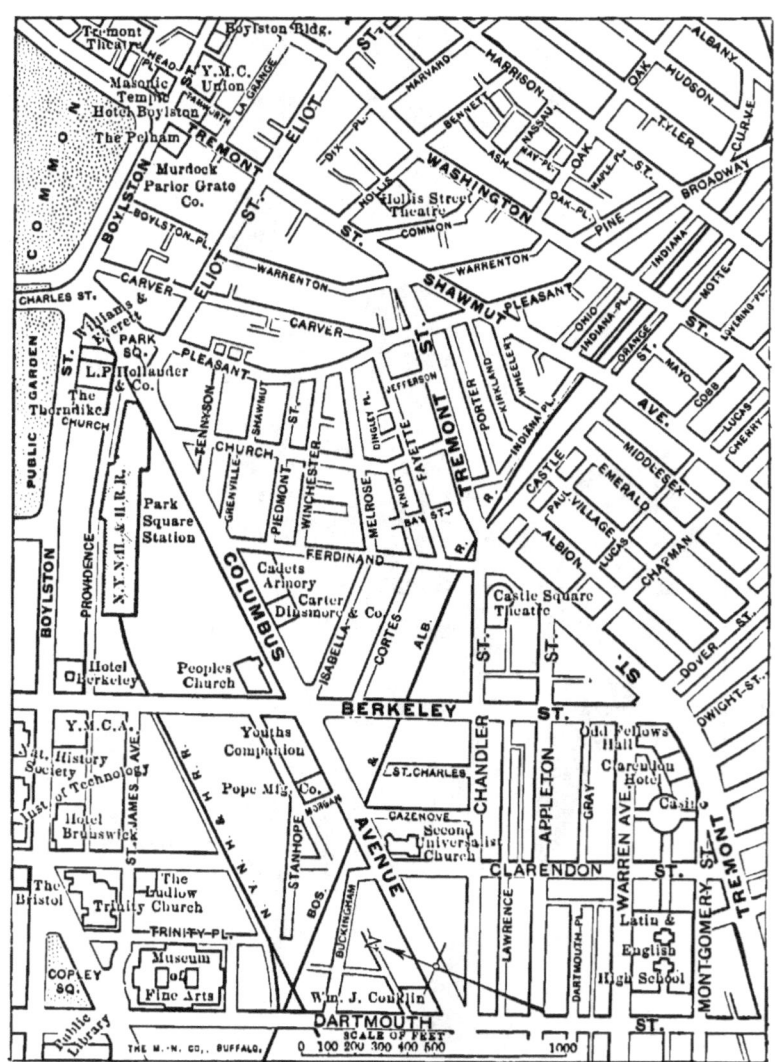

THE SOUTH END.

THE OLD NORTH END.

THIS was an aristocratic Puritan quarter, until the Irish possessed themselves of it, and the sailors and their panderers seized the shoreward parts, so that the district became very squalid and dangerous. Latterly the Italians, Portuguese and Russians have driven out the Irish ; and the bad houses and people along the waterside have been reduced by the police, missionaries and electric lights. Among these prolific Latin and Slav populations remain several Colonial and Provincial landmarks, interesting to all Americans.

Hanover St. (once Orange-Tree Lane), running from Scollay Square, and traversed by many street-cars (to Chelsea Ferry, etc.), is a long and much-winding way, often widened by the city, at enormous cost. It is now broad, busy and active, with many low-priced retail stores, far from aristocracy's haunts — indeed, "The Bowery of Boston." At 19 and 21 is the new extension of the Marston dining-rooms, which run through to

HARVARD BRIDGE, ACROSS THE CHARLES RIVER, BOSTON TO CAMBRIDGE.

Brattle St. The popular American House, a large hotel on the American and European plans, dates from 1835, and stands on the site of Gen. Warren's dwelling. Beyond the crossing of broad Washington St., at Union St. (at the Blue Ball) was Franklin's home for years; and north on Union St. stood the Green Dragon Tavern, the famous patriot rendezvous of Adams, Hancock, Warren, and others, which Webster called "The Headquarters of the Revolution." The Sons of the Revolution erected a tablet on the building occupying its site (No. 84), in 1892. Back in little Marshall St. is the carved Boston Stone, set in the rear wall of a Hanover-Street building, and a landmark since 1737. In this now squalid alley King Louis Philippe long dwelt; and Count Rumford served as an apprentice. Creek and Hatters' Squares are old localities near by. Blackstone St. occupies the bed of the old Middlesex Canal and the earlier Mill Creek.

Salem St. leads from Hanover St., through the Russian quarter, where Hebrew signs appear on all sides, and synagogues are seen, and

UNITARIAN HOUSE.   CONGREGATIONAL HOUSE.   ATHENÆUM.
BEACON STREET AND BOSTON ATHENÆUM.

moujik faces and costumes abound, amid the old homes of the Phipses and other grandees, the true colonial houses, often with projecting upper stories.

Little Italy is the Italian settlement, numbering more than 5,000 persons, about North St. and North Square, where these poor but jocund Latins have two churches (in Prince St. and North Square), newspapers, banks, hotels, clubs, many shops, and a tiny theatre.

North St. in Colonial days was largely occupied by wharf-heads and shipyards, and the Cross, Red-Lion, Ship, Noah's Ark, King's Head, and Salutation Inns. Later, it became a line of sailors' dives, the perilous Whitechapel of Boston. Now, for a long way it has large commercial houses, and the rest of it is only squalid, not dangerous.

North Square had the Mountfort, Shaw, Holyoke, Mather and other aristocratic mansions; Revere's birthplace, still standing, at Nos. 19–21; Pitcairn's barracks; the beautiful estates of Gov. Hutchinson and Sir Charles and Lady Agnes (Surriage) Frankland; the Second (Old North) Church, of the Mathers, pulled down by the British in 1775; and Father Taylor's famous Bethel (now an Italian church). Close by is St. John's parochial school, where 700 girls are taught by the Sisters of Notre Dame. Before its partial redemption from rum and sirens, this region, from North to Salem Sts., and from Richmond to Fleet, was grimly called the Black Sea. Sir David Ochterlony was born on North St.; "Essex" David Porter, on Charter St.; Mather Byles, on Tileston St.; and Charlotte Cushman, on Richmond St.

UNITARIAN BUILDING, BEACON AND BOWDOIN STREETS.

St. Stephen's Catholic Church, at Hanover and Clark Sts., was built in 1805, for a Congregational society (the New North) founded in 1714. Beyond Harris St. (the old White-Bread Alley) is Hanover Avenue (once Methodist Alley), the site of the first Methodist church in Boston, dedicated in 1796, and often preached in (up to 1828) by Lorenzo Dow, Jesse Lee, Asbury, Hedding, Fisk and McKendree.

Opposite the gas-house, on Prince St., is the brick house in which died Major Pitcairn, mortally shot at Bunker Hill, and the nephew of the discoverer of Pitcairn's Island. Cotton Mather dwelt on the site of 298–300 Hanover St.; the Thoreaus (until they moved to Concord), opposite 57 Prince St. The North-End Industrial Home, at North Bennet and Salem Sts., has nearly a score of busy and beneficent departments. At St. John the Baptist's Church, on North Bennet St., is the shrine for the thousands of Portuguese from the Azore Islands dwelling hereabouts. It was built in 1828, by the Methodists. This locality vividly suggests polyglotical suggestions amid puritanical foundations.

At Hanover and North Bennet Sts. is the Boston Baptist Bethel, opened in 1864 in a church built in 1838, on the site where Samuel Mather and John Murray preached.

Copp's Hill, the crest of the North End, in 1632 sustained the windmill for grinding corn; and in 1775 the British battery which destroyed Charlestown stood here. The burial-ground dates from 1659, and is a peaceful spot, overlooking Charles River, and containing the tombs of the noted Mather family, the Eliots, Grays, Lincolns, Snellings, Sigourneys, and others. Some of them bear the marks of British musket-balls, when this was a garrison target-field. The new North-End Park extends from the hill of graves towards the harbor. The streets about the burial-ground have little service, and grass waves over their pavements. The

ASHBURTON PLACE, STATE-HOUSE EXTENSION AND THE OLD MT.-VERNON CHURCH.

houses, mainly owned by their occupants, are humble but neat. The burial-ground is open from 8 to 12, and from 1 to 6.30 daily, and all day Sunday. Descriptive pamphlets are sold, and the purchasers are shown around.

Christ Church, at Salem and Hull Sts., near the burial-ground, is the oldest in town, having been built in 1723; and has a quaint interior, with an organ-case imported from London in 1759, a large clock set up in 1740, cherubim given by an old Provincial privateer, the first monument erected to the memory of Washington; communion-plate, a Vinegar Bible, and other articles given in 1733 by King George II.; the upper "slaves' gallery"; and 33 subterranean vaults, many of which were occupied by dead British officers after Bunker Hill. From the tower window over the clock looking up Hull St., Paul Revere's alarm-lights were hung out, and started the Midnight Ride; and Gen. Gage witnessed the battle of Bunker Hill. The tower contains a melodious chime of eight bells, cast at Gloucester, England, in 1744, and inscribed "We are the first peal of bells cast for the British Empire in North America." They are often rung in chimes, in hymn or ballad tunes; and also (which is quite different) in peals, by a society of English peal-ringers. The Episcopal Church keeps up its service here, amid a careless foreign population.

The Endicott-St. region, crowded with the homes of the poor, is dominated by the enormous Catholic Church of St. Mary (built in 1877, at a cost of $200,000), which has two heavy towers, each 170 feet high. Near by is Cooper St., the scene of the hardest fighting in the Draft Riots of 1863. The armory was defended by militia and regular troops against the assaults and rifle-fire of a vast mob, which was finally scattered by discharges of grape-shot from the artillery.

JOHN A. ANDREW, STATE HOUSE.

KING'S CHAPEL (UNITARIAN), TREMONT AND SCHOOL STREETS.

THE HARBOR FRONT.

STREET-CARS leave Scollay Square for the northern depots every minute. The Lowell station, 700 feet long, built of brick and Nova-Scotia stone, in 1871, has a great double-towered and Louvre-domed head-house containing a lofty marble-paved waiting-hall, and a many-tracked train-house, whose arch spans 120 feet. The Lowell route to New Hampshire, Vermont and Canada was chartered in 1830, and leased by the Boston & Maine Railroad in 1887. The Union Station of all the northern lines, finished in 1894, is conspicuous for its immense granite entrance-arch, one of the grandest in America, and suggested by

HORACE MANN -- STATE HOUSE -- DANIEL WEBSTER.

a Roman triumphal arch. It is 45 feet high, with Ionic columns at the sides. The Eastern Division, chartered in 1836, and leased by the B. & M. in 1883, reaches the coast cities and beaches, Marblehead, Gloucester, Portsmouth, Portland, and the White Mts. The Western Division, chartered in 1833, runs by Haverhill to Portland. The B. & M. has an enormous summer-tourist business, to the beaches and the White Mts. and all parts of the Maine coast and forest.

A short distance southwestward from the Union Station, at the corner of Sudbury and Friend Sts., is the well-known carriage and sleigh manufactory of Ferd. F. French & Co., Limited, successors to William P. Sargent & Co., established in 1851. This concern has supplied the major

UNION RAILWAY STATION, THE "NORTHERN DEPOTS."
CAUSEWAY STREET.

FERD. F. FRENCH & CO., LIMITED, CARRIAGES AND SLEIGHS.
NOS. 14 TO 24 SUDBURY STREET, CORNER OF FRIEND STREET.

part of New England's costly and fashionable equipages of all kinds for the past few generations, and its mammoth salesrooms are filled with innumerable styles of vehicles for all purposes. It has been located at this site for 45 years, and did for a while have a branch establishment at 110 Tremont St., but now transacts its entire business at this one locality.

Just east of the Union Station is the ancient station of the Fitchburg Railroad, chartered in 1842, and running west by the Hoosac-Tunnel route. The station is a dark four-towered granite edifice, resembling a castle, and dating from 1847. In its hall, Jenny Lind gave her thrilling concerts, in 1850, under Barnum's management. All these stations occupy ground redeemed from the harbor.

JOHN HANCOCK'S HOUSE, BEACON STREET.

Commercial St., a short walk from the Fitchburg station (passing near the bridge to Charlestown), winds along the water-front around the North End in true Boston sinuosity, running N. E., S. E., S. and S. W. The Boston Gas Co.'s extensive works here date from 1828. This wharf is near the landing-place of Winthrop's colonists, the colonial ferry to Charlestown and Chelsea, and the debarking point of the 828 redcoats wounded at Bunker Hill, and their dead officers. The slain soldiers were buried on the fatal hill. Passing thence, one gains glimpses up the crowded alleys and humble hill-side lanes of the North End. Following Commercial St. around the bend, we come to the North-End Park, recently constructed to afford the crowded population of this section a bright sea-viewing pleasure-place, and leading up to the venerable Copp's-Hill Burial-Ground. Gray's Wharf early in the century belonged to Lieut.-Gov. Billy Gray, who owned 60 square-rigged vessels, voyaging all over the watery world. Near the foot of Foster St., more than a century ago, stood Paul Revere's cannon and bell foundry.

Aspinwall's Wharf commemorates another illustrious Boston merchant. The Chelsea ferry, from the foot of Hanover St., ascends the Mystic River, with good views of the Navy Yard and East Boston. This sidetrip gives one a chance to rest and enjoy the sea air and shore scenes.

At Constitution Wharf, the live-oak frigate *Constitution*, 44, "Old Ironsides," the pride of the American navy, was built, in 1794-97. She was intended to fight the Algerine corsairs, and attacked Tripoli in 1803-4; but her most glorious services occurred in the war with Great Britain, when she captured the *Guerriere*, *Java*, *Cyane*, *Levant*, etc. Among her officers were Preble, Hull, Decatur, Bainbridge, Stewart, Macdonough, Morris, Porter, Lawrence, Ludlow and Shubrick. This ship was saved from being broken up, when Dr. Holmes begged the Navy Department to

> "Nail to the mast her holy flag,
> Set every threadbare sail,
> And give her to the god of storms,
> The lightning and the gale."

At this wharf also was built the *Boston*, 28, which captured several French armed ships; and the *Argus*, 16, which burnt so many British prizes off the English coast that she was said to have "set the Channel all a-blaze."

Battery Wharf is near the site of the North Battery, constructed in 1646, to command Charles River and the Town Cove, and kept up for more than a century. Four British regiments embarked here for the attack on Bunker Hill; and Lord Howe left 13 cannon in the battery. The steamships for Norfolk and Baltimore sail thence. From Battery St. the North Ferry runs steamboats to East Boston every few minutes. The spacious Lincoln's Wharf has the steamers for Bath and the Kennebec-River ports. Union Wharf bears a line of sombre granite U.-S. bonded warehouses.

Opposite Fleet St. Eastern Avenue runs to the South Ferry to East Boston, down what was once Scarlett's

CHURCH OF THE ADVENT, MT.-VERNON AND BIMMER STS.

Wharf. Here Commercial St. flirts away into the fruit and provision district, leaving the wharves, which are followed thence by Atlantic Avenue, a splendid marginal thoroughfare 100 feet wide, with several street-car and steam freight-railway tracks, and spur-tracks down the wharves. This avenue was made in 1868-70, at a cost of $2,400,000, by building it across the middle of the old docks, with earth taken from Fort Hill, and then filling in the inside parts, which are now covered with imposing commercial structures. It occupies nearly the line of the Barricado, a wharf built in 1673, 2,200 feet long, from the North Battery to the South Battery, to be mounted with cannon to prevent hostile French or Dutch war-vessels from injuring the shipping in Town Cove. Entrances were left for peaceful merchantmen on each side of Long Wharf.

WEST CHURCH, CAMBRIDGE AND LYNDE STREETS.

Lewis Wharf, at 32 Atlantic Avenue, with its long granite warehouses, has the steamships for Yarmouth and Halifax, the Canso ports, Pictou and Prince-Edward Island, and Savannah. This wharf once belonged to John Hancock.

Commercial Wharf is the Boston terminal of the popular International Steamship Co.'s line, which runs to St. John, N. B., via Portland, Lubec and Eastport, making a charming ocean-route to the New England coast and the Maritime Provinces. The fleet comprises three side-wheel steamships, the *State of Maine*, the *Cumberland*, and the *New Brunswick*, providing the modern comforts of traveling. The elegant new steamship *St. Croix*, now under construction, will in many respects surpass all previous efforts of the company. In the spring and autumn this long-established and favorite line runs its steamers tri-weekly, in the summer daily (except Sundays), and in the winter semi-weekly. The trip, for the most part is along the shore, which presents an ever-changing panorama of interesting points. The International Co. affords a pleasant trip to the eastward, reaching numerous pleasure-resorts of

THE "STATE OF MAINE,"—INTERNATIONAL STEAMSHIP CO.
SAILING FROM COMMERCIAL WHARF TO ST. JOHN, N. B., VIA PORTLAND, LUBEC AND EASTPORT.

Maine, and farther still, beyond the international boundary, where lies a vast country under British dominion, full of beauty and crowned with a wealth of interest, replete with the blended romance, story and tradition connected with the earliest settlement of the North-American continent. This country gave refuge to the early voyagers from Europe, at a time when the Pilgrim Fathers of the Old Colony were in leading-strings, and now through two centuries presents its peculiar manners, customs and civilization as an auxiliary charm to the summer tourist from "The States," giving him a taste of Europe to be found on this side of the Atlantic only in this quaint North-East, this country under the shadow of the Crown, this "Land of Evangeline" and the "British Red-coat." Commercial Wharf is also the terminal of the Provincetown line.

This part of Atlantic Avenue is largely occupied by wholesale fish and oyster merchants, and the fishing-vessels float in the adjacent docks. An infinite variety of sea-food may be observed here, and the air is salty and fishy. Huge coils of chain and rope appear by the way; all manner of large and small boats toss about in the slips; and maritime persons and longshoremen placidly observe the lively scene. On the other side is the animated Farmers' Market, mainly used by vegetable and fruit farmers and their wagons, from the suburbs, and a very busy scene at early morning.

T Wharf was a part of the old Barricado, and has a well of excellent water. It belongs to an association of fish-dealers, and is devoted wholly to the fish industry. Boston is the largest fish market in the world. In 1892 more than 90,000,000 pounds of fresh fish were handled by dealers of T Wharf. In 1889 it is estimated that 208,000,000 pounds of fish products passed through the hands of the wholesale dealers of Boston, and, based on value of products as sold, reached an aggregate of $11,100,-259. The number of men engaged in and the yield of all the fisheries of the world, as far as reports are obtainable, are: United States, 200,000 men, value, $50,000,000; Canada, 60,000 men, $17,655,000; England and Wales, estimated yield $23,000,000; Scotland, $8,000,000; Ireland, $1,800,000; Norway, $6,000,000; Holland, $2,000,000; France, 138,-000 men, yield $20,000,000, a grand total of more than $128,000,000 in value, taken in one year. At 21, 22 and 22½ T Wharf, John R. Neal & Co. have a fine museum of models, pictures, implements, etc., illustrating the ancient and modern methods of catching fish and preparing them fresh or otherwise for the markets, and many curious matters pertaining to fishing and packing. This firm ranks eminent among the great fish houses of the country, and besides being enormous handlers of fresh and salted fish they make a specialty of curing haddock which is known over the world as "John R. Neal & Co.'s Star Brand of Finnan Haddie." The Museum is opened free to the public.

Long Wharf was built in 1709-10, as a prolongation of State St., under the name of Boston Pier, 2,000 feet long, with a battery on the end. It became the pride of the town, where the London ships lay, and

JOHN R. NEAL & CO., WHOLESALERS OF FRESH AND SALTED FISH.
VIEWS OF THE NEAL FISHERIES MUSEUM, T WHARF, FOOT OF SOUTH MARKET STREET.

the Royalist governors and armies were sumptuously received on landing. Hawthorne long served here as weigher and gauger. The foreign commerce of Boston, very extensive before the Revolution, and almost monopolizing the American China and India trades for the first half of this century, became nearly extinct between 1850 and 1870. Then the railways from the West reduced their freight rates and improved their terminal facilities, and the local commerce made enormous gains, so that it uses almost a steamship a day from this port to Europe. Boston is second only to New York as a shipping port, with 4,000 vessels entering from or clearing for foreign ports yearly, and an annual import and export trade of $140,000,000. Plans are now under way for the city to buy all the wharves, and replace them with handsome and commodious municipal

CADETS' ARMORY.
COLUMBUS AVENUE, SOUTHEAST CORNER OF FERDINAND STREET.

docks (as in Liverpool and other great ports), whose low charges may invite a still greater maritime traffic. The chief foreign steamships have their docks at East and South Boston and Charlestown.

Long Wharf is the headquarters of the tropical fruit trade, and here the Boston Fruit Company, an association of Boston merchants and West-India fruit-growers, receive their cargoes of bananas, cocoanuts, oranges, lemons, and kindred fruits. The corporation owns nearly 40,000 acres, included in 35 plantations, and deep-water frontage in the harbors of Port Antonio and Port Morant. They own their own lines of steamships, which they operate between those ports and Boston, Philadelphia and Baltimore. Besides carrying their own fruits, they carry some outside freight, and afford passenger accommodations for many tourists visiting the West-India Islands.

Ascending State St. from Long Wharf, one quickly reaches the Custom House, the financial district, the Old State House, and the retail district. Dr. Holmes thus apostrophized Long Wharf:

"Strong right arm of Boston, stretched out o'er the bay,
May the winds waft the wealth of all nations to thee,
And thy dividends flow like the waves of the sea."

Central Wharf has the moorings of the steamships to Philadelphia and to Gloucester.

From India Wharf runs the daily line of new and palatial steamers owned by the Portland Steam Packet Co., the *Bay State* and the *Portland* (each exceeding 2,200 tons), two of the grandest steamers that sail from Boston Harbor. They make the run between Boston and Portland in a night, and charge but $1, the view from the steamers, in either Boston or Portland harbor, morning or evening, being worth the full cost of the trip. It is impossible to obtain a more restful, exhilarating and enjoyable excursion anywhere. These steamers are the largest and finest side-wheel vessels east of Long-Island Sound, and are fitted with every modern appliance for comfort and luxury. Electric lights and bells, steam steering-gear, and first-class appointments are in every department. The passenger dining-rooms are superb, and the meals, on the European plan, are all that can be desired. The company issues through excursion-tickets, by almost every conceivable rail and steamship route, east, west, north and south. The Portland Steam Packet Co. has a record of 50 years' thoroughly satisfactory service, never having lost a life nor injured a person. From India Wharf also sail the freight vessels of the Metropolitan Line, for New York. Howells says of this locality:

"The place was sacred to the shipping of the grandest commerce in the world — these beautiful ships, clean as silver, and manned by honest Yankee crews."

Here the old captains discussed

"The Dutch colonies and coffee; the China trade and tea; the Northwest coast and furs; the Cape and its wines and oil; the pirates that used to harass the early adventurers; famous shipwrecks; great gains and magnificent losses; the splendor of the English nabobs and American residents of Calcutta; mutinies aboard ship; and the idiosyncrasies of certain sailors."

BOSTON FRUIT COMPANY, TROPICAL FRUIT GROWERS.
LONG WHARF, ATLANTIC AVENUE, FOOT OF STATE STREET.

STEAMER "BAY STATE."—PORTLAND STEAM PACKET CO.

SAILS FROM INDIA WHARF. THE LINE MAKES DAILY TRIPS BETWEEN BOSTON AND PORTLAND.

Rowe's Wharf is throughout the summer one of the busiest and happiest of places, for thence every half-hour or so depart the pleasant steamboats for Hull, Hingham, and Nantasket, the favorite summer-resorts of the harbor. Elsewhere are the piers of the Lynn, Nahant, and Plymouth steamers. At Rowe's Wharf is the end of Broad St., the scene of the bloody riots of 1837 between the firemen and the Irish, in which 15,000 persons were engaged. The Irish quarter was sacked by the populace; and it required the advance of 800 State troops, and repeated charges by the Lancers, to avert a general massacre.

Next to Rowe's Wharf is the ferry-house of the Revere-Beach narrow-gauge railroad, whose quaint little trains run from East Boston

CHURCH OF THE DISCIPLES, WARREN AVENUE AND WEST BROOKLINE STREET.

along the shore to Lynn, Ocean Spray, and Winthrop. Near Rowe's Wharf stood the Sconce, or South Battery, erected in 1666, and mounting 35 guns. On Fort Hill, above, stood a larger fortress.

Howells thus portrays the pleasant inner harbor :

"The steamships of many coastwise freight lines gloom, with their black capacious hulks, among the lighter sailing craft, and among the white, green-shuttered passenger-boats; and behind those desperate and grimy sheds assume a picturesqueness, their sagging roofs and crooked gables harmonizing agreeably with the shipping ; and then growing up from all rises the mellow-tinted, brick-built city, roof, and spire, and dome,—a fair and noble sight, indeed, and one not surpassed for a certain quiet and cleanly beauty by any that I know."

The Boston & Bangor Steamship Co. dispatches its fine and seaworthy vessels from Foster's Wharf, at 366 Atlantic Avenue, at five o'clock every afternoon in summer, and semi-weekly in winter. These great steamships, the *City of Bangor, Penobscot, Katahdin,* and *Lewiston,* have accommodations for 500 passengers, with richly-provided dining-rooms and spacious state-rooms. Their voyage gives very interesting panoramic views of the harbor, the receding city crowned with its dome of gold, the European steamships in their docks at East Boston and South Boston, the formidable fortifications frowning over the lower roadstead, and the many picturesque rocky islets which keep the stormy waves from the Puritan harbor. Beyond the tall white lighthouse, they run up along the famous North Shore, with distant views of Nahant and Swampscot, Marblehead and Magnolia, and other popular and fashionable summer-resorts. Before dark, they round the tall twin lighthouses of Thacher's Island, and the gray cliffs of Cape Ann, "the land of rocks and roses;" and stretch away into the dim northern sea, the ancient Gulf of Maine. At

TREMONT STREET, SOUTHEAST CORNER OF ELIOT STREET.

early morning, the vessel enters the beautiful and historic Penobscot Bay, and makes its first port at Rockland, famous for its vast product of lime. The *Mount Desert* and other steamers of this company's fleet connect here for the quaint little ports among the islands, and for the landings about Mount Desert and the remoter eastern coasts. The boat from Boston proceeds up Penobscot Bay and River, making landings at Belfast, Bucksport and other well-known towns, and before noon reaches Bangor, the bright metropolis of Eastern Maine. This line has an immense summer-tourist business, since it furnishes an inexpensive, comfortable and picturesque route to the beaches, headlands and fiords of "hun-

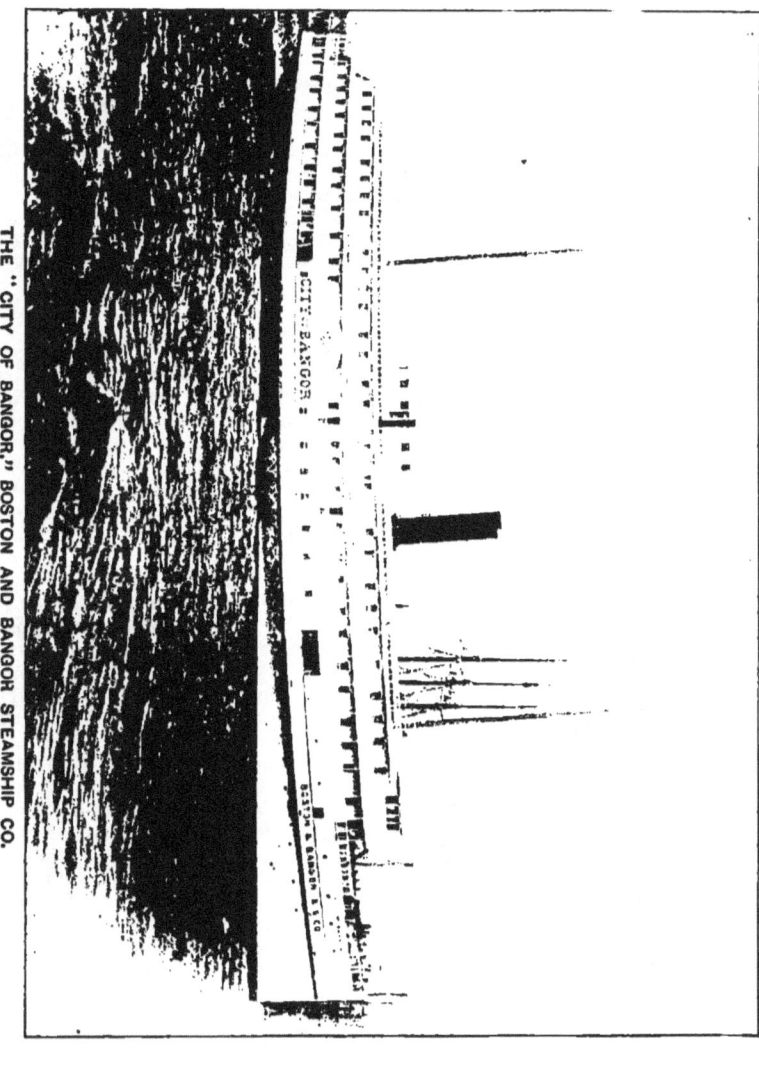

THE "CITY OF BANGOR," BOSTON AND BANGOR STEAMSHIP CO.
SAILS DAILY FROM FOSTER'S WHARF TO BANGOR AND MT. DESERT.

dred-harbored Maine," and to Moosehead Lake and the great forest. The Boston-Bangor steamships began their voyages in 1833, and were for over 40 years known as the Sanford Line, until acquired by the present company, in 1882. The president and general manager is William H. Hill, of Richardson, Hill & Co., the bankers. Snow's Arch Wharf has the steamers for Beverly, Marblehead, and Salem, and for Portsmouth.

Liverpool Wharf (formerly Griffin's) was the scene of the Tea Party of December 16, 1773, when 60 Bostonians, some of them disguised as Indians, boarded the three Indiamen, *Dartmouth*, *Eleanor* and *Beaver*, lying here, and emptied 342 chests of tea into the harbor. Dr. Holmes avers that

> " The waters in the rebel bay
> Have kept the tea-leaf savor;
> Our old North-Enders in their spray
> Still taste a Hyson flavor."

Between Atlantic Avenue and the Congress-St. bridge, at 299 to 303 Congress St., directly facing the harbor, is the great shoe warehouse of the J. B. Lewis Co., whose main factories are at Avon, and whose line of goods, known as "Wear-Resisters," comprises the whole range of boots and shoes of all grades for men, women and children. The business was established in 1858, and its customers extend throughout the Union. The J. B. Lewis Co. are said to be the largest shippers of boots and shoes of any manufacturer selling the retail trade direct from Boston, the centre of the shoe trade of this country.

COLUMBUS STATUE, AT THE CATHEDRAL.

A little farther south Atlantic Avenue reaches Fort-Point Channel to the South Bay, which has many coal and lumber wharves. Across the narrow water are the New-York & New-England Railroad docks and elevators, on land reclaimed from the harbor, and with piers used by European freight-steamships. Atlantic Avenue ends in the wool district (Boston is second only to London as a wool-market), at the foot of Summer St., leading back to the Retail District, and in front of the ugly station of the New-York & New England Railroad. A few blocks south, on Federal St., are the great factories of the Goodyear Shoe Machinery Co , whose patented machines are used in both continents. Kneeland St. has the Old-Colony and Albany railroad stations, a block apart. The Old-Colony (chartered in 1844) leads to Plymouth, New Bedford, Cape Cod, and the steamboat lines to Nan-

J. B. LEWIS CO., WHOLESALE SHOE MANUFACTURERS.
NOS. 299, 301 AND 303 CONGRESS STREET, BETWEEN ATLANTIC AVENUE AND CONGRESS-STREET BRIDGE.

tucket and Martha's Vineyard. The Boston & Albany leads to Worcester, Springfield, Albany and the north, and with its close alliances with the New-York Central, the Lake-Shore and other great roads, it forms the most important route between the East and West. Its through New-York trains, several times daily, are unsurpassed; and its local suburban service at low commutation rates to the Newtons, Brookline, Wellesley and other places is hardly equaled on either continent.

CATHEDRAL OF THE HOLY CROSS, ROMAN CATHOLIC.
WASHINGTON STREET, NORTHEAST CORNER OF MALDEN STREET.

GOODYEAR SHOE MACHINERY CO., MACHINERY MANUFACTURERS.
FEDERAL STREET, SOUTH OF KNEELAND STREET.

BOSTON & ALBANY RAILROAD STATION,
KNEELAND STREET, BETWEEN LINCOLN AND UTICA STREETS.

THE SUBURBS.

THE suburbs of Boston are among the most beautiful in the world. Nature has done much for them, with her great rocky hills, deep forests, shining lakes, far-winding rivers, fragrant salt-marshes, and blue inlets of the sea. Art has also been kind, during nearly three centuries, dotting this rugged paradise with quaint villages, generous country-seats, tall spires, domes, and towers, and beauty-spots of rich flower-coloring. History has dowered the region with the records of the heroic early settlements, of wars with savages and European troops, and of the lives and deeds of many illustrious men. Literature has added her laurels : Holmes

NEW-ENGLAND CONSERVATORY OF MUSIC, FRANKLIN SQUARE.

to the old town, Howells to the modern city, Hawthorne to West Roxbury and Salem, Longfellow and Lowell to Cambridge, Thoreau and Emerson to Concord, Motley to Quincy, and Bynner to Marblehead ; and hundreds of others, poets, romancers, historians and antiquaries. What other city has such a garland of pleasant and historic hamlets and parks, dreaming in comfort and content, in a land of peace?

Sir Charles Dilke has written of the surroundings of Boston :

" In her southern suburbs,— in Roxbury and the hills beyond, and princely Brookline, and Brighton,—Boston may challenge comparison with almost any city in the world. This undulating region, dotted with crystal ponds, superbly wooded, and covered for miles with country-seats in every conceivable style of architecture, is a portfolio crammed with delicious pictures. The velvet turf, golden green in sunshine, the trim buckthorn hedges, the trellised roses, the commingling of pine, elm, maple, larch, chestnut and fir in the groves, the unexpected dells and water-glimpses, the gleam of towers and mellow-tinted house-fronts, far and near, the old avenues, ribbed with Gothic boughs, are among their features, and you can scarcely say that anything is wanting. Although her people are everywhere in the vanguard of all progress, their country has a look of gable-ends and steeple-hats. In all England, there is no city which has suburbs so gray and venerable as the elm-shaded towns around Boston."

Bayard Taylor, with his broad knowledge of the world, said :

" As you approach Boston, the roughest region is yet a region of homes. Man may sometimes deform, but he oftenest improves nature ; and I know no better illustration of the fact than the environs of Boston. The approach to Boston is almost the only picturesque city-view we have on the Atlantic coast. The broad reaches of water, the cheerful suburbs on either hand, the long gently rising brick hill in front, crowned with the dome of the State House, form an imposing and truly attractive picture. . . . Boston, from any side, owing to her elevation, has a stately charm which her prouder sisters do not possess."

CHURCH OF THE IMMACULATE CONCEPTION AND BOSTON COLLEGE, HARRISON AVE. AND CONCORD ST.

CHARLESTOWN.

CHARLESTOWN and Bunker-Hill street-cars leave Scollay Square every few minutes for quaint old Charlestown. Those marked Bunker Hill lead to the monument. Beyond the crowded manufacturing streets, the car crosses Charles River on a long bridge, with the Hoosac-Tunnel Docks on the right front, and the Navy Yard beyond. We soon reach the little park of City Square, with the Waverley House (once a hotel) on the left; and next it the fine City Hall of Charlestown before annexation, now occupied by a branch of the Public Library, and the Municipal Court. The Indian domain called Mishawum was settled by the English before 1629; became a city in 1847; and was annexed to Boston in 1873. The Charles-River Bridge was built in 1786; and the Warren Bridge, in 1828. These railroad bridges for the northern railroads are now approaching completion. S. F. B. Morse, the inventor of the telegraph, was born at Charlestown.

The U.-S. Navy Yard, founded in 1800, covers 87 acres, and has nearly 100 store-houses, machine-shops, arsenals, barracks, rope-walks, shiphouses, etc., with a million-dollar hammered-granite dry dock, a sea-wall, a battery, trees and lawns, parades and avenues. In the stream lies the famous old frigate *Wabash*, now a receiving-ship. Among the war-vessels built here were the *Independence*, 74, *Frolic*, *Vermont*, 74, *Warren*, Farragut's flag-ship *Hartford*, the *Cumberland* and *Merrimac* (afterwards antagonists), the *Wachusett* and *Huron*, and the ironclads *Monadnock*, *Nahant*, *Nantucket* and *Canonicus*. This famous yard is now but little used. Visitors are admitted, and will find it very interesting.

Bunker-Hill Monument was built in 1825-42. Lafayette attended at the laying of the corner-stone, and President Tyler at the final dedication; and Webster gave the orations for both occasions.

PAUL REVERE'S HOUSE, NORTH SQUARE.

The obelisk 220 feet high, and 30 feet square at the base, is of Quincy granite. Two hundred and ninety-five stone steps lead to the observatory chamber at the top, with its venerable Provincial cannon, and superb views over the harbor and sea, the city and suburbs, the inland villages and far blue mountains, Wachusett and Monadnock. The ward Bostonian usually contents himself here with sitting down at the base, and musing over Emerson and Browning, while his Western friends go up the winding stairs. As Dr. Holmes says :

"And Bunker's tall shaft you can climb if you will,
But you'll puff like a paragraph praising a pill."

In the lodge at the base is Dexter's marble statue of Gen. Warren, with other memorials ; and in the main path in 1881 was raised Story's admirable and spirited bronze statue of Col. Prescott, who defended the redoubt. He is in a long seersucker coat and broad farmer's hat, with drawn sword, as when warning his eager men : "Don't fire until you see the whites of their eyes." Col. Prescott marched from Cambridge on the night of June 16, 1775, and fortified this hill-top, which was attacked at dawn by the broadsides of the British fleet, and later by 4,000 Royal troops under Howe and Clinton. The American force, though smaller, and inexpert in war, repulsed two grand assaults, and then were driven from the works, having lost 450 men to the British 1,054. This was the first open battle of the Revolution. The anniversary is a holiday in Charlestown, which was burned during the battle by hot shot from the British battery on Copp's Hill, and by landing-parties of marines and blue-jackets.

MATHER TOMB, COPP'S HILL BURYING GROUND.

The Charlestown Soldiers' and Sailors' Monument, dedicated in 1872, stands on Winthrop Square, the old Training-Field, near "the stone spike that's druv through Bunker Hill." It represents the Genius of America, holding laurels over a soldier and a sailor. The true Bunker Hill, much higher than the battle-ground, is crowned by a conspicuous Catholic church. Not far away extends one of the new parks, with a grand view over the Mystic Valley.

The Charlestown Burial-Ground, reached by the short Phipps St. from Main St., contains the grave of John Harvard, near which the graduates of the University erected a granite memorial, in 1828. The Massachusetts State Prison, built in 1804-05, covers a broad area near Charles River with its gloomy granite structures, crowded with desperate and unfortunate men.

There are many factories in Charlestown, and among them the famous mustard and spice mills of the Stickney & Poor Spice Co., the oldest concern in its line in New England, and with a trade well established throughout the country.

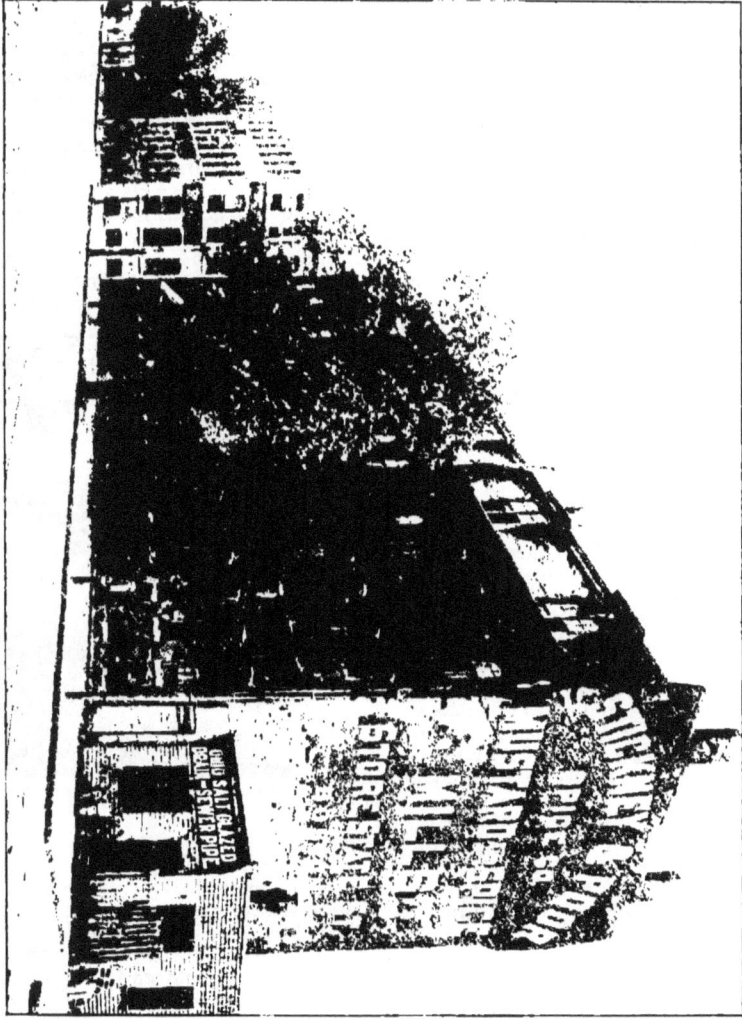

THE STICKNEY & POOR SPICE CO., MUSTARDS AND SPICES.
WORKS: CHARLESTOWN, MASS. OFFICES: 184 AND 186 STATE STREET.

EAST BOSTON.

STREET-CARS run every five minutes from Scollay Square down Hanover St., and across the ferries to East Boston. These steam-ferries are owned and run by the city, and carry yearly 11,000,000 passengers and 1,000,000 vehicles. Some of the street-cars traverse the island on Meridian St. to Chelsea. Noddle's Island (of 663 acres) had but one resident family in 1833, and its only use was for farming, pasturage and picnics. Then the East-Boston Company laid out streets and sold lots, and began an active development. It now has 40,000 inhabitants, with large shipyards, sugar-houses, grain-elevators, dry-docks, iron-works, and other manufactures. Here Donald McKay built the *Great Republic*, the *Sovereign of the Seas*, and other famous ocean-racers. The Atlantic Works, at 70 Border St., build or repair iron ships, and construct steamship engines, boilers and shafting. On the harbor-front are the Cunard and Grand-Junction wharves, where may be seen some of the huge Liverpool or London steamships. Here the chief railways from the West have their tide-water terminals and elevators, with wonderfully ingenious systems of quickly loading and discharging cargoes. On this side of the harbor are the docks which receive gigantic steel freight-steamships like the Warren-liner *Scotsman* and the Cunarder *Sylvania*, each carrying from 7,000 to 9,000 tons of freight. Here also will come the three mammoth Leyland steamships now being built, each 520 feet long, and of 16,000 tons capacity.

COPP'S HILL BURIAL-GROUND, CHARTER AND HULL STREETS.

Maverick Square, the business-centre, is overlooked by the spacious Maverick House, much frequented by steamship officers. Central Square, farther north, on Meridian St., is larger; and from the high ground near the quaint Belmont Square, along Webster Street, interesting views of the harbor are gained. On this square Samuel Maverick, an Episcopal gentleman, had a castle mounting four cannon, called "murtherers," before Winthrop came; and forts arose on the same site in 1776 and 1814. The old Jewish burial-ground, with its Hebrew inscriptions and sea-views, is at Byron and Homer Sts. On the remote east part of the island is the city's Wood-Island Park, covering 80 acres, with lawns, ball-grounds, drives, bath-houses, and fine harbor-views.

SOUTH BOSTON.

STREET-CARS run from Scollay, Park, and Post-Office squares every few minutes to South Boston. In 1804, when it was annexed to Boston, this hilly peninsula had but ten families. It was expected that here would rise the court end of the city, but the growth took quite another form, and it is now a factory-quarter, with 70,000 inhabitants. In this energetic industrial centre skilled artificers make war-ships, elevators, cordage, car-wheels, boilers, heavy cannon, and steel and brass castings, besides refining sugar and oil, and brewing. The South-Boston Iron Co., founded by Cyrus Alger, on Foundry St., covered seven acres, and had the largest iron-works in New-England, with splendidly-equipped shops, famous for their product of ordnance and projectiles. Other foundries may be seen along the water-side; and the sugar-refineries tower high on Granite St.

The Whittier Machine Co.'s works at South Boston are the result of half a century's development. Here are made the passenger elevators — sometimes called the perpendicular railways — which have made possible the lofty structures of to-day. This was virtually the pioneer concern to manufacture passenger elevators, and many of the largest buildings throughout this country, and by far the majority of important buildings in Boston, are provided with the Whittier elevators, which are recognized as having every possible advantage of safety, speed, elegance and durability.

CHRIST CHURCH, SALEM AND HULL STREETS.

The Walworth Manufacturing Company, whose offices are at 14 to 24 Oliver St., and whose works are at South Boston, are manufacturers of steam, water and gas users' supplies, tools, etc., and such specialties as Stillson wrenches, Allston wrenches, Stanwood pipe cutters, Walworth

WHITTIER MACHINE COMPANY, PASSENGER AND FREIGHT ELEVATORS.
WORKS: SOUTH BOSTON. OFFICES: 53 STATE STREET, STOCK EXCHANGE BUILDING.

die-plates, Hall tapping machines and cast iron pipe cutters, Ashley nipple holders and Walworth sprinkler heads. Their business exterds not only throughout this country but into England, Germany and all parts of Europe, Mexico, South America and Australia. Their plant covers many acres, with iron and brass foundries, machine and forge shops, and wharves on tide water, employing 600 men, besides 150 in the warehouse.

Here are huge warehouses; and the New-York & New-England docks and elevators, with great European steamships. The approach to South Boston is squalid; but Broadway, its spacious tree-lined main thoroughfare, soon ascends to a pleasanter region of churches and homes.

The Perkins Institution and Massachusetts School for the Blind, organized in 1832, by Dr. S. G. Howe, in 1839 occupied the Mount-Washington House, a conspicuous sea-viewing summer-hotel, which had

BOSTON HARBOR, NEAR ROWE'S AND FOSTER'S WHARVES.

recently failed; and there, and in later buildings, it remains. When Dr. Howe died, in 1876, the management passed to his son-in-law, Michael Anagnos. Even the deaf, dumb and blind, like Laura Bridgman and Helen Kellar, have been educated into intelligence here, and hundreds of blind youth have been taught self-support, especially by music. There are 30 teachers. Several States support their blind here; and Massachusetts makes a large yearly grant. The library and printery of books in raised letters are the largest in the world. Visitors are admitted Thursdays between 11 and 1.

Independence Square is an open park of 6½ acres, between the fine residence part of Broadway and the harbor. On its low north side are the city House of Correction; and the Boston Lunatic Hospital, built in 1839-46, for 200 patients, with five acres of grounds.

Close to the Perkins Institution is Thomas Park, on Telegraph Hill (whence marine telegraphing used to be done), with a granite monument

WALWORTH MANUFACTURING CO., STEAM, WATER, AND GAS SUPPLIES, ETC.
WORKS: SOUTH BOSTON. OFFICES: 16 TO 24 OLIVER STREET.

telling that on this ridge (then called Dorchester Heights) Washington placed the batteries whose hot fire compelled the British to evacuate Boston. This eminence commands a superb view of the harbor, the Blue Hills, and the city.

The Carney Hospital, on Old Harbor St., is a noble institution, founded in 1865, and run by the Sisters of Charity, but unsectarian as to its contributors and beneficiaries. The buildings are high-placed, and command noble views.

City Point is the chief rendezvous in America for small yachts, and affords a brisk and inspiring sight on a breezy summer day. The Boston

THE OLD FITCHBURG RAILROAD STATION, CAUSEWAY STREET.

and South-Boston Yacht Clubs have their houses here; and near by are the yards where come the celebrated Burgess and other fast yachts. Small restaurants abound hereabouts.

The Marine Park occupies the seaward end, with walks and esplanades and lovely harbor-views. Here Kitson's fine bronze statue of Admiral Farragut was set up, in 1893. A long promenade-pier leads to Castle Island, where there are walks and drives around the walls of Fort Independence, with very noble sea-views. This is the oldest virgin fortress in the world, having never surrendered to a hostile attack. The first battery was erected here by the Puritans, in 1634, and many a shot was fired thence at ships, as well as at Washington's Dorchester-Heights forts in 1776. Scores of distinguished officers have been in garrison here. The present very handsome fort is about half a century old, and has been ungarrisoned since 1880, serving as a depot of supplies, and being kept heavily armed.

One may return to Boston by the Broadway Bridge or Dover-Street Bridge, and regain Scollay Square by the city routes.

DORCHESTER.

DORCHESTER is reached by street-cars from the Old South, across South Boston ; or from Scollay Square or the Granary Burial-Ground, across Roxbury. The Old-Colony and New-York & New-England Railroads have a score of stations in this suburb.

It was settled before Boston, but, being poorly endowed with navigable waters, remained a quiet farming-town, which within a few years was passed by Boston. It once reached to the Rhode-Island line, but several towns were carved out of it, and the metropolis secured the northward parts in 1804. In 1869 the old town was annexed to Boston. It then had 12,000 inhabitants, the present number being 35,000. The picturesque hills, plains, forests and sea-meadows, the broad and tree-shaded old roads, the many fine estates, the interesting and venerable colonial mansions, the cheapness of land, and the easy accessibility to the city have made this a favorite residence-quarter, with countless modern cottages scattered over its 6,000 acres.

The pleasantest and most comprehensive route traverses the attractive Warren St., Roxbury, and enters Dorchester at Grove Hall, near Franklin Park. Thence the line runs for half a league through pleasant semi-rural scenery, passing the gardens of the late M. P. Wilder, the famous horticulturist, and closely approaching Mount Bowdoin, whose summit commands a

UNION STATION, ENTRANCE ARCH, CAUSEWAY STREET.

fine sea-view. Farther on, the noble Blue Hills appear on the right, and the ocean on the left.

The Pierce house is said to be the second oldest house standing in the United States, having been erected in 1635, and continuing in the possession of the Pierce family ever since. Its sides are packed with seaweed, partly as a protection against Indian arrows.

The Second Church, a dignified Puritan temple, dates from 1806. It is Congregational; and Arthur Little holds the pastorate once graced by John Codman. Just beyond is the very fine Henry L. Pierce Public School, of Perth-Amboy salmon brick, built in 1891-92, and accommodating 700 pupils. On this site until lately stood a colonial mansion, where Henry Knox and Daniel Webster dwelt. Nearly opposite the church is the little old Dorchester Town Hall. The car-track stops at Ashmont; and it is twenty minutes' brisk walk thence southward to the quaint valley-hamlet of Lower Mills.

On the harbor-front, and best reached by the Old-Colony Railroad, is the picturesque cluster of villas on Savin Hill; the old Abolitionist village of Harrison Square (founded in 1840), with the house and moorings of the Dorchester Yacht Club; Pope's Hill, where Lucy Stone dwelt; Commercial Point, whose whaling fleets have given place to gas-works; and busy Neponset, with its factories and wharves. Thence a branch railway ascends the Neponset-River valley, passing near the station at Cedar-Grove Cemetery.

Lower Mills station and village are at the picturesque little falls on the Neponset River. This is the seat of Walter Baker & Co.'s immense chocolate-mills. The first water-mill in America was founded here in 1633 by Israel Stoughton, afterwards one of Cromwell's colonels in England. Here are several very ancient houses; and from the villa-crowned Milton Hill, on the south, noble harbor and mountain views are gained. The last station on this branch is at the delightful old rural village of Mattapan, with its quaint stone Church of the Holy Spirit.

Meeting-House Hill (by street-cars from Franklin St., Boston, every 10 minutes) is crowned by the church (built in 1816) of the First Parish (now Unitarian), the fourth on this site since 1670. The first meeting-house, built of logs, with palisades and armed guards, was erected in 1631, at Cottage and Pleasant Sts. On the hill stands a red granite obelisk, bearing the names of the Dorchester soldiers who died in the War for the Union. The Catholic Church of St. Peter is near by. Broad harbor and sea views are had from the hill. Southward, within a mile, is Field's Corner, with the Dorchester post-office, public library, court-house, and police-station. Northward, near Upham's Corner, is the burial-ground, interesting to antiquaries, with monuments as far back as 1638, and the graves of several colonial dignitaries; and near Five Corners is the birthplace of Edward Everett.

ROXBURY.

THE street-car routes described on previous pages lead across the South End to Roxbury. The Washington-St. line is the most interesting, and its cars traverse Scollay Square, and run out by the Cathedral and the New-England Conservatory of Music. A little way beyond is passed the venerable and neglected Eliot Burial-Ground, with the graves of Govs. Thomas Dudley and Joseph Dudley, Chief-Justice Paul Dudley, Gen. Greaton, and others. The parish-tomb contains the bones of six ancient pastors, and of John Eliot, the famous apostle to the Indians. "Rocksberry, because something rocky" (as a chronicler wrote in 1633), was settled in 1630; and gave Gens. Dearborn, Heath, Greaton and Warren to the Revolutionary armies; and Miles, Lee and Amory, Admiral Winslow, and 3,271 soldiers to the War for the Union. It had 2,000 inhabitants in 1775; and 90,000 in 1890. In 1846 it became a city, and was annexed to Boston in 1867. It is a beautifully diversified region of hills and crags, meadows and dales, trees and gardens, amid which wind fine roads, bordered by thousands of happy suburban homes. The fine old Provincial mansions of the Shirleys, Auchmutys and other great families have vanished before this vigorous invasion. The rather somnolent business centre of Roxbury is near the convergence of Washington, Warren and Roxbury Sts. The wooden meeting-house (built in 1821) pertains to the Universalists, and occupies the site of Gov. Dudley's mansion. Up the hill leads Roxbury St. to Eliot Square, on one side of which is the Norfolk House, opened in 1825, and now a comfortable family-hotel and well-known landmark. A short distance beyond, on Roxbury St., are the art works of L. Prang & Co., the art and educational publishers, whose productions are in use over all the continents.

The First Parish Church occupies pleasant grounds on Eliot Square, with an excellent and well-preserved specimen of Puritan architecture, dating from 1804. The society originated in 1632; and for many years had for its pastor the gentle John Eliot, who gave most of his time to preaching to the Indians and translating the Bible into their language. After nearly two centuries of Orthodoxy, the parish became Unitarian; and Dr. George Putnam led it from 1830 to 1876. James De Normandie has been pastor since 1882. In 1775-76 the steeple on this site served as a signal-station for the American army; and the church became a target for cannon-shot from the British lines.

A few minutes' walk along the pleasant Highland St., where E. E. Hale dwells (No. 39) and W. L. Garrison long lived, leads to the handsome white minaret built for a water standpipe (now disused), and a landmark for the southern suburbs. Here stood the Roxbury High Fort, the key of the American siege-lines, built by Gen. Knox in 1775, and levelled by municipal vandals in 1869. Many a cannon-shot flew from these parapets against the Royalist batteries in Boston. Near Highland

L. PRANG & CO., ART PUBLISHERS.
WORKS AND GENERAL OFFICES: ROXBURY, MASS. SALES OFFICES, 859 WASHINGTON STREET.

St. is the Fellowes Athenæum, for which Caleb Fellowes bequeathed about $50,000. It is a public library of 30,000 volumes, including a popular affiliated branch of the Boston Public Library.

Washington-St. cars run out by the venerable Episcopal church of St. James, a stone fane retired among green lawns; Notre Dame Academy, with its charming grounds, and the buildings where the Sisters of Notre Dame teach young ladies; and the New-England Hospital for Women and Children, founded in 1862, with medical, surgical and maternity wards, and a capital nurses' training-school, all under the care of a staff of highly educated women-physicians. Then it traverses the verge of Jamaica Plain, near the Playstead and Glen-Road entrances to Franklin

ROWE'S WHARF AND FOSTER'S WHARF, ATLANTIC AVENUE, FOOT OF BROAD STREET.

Park; and reaches Forest-Hills Cemetery. Street-cars lead from Roxbury's business-centre along Dudley St. to Dorchester, traversing the attractive residence-district of Mount Pleasant.

Warren St., one of the most attractive in this extensive district of homes, is traversed by street cars. Just to one side, on Kearsarge Avenue, is the famous Roxbury Latin School, founded in 1645, by Eliot and Dudley, and prolific in eminent men. It is not a part of the public-school system; and has 150 pupils. The birthplace of Gen. Warren is shown by a tablet upon a stone cottage occupying its site, on Warren St. Close by is the handsome stone church (with costly memorial window) of the Roxbury Swedenborgians. At 216 Warren St. is the house of the Roxbury Club, including nearly 300 well-to-do business men. At Warren and Montrose Sts. stands the grand new Roxbury High School; and at Elm Hill is the handsome All Souls' Church (Unitarian), a quaint stone building, embowered among the trees. Not far beyond is the broad open plaza of Grove Hall, with the late Dr. Cullis's unique home for consumptives, supported by funds received in answer to prayer.

Thence one car-line runs to Mount Bowdoin and Dorchester; and another ascends quickly to Franklin Park.

Franklin Park, the leading feature of Boston's park system, covers about 600 acres, and has cost, since 1870, over $3,000,000. The high and rugged ground on the north has been rather elaborately adorned, in a decorative urban manner, with the superb lawn of the Playstead, broken only by a flagstaff of Oregon pine; the very spacious and high-placed Overlook house, 800 feet long, girt about with flower-fringed battlements of rock; the inchoate driveway of the Greeting; and other features.

A long and handsome masonry wall, with very picturesque portals, red-tiled tops, and bastions of roses, separates this section from the so-called Country Park, where the features have been made more broad, free and natural, with the trellised Italian arbors of Schoolmaster Hill (in old days R. W. Emerson's favorite haunt), the splendid carriage-concourse crowning Scarborough Hill, the long vistas down Nazingdale, the venerable forest of Abbotswood, and other glorious attractions. Firm white roads wind along the rich green pastures, where collie-dogs and shepherds guard flocks of grazing sheep, put here for picturesque effect; and tall elms diversify the sloping glades with their flower-like grace.

BUNKER-HILL MONUMENT, CHARLESTOWN.

At the end of the vistas rise the distant and lofty Blue Hills of Milton, with admirable artistic effects. There are quiet blue ponds, half-artificial labyrinths of wilderness, really remarkable rock-scenery, tennis and ball grounds, refectories, and shelters for rainy hours. The best way to see these attractions is to take the comfortable park-carriages, always in waiting at the gate on Blue-Hill Avenue (at the end of the Boston street-car line). The drivers are familiar with the points of interest. The drive is seven miles long; and the charge is 25 cents for each person.

Franklin Field is a tract of 80 acres, just beyond the park, on Blue-Hill Avenue, changed by the city in 1893-94 from a flower-entangled wet meadow to a vast level lawn, for the drilling of the militia in summer, and the playing of cricket and other games. In winter it is flooded, for skating. The Park and Field were named for Benjamin Franklin, the most illustrious native of Boston, who in 1791 bequeathed the town £1,000, to be loaned out as directed, the accruing fund to be given to Boston, after a century, "for public works to make living more convenient to its people, and more agreeable to strangers resorting thither." In 1891, therefore, the city received nearly $400,000 from this fund, which was first intended to be devoted to the park, but afterwards was set apart for a great trades-school.

PRESCOTT STATUE,
BUNKER-HILL MONUMENT, CHARLESTOWN.

Within 20 years, Boston has generously paid out $15,000,000 for parks, including those at East Boston and Charlestown Heights, Charlesbank, the Fens, Jamaica Pond, the Arboretum, Franklin Park, and the Marine Park at South Boston, with their connecting parkways; and also including her proportion of the cost of the outlying Metropolitan parks, at Middlesex Fells, the Waverly Oaks, the Stony-Brook forest, and the Blue Hills. The landscape-architect was Frederick Law Olmsted.

VIEW OF BOSTON FROM THE HARBOR.

"Boston is more authentic and individual, more municipal, after the old pattern, than any other modern city. It gives its stamp, it characterizes. Even Boston provinciality is a precious testimony to the authoritative personality of the city. Cosmopolitanism is a modern vice, and we're antique, we're classic, in the other thing."—HOWELLS.

FRANKLIN PARK, OF BOSTON'S PARK SYSTEM.
BLUE HILL AVENUE, DORCHESTER DISTRICT.

JAMAICA PLAIN AND WEST ROXBURY.

JAMAICA Plain or Forest Hills may be reached by the Providence Railroad; or else in half an hour by street-cars from the Granary Burial-Ground every five minutes across the South End to Jamaica Plain. The street-cars also reach Forest Hills. The route is along Tremont St. Near Tremont station is seen a region of immense breweries, where Pfaff, Roessle, Burkhardt, and other experts yearly make hundreds of thousands of barrels of lager beer. Quite naturally, a large German population has settled in this fragrant valley. The huge and frequently ornate brick buildings, with their broad yards, indicate a high prosperity in the business of making bitter decoctions of malt. On the right is the lofty Parker Hill; and on the high ground on the left, Prang's lithograph works and the graceful white tower of the Highland stand-pipe. North Heath and Marcella Sts. lead to the much-praised Marcella-St. Home, a municipal asylum for pauper and neglected children under 16, with graded schools and religious services. Another short walk, along Amory St., leads to the Notre-Dame Academy and the New-England Hospital.

SOLDIERS' AND SAILORS' MONUMENT, CHARLESTOWN.

The street-cars cross the Providence Railway on Centre St., a broad and pleasant rural thoroughfare, with spacious estates and shadowy old trees on its sides. The Free Kindergarten for the Blind, a department of the Perkins Institution, has fine brick buildings and several acres of grounds, at Day and Perkins Sts., near the Jamaica Parkway.

Jamaica Plain was first known as Pond Plain. A witty antiquary claims that its present name came from the frequent shouting about its tavern of the

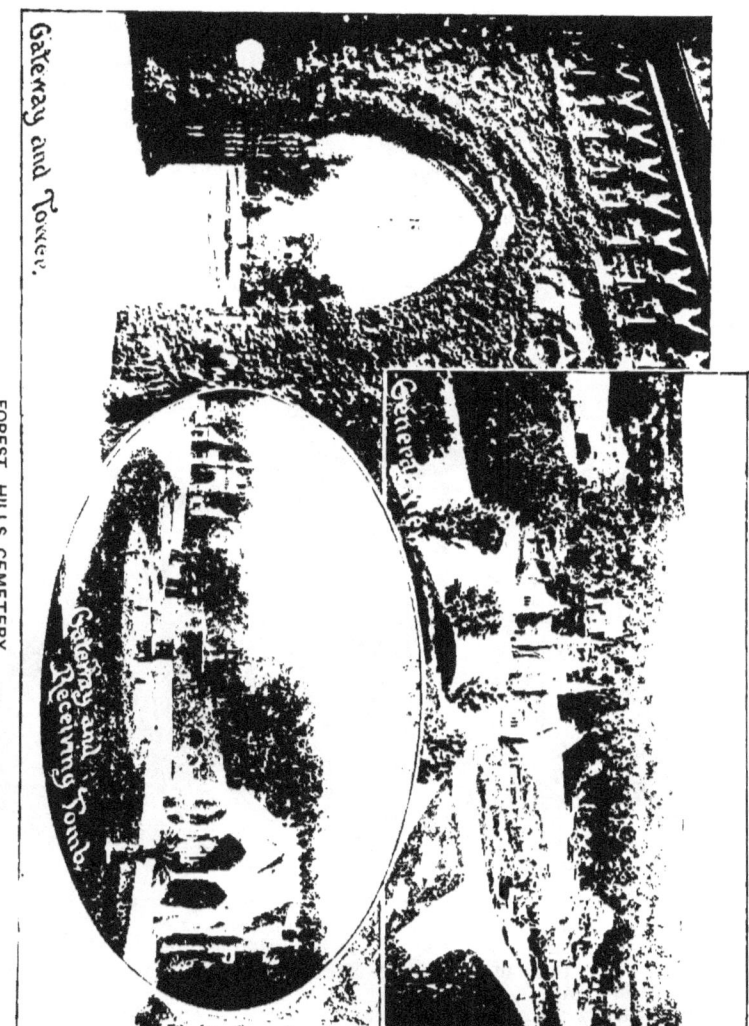

FOREST HILLS CEMETERY.

FOREST HILLS STATION, PROVIDENCE DIVISION, NEW YORK, NEW HAVEN & HARTFORD RAILROAD.

words "Jamaica Plain," meaning that the roystering rustics and thirsty travellers wanted their West-India rum untrimmed by contamination of water or sugar. But sober history claims that the name was given about the year 1680, in honor of Oliver Cromwell's recent conquest of the island of Jamaica from Spain. Govs. Bernard, Hancock and Bowdoin, Com. Loring, "Peter Parley," Parkman, and other well-known persons have had their country-seats hereabouts; and several fine old colonial mansions still survive. The region around Jamaica Pond has many handsome estates, with pleasant and picturesque roads. The street-cars pass Curtis Hall, a large and handsome building built for the town hall, before West Roxbury was annexed to Boston; and the Unitarian Church, a dignified

PERKINS' INSTITUTION AND MASS. SCHOOL FOR THE BLIND, EAST BROADWAY, SOUTH BOSTON.

stone edifice dating from 1854. The society was organized in 1770. Between these stands the Soldiers' Monument, erected in 1871, a tall Gothic granite canopy crowned by a military statue, and enshrining marble tablets with the names of the West-Roxbury soldiers who died in the War for the Union.

Jamaica Park is a beautiful pleasure-ground of 90 acres, reached by Pond St. from the car-line, and made up of the highly diversified shores, hills and woodlands around the deep and crystalline Jamaica Pond. This lakelet of 70 acres, 60 feet deep, used to supply Boston with water, conducted through pipes of hollowed logs. On the village side is Pine Bank, the former Perkins estate; and high on the opposite shore is the estate where Francis Parkman, the historian, spent his summers for many years. His friends have raised a fund to erect a memorial here. A charming parkway, with ponds and meadows, trees and thickets, unites Jamaica Park with the Back-Bay Fens; and another leads to the Arboretum. The beautiful Franklin Park lies close to Jamaica Plain, and may be entered by Glen Road, amid some fine rock-scenery.

The Arnold Arboretum and Bussey Institution, a mile or so south of the village, by South St., is an estate originally of 360 acres, and since much enlarged. This property and a considerable fund were bequeathed in 1842 by Benjamin Bussey, to Harvard University, for a school of agriculture and horticulture. It came into the possession of the University in 1870; and two years later James Arnold of New Bedford bequeathed to Harvard $100,000, to create here an arboretum and a professorship of tree-culture. Harvard maintains these institutions; and the city of Boston constructs and keeps up and polices the roads and paths, and receives in return the use of the domain as a part of its park system, for 999 years. The Bussey Institution has a handsome Victorian-Gothic stone building of 112 feet front, on a far-viewing eminence, for its class-rooms; and a new fireproof brick edifice for the herbarium, library, etc. The Arboretum

FARRAGUT STATUE,
MARINE PARK, SOUTH BOSTON.

is the finest and most extensive and varied collection of trees in the world; and is traversed by charming winding roads and paths, leading upward to the concourse on top of Mount Bellevue, with its vast and impressive prospect.

The Adams Nervine Asylum, adjacent to the Bussey grounds, on Centre St., has 18 acres of pleasant park-land, and is devoted to relieving over-nervous Massachusetts persons, not insane. It was opened in 1880, upon an endowment of $600,000 from Seth Adams, a South Boston sugar-refiner.

Forest-Hills Cemetery, on the other side of the Providence Railway, adjoins Franklin Park, and covers 225 acres. The gateway is one of the finest in the country, and includes several lofty Gothic portals of Roxbury stone, richly mantled with ivy. Its inscriptions, in golden letters are: I Am the Resurrection and the Life; and: He that Keepeth Thee Will Not Slumber. On one side is the handsome stone chapel; and on the hill within rises a noble and lofty bell-tower of stone, not far from the receiving-tomb. In this labyrinth of graves are the last resting-places of Admirals Winslow (of the *Kearsarge*) and Thatcher, Gens. Warren, (slain at Bunker Hill) and Dearborn, E. L. Davenport and John Gilbert, W. L. Garrison and J. F. Clarke, and many other whilom notables. The ground is pleasantly diversified by lakes and far-viewing hills, and the most exquisite landscape-gardening. The soldiers' lot contains Milmore's gigantic bronze soldier, erected in 1867, to commemorate the

MARINE PARK, SOUTH BOSTON.

Roxbury soldiers slain in the War for the Union, whose names are carved on the surrounding walls. They were largely of the 35th Mass., and died at Antietam. The most artistic monument is the relief showing Death staying the hand of the sculptor, executed by D. C. French, and placed over Milmore's grave. Winslow's memorial is a granite boulder from Mt. Kearsarge. The cemetery is easily reached from town by the Providence Railway to Forest-Hills station; and street-cars also run from the station to the city, along Washington St. Mount-Hope Cemetery, to the southward, contains 106 acres, with the Soldiers' Monument of heavy artillery, given by the Government.

Near the Jamaica Plain Station of the Providence Railroad (N. Y., N. H. & Hartford R. R.) is the extensive plant of the B. F. Sturtevant Co., the most eminent manufacturers of blowers and exhaust fans, which

B. F. STURTEVANT CO., BLOWERS, ENGINES, FORGES AND VENTILATING APPARATUS.
WORKS: JAMAICA PLAIN, MASS. SALES OFFICES: 34 OLIVER STREET.

are now so widely used for heating, ventilating, drying, exhausting and other purposes. Here also are made many other Sturtevant machines, steam engines, portable forges, hot-blast heating apparatus, etc.

There are several pleasant suburban villages farther out in West Roxbury. There also is Brook Farm, an estate of 200 acres along Charles River, where Ripley, Hawthorne, C. A. Dana, Margaret Fuller, and others established a socialistic community in 1841. It broke up in 1847. In 1861 the glorious 2d Massachusetts Infantry encamped here,

PIERCE HOUSE ON OAK AVENUE, LEADING FROM ADAMS STREET, IN DORCHESTER.

before departing for Virginia. The estate now pertains to a German Lutheran orphans' home. It is 25 minutes' walk from West-Roxbury station.

LEXINGTON.

LEXINGTON (Boston & Maine R. R., eleven miles out) was the scene of the first battle of the Revolution, when Pitcairn's British light infantry opened a fatal fire on the local minute-men, in line on the Green. The Royalist raiders destroyed a few Provincial military supplies at Concord, 6 miles west, but were hunted back to Boston by the fast-assembling militia, losing 273 men, and barely escaping annihilation. The Lexington Town Hall contains statues of Hancock and Adams, and the Minute-Man of 1775 and the Volunteer of 1861; and many curiosities. The Cary Free Library is in this building. The forest and hill scenery in this region is full of quiet beauty. Theodore Parker was born here.

BROOKLINE AND NEWTON.

THE street-car ride from the Granary Burial-Ground to Chestnut Hill is the most attractive and interesting excursion by land out of Boston. The cars follow Tremont St. to the end of the Common, and then go up Boylston St., past the Common and Public Garden, Trinity Church, the Museum of Fine Arts, and the Public Library, and on to Massachusetts Avenue. Here it passes the Norseman statue and the Harvard Bridge, and turns on to the famous Beacon St., with Charles River on the right. Beyond the sumptuous Charlesgate Hotel, it crosses the Back-Bay Fens, with interesting views all around. Outer Beacon St., generally known as the Boulevard, is one of the most beautiful of American thoroughfares. Within a few years it has been developed from an ordinary suburban road into a parkway of imperial width, with the car-tracks hidden in a grassy and tree-shaded belt in the centre; broad driveways on either side; and pleasant sidewalks beyond. The handsomest equipages in the State traverse this road (but hardly in summer), together with many humbler turn-outs, and endless scattering processions of all manner of cycles.

EDWARD EVERETT HALE'S HOME, 39 HIGHLAND STREET, ROXBURY.

On the heights to the left conspicuously loom the Beaconfield Terrace and similar lines of handsome houses, provided with certain noteworthy communistic features to enhance their luxury.

Longwood is an idyllic hamlet just to the left of the Boulevard, with many patrician homes under its overarching trees, grouped around the handsome Gothic Episcopal Church of Our Saviour, with its stone spire, rich stained-glass windows, and broad surrounding lawns. A little way beyond is a stone chapel, built and maintained by the Sears family as a memorial. The luxurious cottages and fragrant gardens, the quiet and refinement of Longwood have long made it a hoped-for ideal for young persons contemplating matrimony; wherefore one of its little streets has

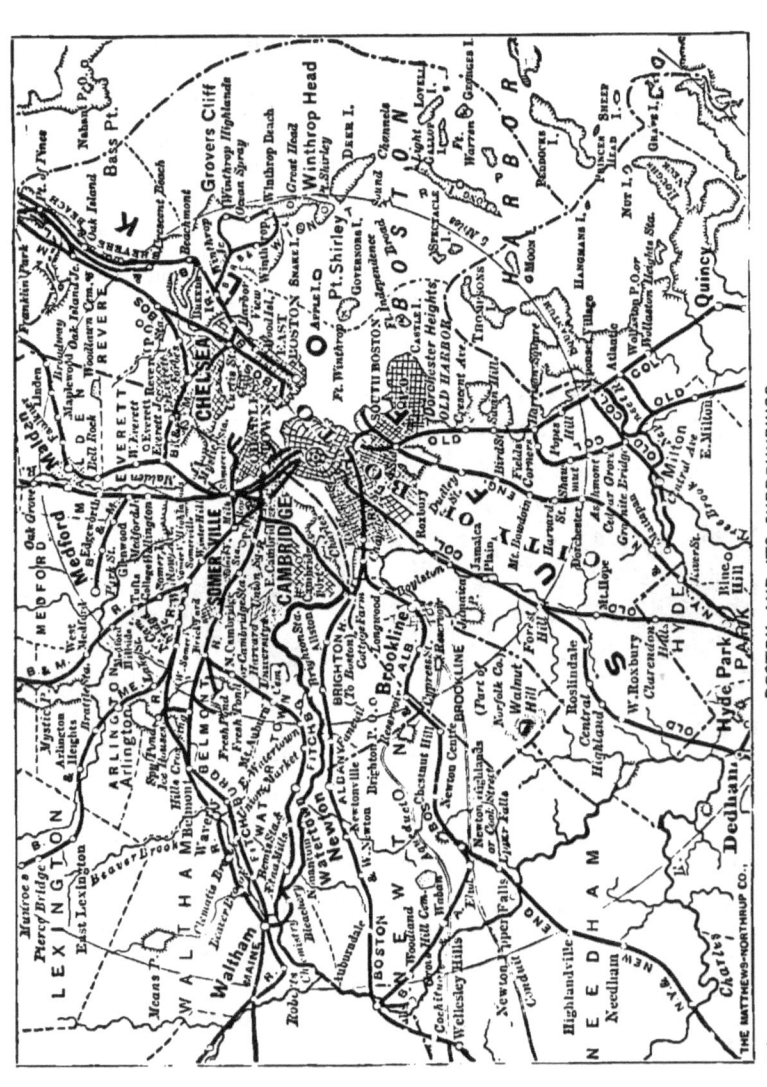

BOSTON AND ITS SURROUNDINGS.

borne the popular appellation of "Honeymoon Row." The Fenway and Riverdale park strip, connecting the Back-Bay Fens with Jamaica Park, occupies the valley to the eastward, with pleasant walks and rambles. Corey Hill rises from the Boulevard on the right, and has many houses. It commands one of the finest views in Eastern Massachusetts.

Chestnut-Hill Reservoir, five miles from the Boston City Hall, in Brighton, is the usual terminus of the Boulevard rides. It has 125 acres of water-surface, containing 730,000,000 gallons, and receiving in its two sections the waters from Cochituate Lake and the Sudbury River, either separate or blended, according to desire. The colossal and ingenious pumping machinery, in a large stone building near the Boulevard, will reward inspection. The reservoir is encircled by a splendid macadamized

ROXBURY HIGH SCHOOL, WARREN AND MONTROSE STREETS, ROXBURY.

driveway, 60 or 80 feet wide and two and one half miles long, traversing beautiful grounds and overlooking this beneficent artificial lake, whose irregular curving shores increase the beauty of the scene. Commonwealth Avenue passes near the northern side, in its magnificent course from the Boston Public Garden far out into the Newtons. Beyond the reservoir is the patrician hamlet of Chestnut Hill, the home of the Lees, Lowells, Shaws, and Saltonstalls ; and still farther out is the venerable village of Newton Centre.

Brookline proper, the chief business-centre of the town, may be reached by turning from the Boulevard to the southward down Harvard St., passing the very handsome Harvard Congregational Church. Here is the

UNITARIAN CHURCH AND SOLDIERS' MONUMENT AT JAMAICA PLAIN.

spacious stone Town Hall; and also the Public Library (of 30,000 volumes), with several churches and many stores. This town, with upwards of 12,000 inhabitants and enormous wealth, has at several elections refused to be annexed to the metropolis, preferring its own local administration, although nearly surrounded by Boston. Its pleasant valleys and noble hills are traversed by the finest of streets, which it is the fashion here to call "roads," as Gardner Road, Lanark, Chiswick and Selkirk Roads, etc.; and here are the secluded country-houses of scores of wealthy families. In the remoter rural region is the estate of the fashionable Country Club, made up of 600 swell Bostonians, who find here capital facilities for riding, golf, tennis, shooting, polo and other athletic sports, and good dinners withal.

Newton, "the Garden City," has a dozen picturesque Albany R. R. stations. There are also street-car lines from Boston to Newton, across Cambridge or Brookline and Brighton. Newton has 25,000 inhabitants, in 15 beautiful villages, amid much pleasant scenery of hills and forests, lakes and winding streams, meadows and upland plains. It has a handsome Public Library (50,000 volumes), the Baptist Theological Seminary, the Lasell Seminary, Lee's fine Woodland-Park Hotel, delightful boating on the Charles, just below where it is spanned by the graceful Echo Bridge, one of the most wonderful pontifical constructions in the world. It is the home of the Rev. Dr. S. F. Smith, who wrote "America."

One may return from Brookline or to Boston quickly by the Albany Railroad; or more leisurely by the electric cars.

SOLDIERS' MONUMENT, MOUNT HOPE CEMETERY.

BRIGHTON.

BRIGHTON was settled, as Little Cambridge, in 1635; became a parish in 1779; a town in 1807; and by annexation a district of Boston in 1874. It then had 3,000 inhabitants, which had increased to 12,032 in 1890. The town sent 365 soldiers to the War for the Union, exceeding its quota. The slaughtering business, founded in 1775, and the nursery, flower and fruit business, founded in 1810, were long the chief features here, but although these have since grown greatly in volume, they have been in a way set apart; and Brighton's foremost advance is as a place of rural and suburban homes for Boston business men. The unusual fertility of the soil, the beauty of the hills and glens, and the inimitable excellence of the roads are valuable traits toward this development.

HARVARD CONGREGATIONAL CHURCH, HARVARD ST., BROOKLINE.

Brighton may be reached in a few minutes by the Albany Railroad. A slower, pleasanter and more expensive way is to drive out from Boston, by Beacon St. and the famous Mill-Dam road, the favorite speedway for fast horses. Here, in winter, in May and June, and in autumn the finest teams in Boston may be seen, with the best roadsters and most expert drivers, a truly inspiring spectacle. The street-cars from Boston to Brighton depart every 15 minutes from Bowdoin Square, down Cambridge St. and across Charles River by the long West-Boston Bridge, with charming views of the broad stream and its bordering cities and hills. Traversing the uninteresting streets of Cambridgeport, we leave Massachusetts Avenue, the main route to Harvard, at Central Square, and turn on to River St., and soon see, on the right, the famous printing-house of the Riverside Press, and the works of the Dover Stamping Co. Just

CHESTNUT HILL RESERVOIR.

beyond, the car again crosses Charles River, and enters Brighton, not far from the famous old Beacon-Park race-course.

Allston, at the western end of the Mile-Ground pleasure-drive, is a modern suburban village, named for Washington Allston, the illustrious artist, whose studio was across the river, in Cambridgeport. Here are the spacious car-shops of the Albany Railroad.

Brighton Centre, a mile farther on, by the street-cars, has been for

CHESTNUT HILL RESERVOIR, PUMP HOUSE.

many years the foremost cattle-mart of New England.

Oak Square, the end of the car-line, is close to Bigelow Hill, which commands an interesting and extensive view over the Charles-River valley and far beyond. Not far distant is St. John's Ecclesiastical Seminary, with its vast and fortress-like Norman walls and towers of stone, rising on an eminence near two pleasant ponds. This finely-equipped institution for educating Catholic priests was built in 1881–85, and is conducted by Sulpician fathers. It has 120 students. On Lake St. is the Sheltering Home for Animals, founded in 1884 by Ellen M. Gifford; with a fine brick administration house and many kennels and yards for homeless dogs and cats, who are painlessly killed if hopelessly sick, medically treated if curable, copiously fed, and sold or given to good masters.

CAMBRIDGE CITY HALL, AT CAMBRIDGEPORT.

The Abattoir, on the navigable Charles River and two railways, was founded in 1873, after careful studies of the best European methods, at a cost of $500,000; and can slaughter daily 300 cattle and 3,000 sheep. Tight floors, scientific sewerage, prompt rendering, a free use of ice and water, and regular inspections by the Board of Health make this establishment at once efficient and inoffensive. No private slaughtering is allowed. 1,500,000 animals are received here yearly.

Street-cars lead from Allston or Brighton to the Boulevard, in Brookline, connecting with the cars thereon for Chestnut Hill or Boston.

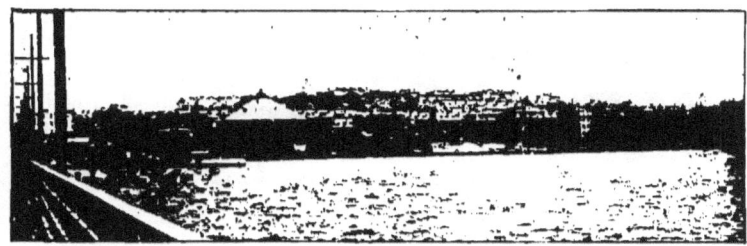

BACK-BAY DISTRICT, ACROSS THE CHARLES RIVER, FROM THE WEST-BOSTON BRIDGE.

CAMBRIDGE, HARVARD AND MT. AUBURN.

CAMBRIDGE, the most famous university town in America, may be reached by the street-cars from Bowdoin Square across the West-Boston Bridge, or from the Granary Burial-Ground across the Harvard Bridge, or by cars from Park Square. In any case, a fine view of the Charles-River Basin may be enjoyed from the long bridges. The West-Boston Bridge and its prospects are frequently exploited in the writings of Longfellow, Lowell, and Holmes.

PUBLIC LIBRARY, CAMBRIDGE.

As Howells says: "It is a joy in every nerve to ride out over the Long Bridge at high tide, and looking southward to see the wide crinkle and glitter of that beautiful expanse of water, which laps on one hand the granite quays of the city, and on the other washes away the reeds and wild grasses of the salt meadows. A ship coming slowly up the channel, or a dingy tug violently darting athwart it, gives an additional pleasure to the eye, and adds something dreamy or vivid to the pleasure of the scene. It is hard to say at what hour of the summer day the prospect is loveliest, and I am certainly not going to speak of the sunset as the least of its delights."

The newer Harvard Bridge is more artistic, and the route thereto leads through the charming Back-Bay District, past the Public Garden, Trinity Church, the Public Library, and the Art Museum. It might be well to go one way and return by the other. There is a fourth route, crossing the Canal Bridge to East Cambridge, and thence following Cambridge St. Each of these lines reaches Harvard University. East Cambridge and Cambridgeport contain extensive factories, where sugar, furniture, pumps, organs, boxes, provisions, and many other articles are made or prepared by large industrial populations. East Cambridge has the court-house and jail of Middlesex County. Here are the spacious pork-packing works of John P. Squire &

MANUAL TRAINING SCHOOL, CAMBRIDGE.

GINN & COMPANY, EDUCATIONAL PUBLISHERS.
THE ATHENÆUM PRESS. — PRINTING ESTABLISHMENT: CAMBRIDGEPORT. OFFICE: 7 TO 13 TREMONT PLACE.

REVERE SUGAR REFINERY CO., SUGAR REFINERS.
REFINERIES: EAST CAMBRIDGE. OFFICES: BROAD AND CENTRAL STREETS, BOSTON.

JOHN P. SQUIRE & CO., (INCORPORATED,) PROVISIONS.
PACKING HOUSES: EAST CAMBRIDGE. OFFICES: 25 FANEUIL-HALL MARKET, BOSTON.

Co., employing 1,000 persons, where visitors will be interested in seeing the rapid and, it may be so called, the humane processes of procuring and preparing meats for mankind.

The Revere Sugar Refinery, established in 1872, has an extensive plant at East Cambridge, and is celebrated for producing only the very best qualities of sugars, using exclusively the highest grades of sugar cane, and totally avoiding the use of beets. The products, universally known as "Revere sugars," are sold by Nash, Spaulding & Co., of Boston, who are the main owners of the refinery.

On First St. the eminent school-book firm of Ginn & Co. are establishing a model industrial community, made up of their mammoth brick and stone printing-house, and the comfortable new dwellings of their employees. The text-books of Ginn & Co., in ancient and modern languages, covering the whole field of education, rank as the peers of any in the world. On Hampshire St. are the numerous buildings and offices of the Geo. G. Page Box Company, by far the largest and best-equipped concern in its industry in New England. The variety in shapes, sizes, and qualities of the boxes turned out here for its myriad of patrons is almost incredible.

The Riverside Press, less than a mile from Harvard University, on the banks of Charles River, was founded in 1851 by H. O. Houghton, and has four acres of grounds, with handsome buildings and 600 employees. Here are printed the several thousand books bearing the imprint of Houghton, Mifflin & Co., a publishing house not surpassed in the world. The first printing-press in America was set up at Harvard College in 1639.

WASHINGTON ELM, AND SHEPARD CHURCH, CAMBRIDGE.

Four beautiful public buildings of Cambridge are essentially the philanthropic gifts of F. H. Rindge, a former resident, whose father, Samuel B. Rindge, left a vast estate. They include the City Hall, a

GEORGE G. PAGE BOX CO.'S BOX MANUFACTORY.
NOS. 3 TO 13 HAMPSHIRE STREET, CAMBRIDGEPORT.

noble and stately stone edifice, on Massachusetts Avenue, with a tower which would do honor to Florence; the Public Library, a very attractive round-arched stone building, at Broadway and Trowbridge St., containing over 50,000 volumes; the High School, an imposing stone and light pressed-brick structure, opposite the Public Library, for which Mr. Rindge donated the land; and the Manual Training School, a quaint brick building thoroughly equipped for its varied instructions, the whole cost of which, as well as its maintenance, is borne by Mr. Rindge. These three institutions form valuable adjuncts to Cambridge's Public Schools.

Harvard University, the illustrious institution which has made Cambridge known in all civilized lands, is in that part of the city known as Old Cambridge. The College Yard includes 22 acres.

The Legislature in 1636 appropriated £400, or an entire year's tax of the Colony, for a school at Newtown (Cambridge); and two years later John Harvard, a young non-conforming curate of Charlestown, died,

WASHINGTON'S HEADQUARTERS, LONGFELLOW'S HOME, BRATTLE STREET, CAMBRIDGE.

and bequeathed £800 and his library to the new institution, which by legislative act then received his name. By degrees, and with very hard work, the college has freed itself from State and Church, and accumulated property estimated at $12,000,000, while gaining a paramount place in education. The schools of medicine, dentistry, and veterinary medicine are in Boston; that of agriculture in West Roxbury; and the academic, scientific, law, divinity, and graduates' schools, in Cambridge. Each school has its own funds and faculty. In the summer vacation the College Yard is deserted, and outside falls "the elmy quiet of the dear old Cambridge streets," extending Arlington-ward along Massachusetts Avenue, which Howells called "not only handsome, but probably the very dullest street in the world."

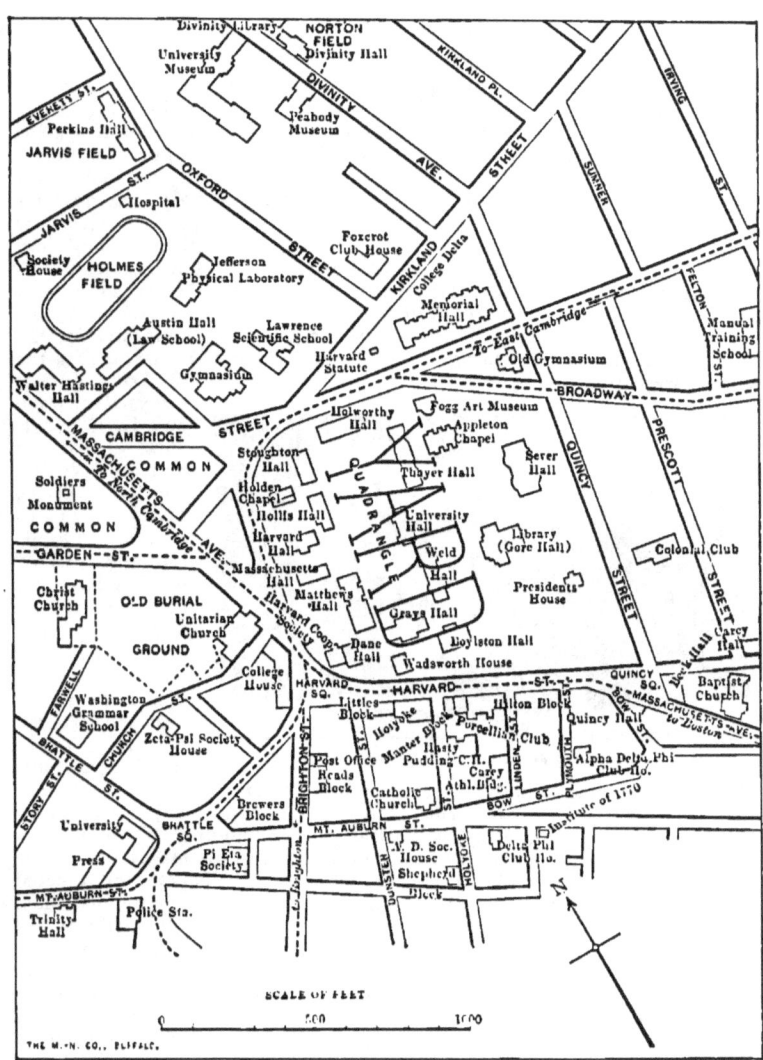

HARVARD UNIVERSITY: COLLEGE YARD AND VICINITY.

The main entrance to the College Yard is from the western side, through the antique Johnston gateway, designed by McKim, Mead & White. Pertaining to Harvard University are too many buildings to be enumerated here. The venerable Massachusetts Hall, erected in 1720, a barrack for American troops in the Revolution, a dormitory for over a century, is now occupied by lecture-halls. Parkman roomed here. Harvard Hall, with a quaint belfry, was erected in 1765, and now has lecture-rooms, etc. Matthews Hall, a handsome Gothic dormitory, was erected in 1872, at a cost of $120,000. Dane Hall, a little brick building, was from 1830 to 1885 the seat of the Law School. The granite Boylston Hall contains chemical laboratories and collections. Grays Hall, built of brick, in 1863, has 52 suites of dormitories. Wadsworth House (1726), a brown wooden building fronting on Massachusetts Avenue, was for 123 years the home of the Harvard presidents. College House, across the square west from the yard, was the domicile of Evarts, Dana, Justice Gray, Rockwood and G. F. Hoar, Prof. Goodwin and Joseph H. Choate. Gore Hall, a gray-granite Gothic building, erected in 1838, and later enlarged, contains many interesting pictures and busts, and the University Library of 450,000 volumes. Only the Congressional

"ELMWOOD," JAMES RUSSELL LOWELL'S HOME, CAMBRIDGE.

and Boston Public libraries exceed it in number; and even these have fewer unduplicated books. Weld Hall is a Mansard-roofed brick dormitory. University Hall (1815) is a white-granite building, with university offices. Sever Hall, with its recitation and lecture rooms, is one of the notable architectural works of H. H. Richardson. Thayer Hall, erected in 1870, at a cost of $115,000, has 68 dormitory suites. The round-arched yellow-stone Appleton Chapel is where the students voluntarily attend religious services. The Fogg Art Museum, with its rounding walls and heavy pillars, is to contain the art-treasures of the university. Holden Chapel, built in 1744, has been later used for instruction and elocutionary practice. Between Hollis and Harvard is the Class Tree, around which half a century of classes about to graduate have enjoyed their peculiar frolics in the presence of their hosts of friends. Holworthy, Stoughton, and Hollis Halls, three ancient brick dormitories, have had many famous

HARVARD UNIVERSITY BUILDINGS.
HARVARD SQUARE, OLD CAMBRIDGE.

occupants. In the demure Hollis Hall (1763), Emerson, Sumner, Thoreau, Felton, Hillard, Cushing, E. R. Hoar, G. T. Bigelow, A. P. Peabody, Horatio Greenough, Everett, W. H. Prescott, C. F. Adams, B. R. Curtis and Wendell Phillips roomed when Harvard students. Stoughton Hall (1805) was the domicile of Holmes, President Quincy, Phillips Brooks, A. H. Everett, Judge Preble, and E. E. Hale.

Memorial Hall, built by the alumni in 1870–76, at a cost of $422,000, is of brick and sandstone, 310 by 115 feet, with a conspicuous tower 200 feet high, visible for miles. At the east end is the classical Sanders Theatre, for public exercises and concerts; and under the tower is the Memorial Transept, 115 feet long and 58 feet high, with marble tablets bearing the names of 136 Harvard men who were slain in the War for the Union. The immense dining-hall (larger than any in England), where more than 1,200 students eat daily, stretches thence westward, 164 by 60 feet, and 80 feet high, with a grand timber-roof; a lofty wainscot, embellished with scores of portraits of New-England worthies, by artists like Copley and Stuart, Hunt and Vinton, Powers and Crawford (catalogues near entrance); many very costly memorial stained-glass windows, erected by various classes; and a magnificent western window, emblazoned with the arms of the Republic, the State, and the University. Outside the Memorial-Hall cloister is the fine bronze ideal statue of John Harvard, by D. C. French, erected in 1884.

SPHINX, MT. AUBURN CEMETERY, CAMBRIDGE.

Divinity Avenue leads from the northern side of Memorial Hall to the Divinity School (unsectarian; but Unitarian in tone), with its pretty library-building; and the enormous Agassiz Museum of Comparative Zoölogy, and the Peabody Museum of American Archæology and Ethnology, etc., with several acres of floor-space, and millions of curiosities. North of the College Yard is the noble Romanesque Austin Hall, designed by H. H. Richardson for the Harvard Law School; the modern colonial Hemenway Gymnasium, with its perfect equipment; the plain brick Jefferson Physical Laboratory, Lawrence Scientific School, and other departments, together with several fine dormitory buildings. Half a mile westward are the many structures of the Observatory and the Botanic Garden, with several acres of grounds, on a pleasant hill.

Radcliffe College, on Garden St., with its library, laboratories, etc., is the headquarters of 400 women students, who have similar courses and the same instructors as the Harvard students, with access to the museums, laboratories and libraries, and diplomas countersigned by Harvard University.

THE "OLD SHIP" AT HINGHAM.

Cambridge Common covers a broad area near the University, with many trees, a bronze statue of John Bridge, one of the Puritan pioneers, and a lofty monument to 346 Cambridge soldiers who died in the War for the Union. At its base are several British cannon, trophies of the Revolution. On the west side of the Common, in front of the Shepard Congregational Church, standing in the road, and marked by a tablet, is the elm-tree (300 years old) under which Washington took command of the American army, July 3, 1775. As Dr. Holmes sings:

"O George the Third; you found it true
Our George was more than *double you*,
For Nature made him so."

Nearly opposite the college gateway is the venerable First Church (Unitarian), used for many years for the Harvard graduation exercises, and in whose yard Allston is buried. Westward is Christ Church (Episcopal), built before the Revolution, and attended by Washington.

YACHT CLUB HOUSE, HULL, IN BOSTON HARBOR.

The Episcopal Theological School, westward on Brattle St., surrounds a grassy quadrangle, with its beautiful Gothic stone dormitories, class-rooms, refectory and library, and the exquisite St. John's Church. This institution dates from 1867; and has 40 students.

Longfellow's house, just beyond the Episcopal School, on the same side of Brattle St., is the most famous private house in America (Mount Vernon being public). It is a comfortable mansion, set in broad grounds, amid fine elms. Built in 1759, it was deserted by Col. Vassall, its Tory master, in 1775, and occupied by Washington (and his wife) as head-quarters during the eight months of the siege of Boston. Longfellow came here as a boarder in 1837; became possessed of the house later; and died here in 1882. His family now dwells here. Washington's office and Longfellow's study were in the room on the first floor to the right of the

NANTASKET BEACH AND THE ATLANTIC HOUSE IN BOSTON HARBOR.

door (as you face the house); the officers' room and library being back of it; and the drawing-room on the other side of the front door. Admirers of the poet have established a memorial park in front of the house, keeping open the view to Charles River. Across Brattle St. from the Longfellow house, but nearer the University Press, is the Vassall mansion, built about 1700, and in 1775-76 the headquarters of the medical staff of the army, and a hospital for the wounded from Bunker Hill.

Farther on is the home of John Bartlett, whose "Familiar Quotations" has run through many editions.

Lowell's house, "Elmwood," is some way beyond Longfellow's, on the same side of Brattle St. This also was built before the Revolution, and deserted by its Royalist owner, Lieut.-Gov. Oliver. Lowell, the poet and essayist, dwelt here many years, and wrote some of his best works in a far-viewing third-floor room. He died here in 1891. The family of Ole Bull were tenants here.

Mount-Auburn Cemetery, one of the most beautiful, and the first garden cemetery, in the world (opened in 1831), lies beyond Old Cambridge (street-cars). It may be reached most quickly by the Fitchburg Railway from Boston. On the north is the charming park around Fresh Pond ; on the south, Charles River winds seaward. Note the ponderous Egyptian entrance ; the statue of Hosea Ballou ; the bronze statue of Bowditch, to the right, inside ; the grand Sphinx, commemorating the slain National soldiers in the War for the Union ; and the handsome Chapel, in which are Greenough's statue of Winthrop, Crawford's of James Otis, Randolph Rogers's of John Adams, and Story's of Joseph

NANTASKET BEACH, IN BOSTON HARBOR.

Story. Phillips Brooks's grave is not far from the Chapel, on Mimosa Path. On the left of the entrance-gate is James Russell Lowell's grave ; and above it, on Indian Ridge, the marble sarcophagus of Longfellow. Francis Parkman is farther east, on Indian Ridge ; and Oliver Wendell Holmes on Lime Avenue, beyond. Agassiz is covered by a rough stone block, on Bellwort Path ; and elsewhere are the monuments to Channing, Spurzheim, Felton, Fields, Prescott, Palfrey, Ticknor, Sparks, Fanny Fern, Burlingame, Rufus Choate, Asa Gray, N. P. Willis, Dorothea L. Dix, and John Murray, the founder of Universalism in America. The highest hill is crowned by a far-viewing tower, near which are the last resting-places of Edwin Booth, Charlotte Cushman, Everett and Sumner. The beauty of this wide area of hills, vales and ponds has been improved by landscape-gardening, fine trees and rich flowers. The cemetery is open to visitors, except on Sunday, from 7 A. M. until sunset.

BOSTON HARBOR.

VERY comfortable steamboats leave Rowe's Wharf many times daily, in summer, for Hull, Hingham and Nantasket. It is often quite refreshing, on a hot day in town, to make this little salt-water journey, especially if the wind is east, and the steamer uncrowded.

After the boat is well into the stream, and past the yachts moored on the Upper Middle Shoal, the Navy Yard and the big English steamships at East Boston appear on the left; and on the right South Boston swells upward, from the docks and factories near the water, to the Blind Asylum on the heights. Farther out are the fine gray walls of Fort Independence. On the opposite side of the channel rise the high bluffs of Governor's Island, granted to Gov. Winthrop in 1632, and held in his family till 1808. The ponderous bastions and traverses of Fort Winthrop, and its formidable citadel mounted with long Parrott guns, now occupy the hills, with connected water-batteries. Beyond this embattled island, well in-shore toward the pleasant peninsular town of Winthrop, is Apple Island, marked by its tall elms. On the other side of the ship-channel, back of Castle Island, appear the ancient yellow brick buildings and dark groves of the Farm School, on Thompson's Island, where 100 indigent boys are given book, farm, and industrial instruction, with a care for their morals, manners and sports. When grown up, places are found for them. The institution dates from 1814, and occupied this spacious and pleasant island (an Indian trading-post in 1626) in 1835. Next, near the channel, come the high bluffs of Spectacle Island, where for 38 years the dead horses of Boston have been converted into useful products. Next our course lies across President Roads, with Deer Island on the left front, bearing the municipal House of Industry, the House of Reformation for Girls, a truant-school, and other places of detention. It was once a deer-haunted forest of 200 acres; and afterwards a prison for hundreds of Indian captives. A light-house occupies one of its headlands.

Long Island, 1¼ miles long, with several sea-gnawed bluffs, has a spacious modern brick building for the city's paupers. On the heights at the seaward end is a round white lighthouse, and also a battery for the defense of Broad Sound. The sea-wall

THE "MINUTE MAN" AT CONCORD.

below cost $150,000. A picturesque village of Azore-Island fishermen occupied the eastern bay until 1885, when they were evicted by the city.

Beyond Long Island is the green bluff of Gallop's Island, with the neat white hospital and other buildings of the Quarantine station; the low plain of Lovell's Island, with the wharf and spare buoys of the U.-S. Lighthouse service; the weird black beacon of Nix's Mate, with its grisly legends of oldtime pirates; and Rainsford Island, the seat of city almshouses. Outside lies a range of seven rocky islets, several of which are inhabited by groups of daring fishermen. One of them carries the tall white tower of

TUCKER'S LANDING, MARBLEHEAD.

Boston Light, built in 1783, on the site of one blown up by British marines in 1776. There was some hard fighting hereabouts during the Revolution. The Bug Light rises out of the water from a long gravelly bar, standing on spidery iron pillars, but snugly inhabited, and flashing a red light over the sea at night.

Fort Warren, built in 1833-50, on George's Island, has a garrison of Federal artillerists, and commands the narrow entrance of the harbor with an armament of 400 cannon. The handsome granite walls are partly hidden by modern earthworks and water-batteries of enormous thickness. The barbette guns are visible, and the sentries at the main gate, and the bright garrison-flag. Fort Warren was fully garrisoned during the War for the Union, and held in durance thousands of Confederate prisoners, including Alex. H. Stephens, Mason and Slidell, Buckner, and many generals, besides disloyal civilians from the Border States.

Farther on, after a view out to sea, down Nantasket Roads, the steamboat rushes through the narrow Hull Gut, with the lonely bluffs of

Peddock's Island on the right, and on the other side the much-frequented Hotel Pemberton.

Hull, with its steamboat-piers, Hull Yacht-Club house, hotels great and small, and many summer-cottages, lies in the very breath of the sea, surrounded by salt water. Back of it rises Telegraph Hill, bearing the remains of a fort planned by Lafayette, and long garrisoned by French troops and Massachusetts militia. Many a heavy round shot from this sea-viewing eyrie crashed into His Majesty's frigates in Nantasket Roads, or hurtled out to check British blockaders venturing too far inward. Hundreds of our French allies lie buried on the lower eastern slope of the

ECHO BRIDGE, BOSTON AQUEDUCT, NEWTON UPPER FALLS.

hill. Hull was settled some years before Boston; and earlier in this century was enlarged by mariners from the Dalmatian coast of the Adriatic, and similar outlandish places, whose descendants remain in the quaint hamlet. Lord Nelson cruised off here, on blockade-duty. Scores of fatal wrecks have occurred on the perilous rocks outside of Hull.

Nantasket Beach is reached from Hull by the steamboat crossing Hingham Bay and ascending the serpentine Weir River; or by a railway, running along the sea-bounds. It is a fine expanse of gray sand, several miles long, between the ocean and the harbor, beaten by a light surf, and affording opportunity for safe bathing. Above the high-tide line are groups of hotels, restaurants, chowder-houses, and bathing-houses, where Anglo-Saxon-Celtic-Latin-Slav Boston sends tens of thousands of her citizens on torrid summer days. It is a grand place for "a good time" in a democratic way. Inland people who would appreciate the mystery and magic and awe of the sea will find less human distraction at a lonely beach like the Humarocks, down in the Old Colony, or on the lofty and picturesque wave-beaten rocks of East Point, at Nahant.

Hingham, visited by some of the harbor-boats, is a quaint and venerable village, once well-known in maritime commerce, but now mainly regarded as a place of summer-homes, and the campground of the Cadets. The church known as the "Old Ship," built in 1681, and still used by the First Parish, has a long steep roof running up on four sides to a balustraded platform and a narrow pointed belfry. It is said to be the oldest church in continuous use in New England. Back of this building is the grave-yard, on a terraced hill, with tall monuments "To the Early Settlers of Hingham," and the 76 soldiers who died in the War for the Union; the tomb of Gen. Lincoln (a native of Hingham), who commanded the Army of the South in 1778-80; and a noble statue over the grave of War-Governor Andrew. Pleasant roads lead inland by Liberty Plain to Queen Anne Corner and Assinippi; and seaward to the grand Jerusalem Road, following the rocky coast for miles, and lined by broad patrician estates. Govs. Andrew and Long were residents of Hingham. R. H. Stoddard was born here.

A large illustrated book has been written about the Indian, colonial and subsequent legends and picturesque occurrences on and about the harbor islands. No other American bay has such a wealth of history, tradition and poetry. None on the North Atlantic coast surpasses it in natural beauty. Here is the yachting headquarters of the Western World, for though New York has

POWDER HOUSE AT SOMERVILLE.

richer yachtsmen and more costly boats, the Yankee bay has a vastly greater number, and very many more men who find delight in blue-water sailing. As to their quality, the old *America* (that won the cup), the *Puritan*, *Mayflower* and *Volunteer*, were all Massachusetts yachts. The harbor has more yachts, more regattas, and more yacht clubs (23; with 3,000 members) than any other in the world.

Plymouth (Old Colony R. R.; 37 miles) is a quiet provincial seaport of 8,000 inhabitants. Plymouth Rock, "the corner-stone of the Republic," is a boulder down near the harbor, protected by a lofty granite canopy, whose upper part contains the bones of the pilgrims who died in the bitter winter of 1620-21. The National Monument to the Forefathers is an immense and noble marble and granite memorial.

FORBES LITHOGRAPH MANUFACTURING CO., ART AND COMMERCIAL LITHOGRAPHERS.
WORKS: CHELSEA, MASS.   BOSTON OFFICES: 181 DEVONSHIRE STREET.

WELLESLEY COLLEGE, FOR HIGHER EDUCATION OF WOMEN.
WELLESLEY, MASS., ON THE BOSTON & ALBANY RAILROAD.

CHELSEA, CONCORD AND WELLESLEY.

CHELSEA, reached by steam and street-cars from Boston and Charlestown, across the Mystic River, passing the handsome U.-S. Naval Hospital (a granite building erected in 1836-65, with 75 acres of grounds), is a city of 30,000 inhabitants, with the noted Low art-potteries and tile-works, and rope-walks and other industries, the most famous of which is the vast establishment of the Forbes Lithograph Manufacturing Co., whose art and commercial productions are unsurpassed in America or Europe, and whose customers cover the continent. The Mass. Soldiers' Home, with hundreds of disabled veterans, crowns Powder-Horn Hill, overlooking the sea and harbor, and all the northern suburbs. Woodlawn, two miles out, is the chief cemetery in the northern suburbs, and has beautiful avenues and monuments, the far-viewing Chapel and Elm Hills, and the curious Gingko trees.

NORUMBEGA TOWER, CHARLES RIVER.

CONCORD, 20 miles from Boston by the Fitchburg Railroad, contains the former dwelling of Emerson; the Wayside house, where Hawthorne dwelt; the old home of Louisa M. Alcott; the Old Manse, Emerson's and Hawthorne's home for years; and the graves of Emerson, Thoreau and Hawthorne, on a hill in Sleepy-Hollow Cemetery: Emerson's, with a rose-quartz boulder; Hawthorne's, a low marble headstone over a myrtle-clad grave, with arbor-vitæ hedges; the blue-granite headstone of Thoreau; and the five low marble stones over A. B. Alcott and his daughter Louisa and her "Little Women." Just beyond the Old Manse is the bridge about which began the battle of April 19, 1775, when 400 minute-men drove away three companies of British light infantry. The bodies of the slain Royalists lie buried near the bridge, on the further side of which is D. C. French's noble bronze statue of "The Minute-Man." The Public Library, besides its 20,000 books, has many curiosities, with fine paintings and busts. Channing, Hoar, Sanborn, Everett, Mann, Margaret Fuller and G. W. Curtis were dwellers in Concord.

WELLESLEY (Albany R. R.; 14 miles) is celebrated for its college for women, whose picturesque main building, 475 feet long, was designed by Hammatt Billings, "the artist-architect." There are several other fine edifices, rich art-collections, and an immense library. The college dates from 1875; has about 1,000 students and 300 acres of beautiful grounds bordered by Lake Waban and the superb Hunnewell gardens.

THE END, NOT OF THE STORY, BUT OF THIS BOOK.

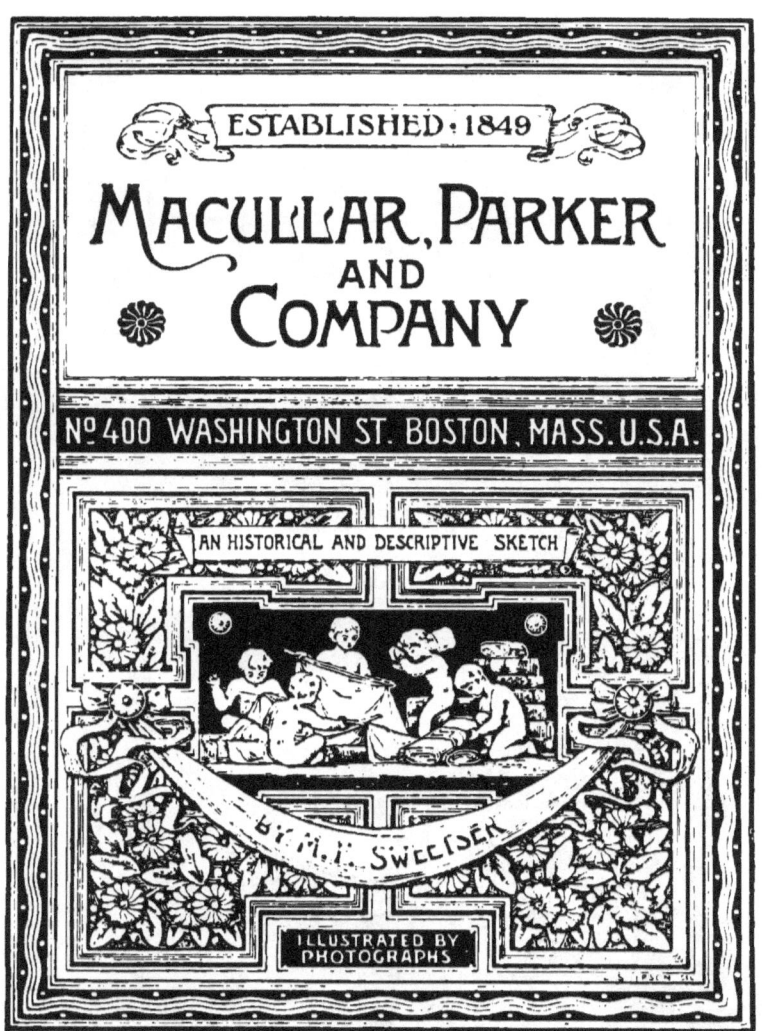

CLOTHING AND FURNISHING GOODS. — MACULLAR, PARKER & COMPANY.
MAIN FLOOR, NO. 400 WASHINGTON STREET.

MACULLAR, PARKER & COMPANY.
A Utopian Industrial Establishment.

Howells's Altruria and Bellamy's Utopia are approached in the happy independence of nearly a thousand working men and women in the industry told about in these pages. And this result is gained, not by governmental socialism or posing philanthropy, but by a wise observance of natural and business laws. The heads devote their time, thought and policy to providing means, materials and a market; the hands collaborate by using the materials with such skill and faithfulness that the market is always ready for more. The hours for work are as short and the holidays and half-holidays are as frequent as in any place of extensive business. The two groups — the men at the head, and the guild of handworkers — regard each other with mutual esteem and respect, and form a prosperous and contented industrial community. It is well worth while for our myriads of visitors from other cities to spend an hour or two in this mercantile college, and see what Boston does toward solving certain vexed problems of the day.

It is well known that a large portion of the ready-made clothing worn in America is put together in the sweaters' shops, in crowded and filthy tenement-houses. The makers are half-civilized foreigners, ground down to the edge of starvation and illness. It is impossible here to give details as to the unspeakable squalor of these sweat-shops, or to suggest the general peril attendant upon wearing garments made amid such surroundings. Legislative investigations, the eloquence of many pulpits, the search-lights of the public press, have revealed these dire iniquities.

In this house, however, there are no germ-factories, no haunts of poisonous bacteria, no sources of multiplying microbes. Here are workrooms covering a tenth of an acre each, exceptional in neatness, with pure air and bright sun-light, and populated by healthy and happy workers. There is an open invitation for all persons to visit these halls during business-hours; and many avail themselves thereof, to see the workings of a vast ideal industry, in the heart of a metropolis.

This establishment is in a sense a commonwealth. Its continuous success has been largely based upon the continuous comfort and efficiency of its employees, quite a considerable number of whom have been at work for this firm constantly during periods ranging from ten to forty years.

OF THE WORKSHOPS.—MACULLAR, PARKER & COMPANY.
FOURTH FLOOR, NO. 400 WASHINGTON STREET.

The appointments of the work-rooms as to light, air, and general equipment have been so perfected that it seems as if nothing need be added for the comfort and content of the toilers. Nowhere is there a dark, obscure or unclean corner. The ventilation is ensured by the best processes, flooding the rooms continually with fresh pure air. The best of New-England sunlight pours in through scores of great windows. In summer the rooms are cool; in winter, abundant warmth is furnished. There is an elevator to convey the people to their places of labor; and plentiful facilities are given for warming their mid-day luncheons, if they prefer not to go outside for them.

The history of an industry like this, materially more important than many of the so-called public institutions, is full of interest and suggestiveness. Here an army of trained men and women, large enough to make a mediæval guild, earns the wherewithal to comfortably support a population equal to that of a goodly village; and the production of the materials used in their work supports other villages in England and Scotland, France and New England. This great and far-reaching business found its origin in inland Worcester, about the middle of the century, when two young men formed the firm of Addison Macullar & Co., for the sale of ready-made clothing. Their fair methods and accurate perceptions soon won so much success that they sought a broader field of development; and therefore removed to Boston, in 1852. Here they found an equal success; and the opening out of the business required several successive moves, from Ann St. to Milk St., and thence to the site of the old Washington Coffee-House, on Washington St., and thence to the building previously occupied by Warren's dry-goods emporium. Here they remained from 1860 to 1864, and then transferred this ever-growing trade to its present site, at No. 400 Washington St., which it has now held for nearly a third of a century. By this time the firm name was Macullar, Williams & Parker, which in 1879, was changed to the present style of Macullar, Parker & Company.

The establishment is in the centre of the retail district, where Franklin and Summer, Bromfield and School Sts. draw their thousands of busy shoppers every day. The sales-rooms are each 220 feet long, so that if Bunker-Hill Monument were taken down and laid in either of them, the doors could be shut upon both ends at the same time. The street-floor of 400 Washington St. is devoted to fine garments for men and boys, a vast stock, continually drawn down by the daily sales, and as often replenished by the newest and most fashionable styles. These garments are manufactured from choice and thoroughly tested materials, in the spacious work-rooms overhead, where several hundreds of the happiest, most

YOUTHS' AND BOYS' CLOTHING AND FURNISHING GOODS.—MACULLAR, PARKER & COMPANY.
REAR OF STREET FLOOR, NO. 400 WASHINGTON STREET.

skilful and most contented operatives in the United States are kept busy. The whole work is simplified to the extreme, and as each operative being kept at the same kind of work all the time, the most efficient skill is obtained. The patrons include the better class of men of New England, members of the learned professions, visitors from other cities, and the country gentry,—in fact, those classes who cannot content themselves with slop-shop garments.

It was Ralph Waldo Emerson who said that "The consciousness of being well-dressed brings a peace of mind which revealed religion cannot give." A saying not without value, as showing the importance of proper and appropriate garments. How extensive has been the sartorial range of development, from the light and inexpensive summer suit of fig-leaves worn by Adam down to the superb scarlet silk robes, with a train ten feet long, in which Cardinal Gibbons swept down through the chancel of Boston Cathedral, in May, 1895! In these latter days, for an intelligent man to be ill-dressed causes remark, as when an eminent statesman of the war time said: "President Lincoln's trousers may bag at the knees, but his statesmanship doesn't." Longfellow, Lowell, Holmes, Aldrich, and others to whom Boston looks up were among the most carefully clad men of their time (and all, excepting perhaps Lowell, were constant patrons of this house). And since the evolution of humanity, as well as the laws and the climate, compel us to wear curiously fashioned fabrics of cloth, it is well to drape these corporeal temples with skill and good taste. Here, then, we find the various articles of costume, planned on the advanced lines of contemporary taste and fashion, constructed of the finest and most durable materials to be found in America or Europe, and put together with a trained mechanical skill and an observance of details which ensures unusual durability. Scores of thousands of men visit Boston to quicken their hearts with new and invigorated ideas of true patriotism, religion and fraternity. It may be well, also, to secure a further memorial of this well-groomed old Puritan City, by clothing the temples in which those earnest hearts dwell in habiliments of taste and strength.

Thoroughness and precision have prevailed in every detail for half a century. To sell an unsatisfactory garment bearing their name would be more serious for them than for the purchaser. Some fabrics are better and costlier than others, but all are good. Figuratively speaking, buttons sewed on here are as firmly anchored as the Pyramids; seams are as solid as electric-welded metals. The garments will, during years of use, lose their touch with fashion, or become tiresome to the wearer, but they always satisfy the reasonable patron, for the work of building has been

CUSTOM TAILORING DEPARTMENT: MACULLAR, PARKER & COMPANY.
STREET FLOOR, NO. 898 WASHINGTON STREET.

honestly and well done. It may be, that the vast array of clothing in the white Corinthian halls at 400 Washington St. may not contain the exact color, or pattern, or fit to suit some special cases. In that event, there is a great custom department, covering an equal area, and under the same ownership, containing cloths of an almost limitless variety as to color, design and texture, to be made up on order, with the certainty of an accurate fit, in any desired form.

The building at 400 Washington St. went down in the Great Fire of 1872, but its grand white-marble façade withstood the utmost fury of the sea of flames, and stood like a monument to the ruined city, until its removal for the widening of the street. Upon the same site, the firm built, restoring the original front, a new and extensive structure, planned in every way with singular care and thoughtfulness, for the purposes of a safe, light, airy and commodious manufactory and sales-room for clothing. It seemed as if this huge edifice would serve the utmost purposes of the business forever; but its good repute spread more rapidly than its plant.

Such a volume of trade poured in from all over the States and Canada, that the manufacturing operations became pinched for room, and the upper stories of the building next to the northward were opened to relieve this pressure. In 1884, the adjoining building was annexed for the custom department, whose books contain the names of many of the foremost gentlemen of the Eastern States. At No. 400 is the men's furnishing goods department, in itself a good-sized establishment. A large and fully equipped department for boys' clothing of high grade is conducted to the manifest external improvement of thousands of junior Bostonians.

An important department is that for selling piece goods and tailors' trimmings at wholesale. Travelling salesmen employed by the firm visit all the most important cities and towns of the Northern States, with samples, and supply the wants of large numbers of the best merchant-tailors. The making of a full line of superior grades of white vests, which are supplied to the foremost tailors and clothiers of this country, has been a specialty here for many years.

The assortment of woolen piece goods includes the finest that are made the world over. The firm has an agency in London, to secure the best and most fashionable English, Scotch and Continental cloths, from season to season, so that the materials worn here may be the same as those in contemporary favor in London and Paris.

Thus it is that this great house with its wide-spread ramifications, its model workshops, its honorable methods, its high-grade productions, its long-established success, may well be regarded as an ideal industry.

WHOLESALE WOOLENS AND TRIMMINGS.—MACULLAR, PARKER & COMPANY
MAIN FLOOR, NO. 81 HAWLEY STREET.

MACULLAR, PARKER & COMPANY.
SECTIONAL VIEW OF MAIN BUILDING FROM 400 WASHINGTON TO 81 HAWLEY STREET.

SPECIAL OFFER

To the Visiting Delegates.

WE shall take pleasure in making the concession specified on the other side — the pair of Minton tiles for seventy-five cents. These are indestructible souvenirs of Boston, and commemorate two of the most historical structures of this country. They were made by the famous Mintons, of England, exclusively for us, and obtainable nowhere else.

Macullar, Parker & Company,

400 Washington Street,

———— BOSTON.

SEE OTHER SIDE.

Interesting Boston Souvenirs.

INDESTRUCTIBLE BY TIME.

Six-inch Tiles, made by MINTON, bearing
beautiful representations of

The Old John Hancock House in 1863,

just prior to its demolition, and

The Boston State House in 1818,

as it appeared, when cows were pastured
on the Common.

Price, 50 cents Each, or the Pair for 75 cents.

To be found only at No. 400 WASHINGTON STREET,

☛Macullar, Parker & Company.

INDEX.

The black figures (**163**) indicate illustrations; Italic figures (*158*) maps; plain Roman figures (258) ordinary references, and black titles (**Historical**) chapters.

Abattoir, 245.
Abbey, Edwin A., 146.
Abbott-Lawrence Mansion, 94.
A. B. C. F. M., 159.
Abolition Riots, 14.
Adams, Charles Francis, 165.
Adams House, 108, **109**, *108*.
Adams, John, 26, 160.
Adams, John Quincy, 26, 101.
Adams Nervine Asylum, 235.
Adams, Sam., 26, 92, 99, 162, **187**.
Adams (Sam.) Statue, **17**, 19, **22**.
Adams Square, **17**, 19, **22**.
Adath Israel Temple, 176.
Advent, Church of the, 166, **196**.
Adventists, 14.
Advertiser, the, *52*, 125, **127**, 128.
Agassiz, Louis, 140, 259.
Agassiz Museum, 256, *253*.
Aged Women, Home for, 165.
Albion Building, 90.
Alcott, A. B., 99, 266.
Aldrich, Thomas Bailey, 165.
Algonquin Club, 150, **176**, *157*.
Allen Gymnasium, 153.
Allston, 244.
Allston, the Painter, 76, 142, 244, 257.
America, the Yacht, 263.
Am. Academy Arts and Sciences, 160.
American Bombardment, 9.
American House, **187**.
American Loan & Trust Co., *21*, 34, **36**, *52*.
American Peace Society, 159.
American Waltham Watch Co., 5, 112.
Ames Building, *10*, **15**, **16**, **17**, *52*, **56**.
Ames Plow Co., **25**.
Ancient and Honorable Artillery Co., 26.
Andrew, Gov. John A., **17**, 26, 97, 156; Statue, **191**, 162.
Andros, Sir Edmond, 76.
Annexations, 9.
Antenomians, 9.
Appalachian Mountain Club, 94.
Arch St., 66, **67**, **69**.
Archway Bookstore, *10*, *52*, 116, *91*.
Aristides, 166.
Arlington-St. Church, 138, *157*.
Armenian Sympathy, 22.
Army and Navy Monument, **95**, **131**, 97.
Arnold Arboretum, *158*, 235.
Art Club, the Boston, *157*, 148, 156, **168**.
Art Museum, Boston, *157*, 142, **144**, *186*.
Art School, Mass. Normal, *157*, 150, **181**.

Art School, 142.
Ashburton, Lord, 22.
Ashburton Place, 160, **190**.
Ashmont, 225.
Asiatic commerce, 9.
Aspinwall's Wharf, 196.
Athenæum, the Boston, *10*, 160, **188**.
Athenæum, the Fellowes, 228.
Athenæum, the Howard, 168.
Athenæum Press, **247**.
Athletic Assn., Boston, *157*, 153, **184**.
Atlantic Avenue, 76, 197, 199.
Atlantic Monthly, 94.
Attucks (Crispus) Monument, 94, 101.
Auburndale, 148.
Back Bay: *156*, 169, Birdseye View, **161**, Cambridge View, **245**.
Back Bay District, 130, 158, **161**, map of, *157*; names, 150.
Back Bay Fens, 148, 156, *158*, 235.
Baldwin, William H., 104.
Ball, the Sculptor, 134, 138, 162.
Bancroft, George, 76.
Bangor Steamers, 206, **207**.
Baptist Bethel, 90.
Baptist Church, 9.
Baptist Headquarters, 90.
Baptist Tabernacle, 168.
Baptist Theological Seminary, 242.
Bar Association, 48.
Barnes (F. G.) & Appleton, **30**.
Barnes & Dunklee, 140, **141**.
Barnum Museum, 195.
Barricado, the, 197.
Bartlett's Familiar Quotations, 259.
Bartol, Rev. Dr. Cyrus A., 165, 167.
Barton, Wm. A., 54.
Base-Ball Grounds, 180.
Bates Hall, 146.
Batterymarch St., 48, 66.
Battery Wharf, 196.
Battle-flags, 162.
Bay State Gas Co., 101.
"Bay State" Steamship, 202, **204**.
Beacon, the old, 162.
Beacon Hill and West End, 159-168.
Beacon Hill, 7, 150, 167.
Beacon St., 1, 56, 90, 95, 96, **161**, **163**, **188**.
Beecher, Henry Ward, 86.
Beethoven Statue, 92.
Bellevue Hotel, 160.
Bendall, Edward, 11.
Berkeley Hotel, *156*, *157*.
Berkeley Temple, 176.

279

Berkshire Life Insurance Co., **53**, 54, **51, 50.**
Bigelow, Kennard & Co., *106*, 108, **109**, 110.
Bishop's Alley, 80.
Blackstone Square, *158*, 170, 180, 182.
Blaxton, William, 166.
Blind Alley, 80.
Blind Asylum, 221, 260, **234.**
Blue Hills, 229.
Booth, Edwin, 83, 108, 130, 150, 165, 259.
Boston & Albany Railroad, *2*, 74, 210, **212**, 80, 180.
Boston & Bangor Steamship Co., 74, 206, **207.**
Boston & Maine Railroad, 192.
Boston and Surroundings, map, *240.*
Boston College, 183, **214.**
Boston Daily Standard, *91*, 112, **115**, 125.
Boston Fruit Co., 202, **203.**
Boston Gaslight Co., 101, 195.
Boston Harbor, 260-263, 221.
Boston Ice Co., 39.
Boston in 1857, 4.
Boston Library, 130.
Boston. the name, 7.
Boston Proper Map of, *2.*
Boston Safe Deposit & Trust Co., **55**, **59.**
Boston Stone, the, 187.
Boston Storage & Warehouse Co., 153.
Boston Theatre, 104, **109**, *106.*
Boston Traveler, *10*, **122**, 123, 28, *52*, 125.
Boston University, 14, 70, 159, 165.
Bostonian Society, 28.
Botolph's Town, 7.
Bot's Town, 7.
Boulevard, 239.
Bouvé, Crawford & Co., Corpn., *52*, *106*, 104, **105**, **129**, 82.
Bowditch, Nathl., 75.
Bowdoin Square, 11, 168.
Bowdoin-Sq. Theatre, 168.
Boylston Building, **105**, *106*, *181.*
Boylston Hotel, 101, **103**, *106*, *186.*
Boylston St., 133, **139.**
Boylston St. from Berkeley to Dartmouth, **139.**
Boylston Market, 104.
Bradlee, N. J., 54.
Bradstreet Company, the, 70, **71**, 74, **72.**
Brattle Square Church, 17, 148.
Brattle Street, **12**, 17, 10, **20.**
Brazer's Building, 28, **30**, *52.*
Brazer Inn, 32.
Brewer, (Gardner) Fountain, 97, **96.**
Bridewell, the, 92.
Briggs, Richard, *10*, *52*, *91.*
Brigham's Restaurant, **107.**
Brighton, 243-245, 9, 213.
Brimstone Corner, 92.

Brine, Wm. H., 12.
British Coffee House, 40.
British Garrison, 9, 48, 120, 169.
Broad St., **41**, **42**, **46.**
Broadway National Bank, *52*, 66, **67**, **91.**
Bromfield-St. Methodist Church, 92.
Brook Farm, 238.
Brookline and Newton, 239-242.
Brookline, 170, 213, 239-242, 148.
Brooks, Phillips, 86, 97, 140, 142, 256, 259.
Bug Light, 261.
Brunswick, the Hotel, *157*, 140, **141**, *186.*
Bulfinch, 22, 70, 162
Bull, Ole, 99, 259.
Bunch-of-Grapes Tavern, 40.
Bunker Hill, 3, 189, 191, 195, 215.
Bunker-Hill Monument, *2*, *158*, **229**, **230**, 215.
Burditt & Williams, 19, *21*, **23**, **22.**
Burlingame lying in State, 22.
Burnham Antique Bookstore, **121**, 123.
Burnham T. O. H. P., 86, **121**, 123.
Business District, 11.
Bussey Institution, 235.
Butler (W. S.) & Co., *10*, *91.*
Bynner, the Novelist, 48, 213.
Cadets' Armory, 172, **201**, *157*, *186.*
Cambridge, Harvard and Mt. Auburn, 246-259, *253.*
Cambridge, 166, 168, 184.
Cambridge, City Hall, 251, **245.**
Cambridge Common, 257.
Cambridge Elm, 257. **250.**
Cambridge High School, 252.
Cambridge Manual Training School, 252, **246.**
Cambridgeport, **44**, 246.
Cambridge Public Library, 252, **246.**
Camera Club, 92.
Carney Hospital, 223.
Carter Building, *52*, *125.*
Cass Statue, 134, **137.**
Castle Island, 9, 223, 260.
Castle Square Theatre, 176, *186.*
Cathedral Building, 70, **73**, 74.
Cathedral of the Holy Cross, 70, **170**, 210, 178, 181, 182.
Cavalry Battalion, 142.
Central Burying-Ground, 94.
Central Congregational Church, *157*, 138 **161**, **139**, **164.**
Central Street, 40, **46**, **47**, **49**, *21.*
Central Wharf, 40, 202.
Chamber of Commerce, **47**, *21*, 40.
Change Avenue, 32.
Channing, Wm. E., 22, 138.
Charity Bureau, 168.
Charlesbank, 166.
Charlesgate, 156.
Charles River, 11, 130, 150, 169, 187, 242.
Charles II., 17.

Charles St., 95, 96, 131, 165.
Charles-St. Methodist Church, 165.
Charlestown, 215-217.
Charlestown, 157, 9, *158*, 195, 216; Soldiers' and Sailors' Monum't, 216, **232**.
Chauncy-Hall School, 148, *157*.
Chelsea, Concord and Wellesley, 266, 70, 187, 196.
Chesbro, F. A., 54.
Chester Square, *158*, 184.
Chestnut Hill Reservoir, 241, **244**, 148.
Chickering Hall, 101.
Chickering, Jonas, 176.
Chickering & Sons, 5, 101, 176, **177**.
Children's Hospital, 153.
Children's Mission, 176.
Chinese, 104.
Choate, Joseph H., 254.
Choate, Rufus, 17.
Christ Episcopal Church, 190, **219**.
Christian Endeavor, Gen'l Society of, 104, **107**, 134.
Christian Leader, 101.
Christian Scientists, 156.
Church of St. Peter (Cath.), 225.
Church of the Disciples, 174, 180, **205**.
Church of the Messiah, 153.
Church of the Unity, 180.
"City of Bangor," Steamer, 206, **207**.
City Hall, *10*, 14, *52*, 74, 86, **88, 123**, 128.
City Hospital, 184, **185**.
City Point, South Boston, 243.
Claflin, William, 97.
Clarendon-St. Baptist Church, 178.
Clarke, James Freeman, 9, 86, 160, 174.
Clarke (W. B.) & Co., **119**.
Clark's Boston Tavern, 116, *52*, *10, 91*.
Clark's Hotel, 108, **109**, *106*.
Clark, Ward & Co., *52*, 60, **64**.
Clearing House, *21*, 34, **39, 40**.
Clinton, Gen., 26.
Cochituate Lake.
Cole, Samuel, 32.
Collins & Fairbanks, 112, 116, **117**, *91*.
Colonial Charter, 9.
Columbia Theatre, 181.
Columbus Ave., 131, **159**, 169, 170, **171**.
Columbus Statue, 166, **208**, **210**, 182.
Comer's Commercial College, **107**.
Commerce, 9, 201.
Commercial Cable Co., **41, 42**.
Commercial National Bank, **47**.
Commercial Street, **25**, **43**, **44**, 195, 197.
Commercial Wharf, *2*, 197.
Common, the, 93, 94, **95**, **96**, 97, 99, 165.
Commonwealth Avenue, **152, 161**, *157*, 148, **169**, **170**, **172**, 241, *158*.
Concord, 266, 3-Minute Man, **260**, 266.
Congregational House, *10*, 159, **188**.
Congress Street, 28, **56**, **58**, **59**, 31, **32**, **33**, 34, 48, **50**, **51**, **53**.

Conklin, William J., *186*, 174, **175**.
"Constitution," U. S. Frigate, 196.
Constitution Wharf, 196.
Copeland, Charles, 90.
Copley, John S., 142, 164.
Copley Square, *157*, 140, **141, 142, 143, 144, 145**, 150, *158*, *186*.
Copley Square Hotel, *157*, 153, **154**.
Copp's Hill Burying Ground, 190, **216, 218**, 195.
Cordley (F. R.) & Co., *21*, **39**, **40**.
Corey Hill, 136, 241.
Corn Court, 32.
Cornhill, **12**, 17, **18**, *10*.
Cotton Hill, 164.
Cotton, John, 86.
Country Club, 242.
Court House, *10*, **13**, **12**, **14**.
Court House, the Old, 14, *10*.
Court Square, 128, *10*.
Court Street, 11, **12**, **16**, 17, **18**, *10*.
Cowdin, 26.
Cow Lane, 80.
Cowley Fathers, 162, 167.
Cradle of Liberty, 22.
Crawford House, *10*, 19.
Crawford Shoe Store, *52*, **106**, 104, 128, **105**, **129**, *82*.
Cromwell, 17.
Cromwell's Head Tavern, 90.
Crosby, C. A. W., **111**.
Crowell (Thomas Y.) & Co., **76**, **78**.
Curtis & Motley, **39**.
Cushman, Charlotte, 90, 189, 259.
Custom House, *21*, 32, **40**, **41**, **43**, **45**, **46**, 202.
Custom House, the Old Colonial, 28.
Dame, Stoddard & Kendall, *52*, 116, **118**, *91*.
Damrell & Upham, **124**, **125**.
Davenport, A. H., **19**.
Davis (Curtis) & Co., *21*, **40**, **44**.
Deaf-Mute Schools, 153.
Dearborn, Gen., 26, 32.
Debt, 9.
Declaration of Independence, 54, 90, 92.
Deer Island, 260.
Deland, Margaret, 165.
D'Estaing, Count, 22, 26.
De Joinville, Prince, 22.
Destitute Catholic Children's Home, 183.
Devonshire Street, **27**, **29**, **30**, **51**, **53**, 60, **63**, **64**, **65**, 66, 70, **71**.
DeWolfe, Fiske & Co., 112, *52*, *10*, *91*.
Dickens, Charles, 90, 99.
Dilke, Sir Charles, 213.
Diocesan House, 164.
Dispensary, Boston, 180.
Ditson (Oliver) Co., 112, 123.
Doane (Francis) & Co., *21*, **40**, **42**.
Doane Street, 49.

Dock Square, 10, **22, 23.**
Doll & Richards, *10*, 92. **93.**
Dorchester, 224-225, 9, 136.
Draft Riots, 101.
Drowne, Deacon Shem, 26.
Dyer, Col W. H., 54.
East Armory, 183.
East Boston, 218, 196.
East Cambridge, 26, 246.
Echo Bridge, Newton Falls, 242, **262.**
Election Sermons, 120.
Elgin, Lord, 22.
Eliot Burial-Ground, 226.
Eliot, Charles W., 97.
Eliot, John, 226.
Elks Building, 108.
Elmwood, 259, **254.**
Elysium Club, 153.
Emancipation Statue, 131, **159, 160.**
Embargo, the, 24.
Emerson (D. R.) & Co., 99, *91, 108*.
Emerson, Ralph W., 76, 86, 123, 148, 213, 216, 266.
Emmanuel Episcopal Church, 138, 156, *157*.
Endicott-Street Region, 191.
English Settlers, 7.
Episcopal Theological Seminary, 258.
Equitable Life Assurance Soc., 54, **63.**
Equitable Life Building, *52*, 54, **57**, 60, **62, 63, 64,** *74*.
Eric (Leif) Statue, 148.
Essex Street, 80.
Estes & Lauriat, 123.
Ether Monument, 134.
European Commerce, 9.
Everett, Edward, 22, 26, 94, **128,** 146, 266 ; Statue, 134, 250.
Exchange Club, 48, **60, 66.**
Exchange Place, 34, 48.
Exchanges, 26, 35.
Exchange Street, **29, 35.**
Express Office, 70.
Eye and Ear Infirmary, Mass. Char., 166.
Fairbanks, Brown & Co., 60, **61.**
Fairbanks Company, *52*, 60, **61.**
Fall-River Line, 131.
Faneuil Hall, 19, *21*, **22, 23, 24,** 26, 32.
Faneuil Hall Market, 24, **25,** 26.
Faneuil-Hall Square, **24, 25.**
Faneuil, Peter, 22, 24, 86, 92.
Farlow Building, *21*, 40.
Farmers' Market, 109.
Farragut Square, 48.
Farragut Statue, 223, **235.**
Federal Constitution Ratification, 80.
Federal Courts, 09, 48.
Federal Square, 48.
Federal Street, **57, 58,** 61, **62, 63,** *66*.
Federal Street Theatre, 70, 76.
Fenway, 241.

Field's Corner, 225.
Filled Land, 9, 26, 40, 76, 195.
Fire of 1872. **6, 8,** 66.
Fire, 1889 (Thanksgiving Day), 80.
Fire, 1893 (March 10), 80.
First Baptist Church, *157*, 148, **149,** 156, 160.
First Catholic Church, 90.
First Church, 28, 140, *157*, **165.**
First Episcopal Church, 86.
First Masonic Lodge, 101.
First Methodist Church, 189.
First National Bank. *52*.
First Newspaper, 108.
First Parish Church, Roxbury, 226.
First Presbyterian Church, 172.
First Spiritual Temple, 150, **182.**
First State Library, 162.
First Theatre Play, 40.
First Underwriter, 48.
First Unitarian Church, 86, *157*.
First Washington Monument, 190.
Fisheries Museum, 199, **200.**
Fish Industry, 199.
Fisk (Harvey) & Sons, *21*, 34, **38.**
Fiske Building, *21*, 40, **56.**
Fitchburg Station, *2*, 195, **223.**
Five Cents Savings Bank, *10*, *91*.
Forbes Lithograph Mnfg. Co., 70, 266, **264.**
Foreign Consulates, 40.
Forest-Hills Cemetery, 235, **233,** 228, 232.
Fort Hill, 9, 76, 197, 205.
Fort Hill Square, **80,** 76, *158, 74*.
Fort Independence, 223, 260.
Fortifications, 9.
Fort Point Channel, *2*, 181, 208, *74*.
Fort Street, 80.
Fort Warren, 261.
Fort Winthrop, 260.
Foster's Wharf, *2*, *74*, 206, **228, 221.**
Fowler, E. R., 54.
Franklin, Benjamin, 230, 160, 187 ; birthplace, 120.
Franklin Field, 229.
Franklin Park, *158*, **231,** 229, 156, 170, 228, 235.
Franklin Square, *158*, 182, **213.**
Franklin Statue, *10*, 90, **123, 88.**
Franklin Street, **58,** 66, **69,** 80.
Freeman Place Chapel, 160.
French, Daniel C., 48.
French (Ferd. F.) & Co. Ltd., 192, **194.**
French Huguenot Church, 90.
French restaurants, 176.
Frog Lane, 130.
Frog Pond. **96, 95,** 94, 97.
Frost & Adams, *10*, **17, 18.**
Fruit and Produce Exchange, 26.
Garrison, Wm. Lloyd, 22, 148, 150 ; statue, **137.**

Gaugengigl, I. M., 83, 90.
Gay (Aaron R.) & Co., **42.**
General Theological Library, 162.
German Catholic Church, 176.
Gifford Home for Animals, 245, 243.
Gilman, Arthur, 156.
Ginn & Co., *10*, 159, 250, **247.**
Girls' High Latin School, 180.
Globe, the Boston, *52*, 125, **127,** 128.
Globe Theatre, 104.
Glover (Gen. John) Statue, 148, **172.**
Golden Rule, 104. **107.**
Goodyear Shoe Machinery Co., 74, 76, 208, **211.**
Governor's Island, 260.
Granary Burial Ground, *10*, **92, 125,** 128, 160.
Grand Opera House, 181.
Grant, Robert, 83.
Grant, Pres't U. S., 140, 168.
Gray's Wharf, 195.
Green Dragon Tavern, 101, 187.
Greenleaf (C. H.) & Co. 150, **151, 152.**
Greenough, R. S., 12, 90.
Grove Hall, 228.
Hale, Edward E., 86, 97, 128, 150, 178, 256 ; house, **239,** 226.
Hamilton (Alex.) Statue, 148, **172,** 138.
Hamilton Place, 62.
Hancock, Gov. John, 12, 24, 26, 54, 60, 86, 92, 160, 162, 187, 197 ; House, 164, **195.**
Hancock (John) Life Building, 60, **63.**
Hancock National Bank, 48, **50, 51,** *52*, **53, 56,** *74*.
Handel and Hayden Society, 92.
Hanover Street, 19, **20,** 187.
Harbor Front, 192-212, **4,** 32, **230.**
Harvard Bridge, 156, **161, 187,** 246.
Harvard Church at Brookline, 241, **243.**
Harvard Dental School, 167.
Harvard, John, 216, 252, 256.
Harvard Medical School, *157*, 153, **183.**
Harvard Musical Association, 165.
Harvard Observatory, 48.
Harvard University, *253*, 252, 153, 235, **255,** 246, 250; map of vicinity, *253.*
Haven, Franklin, 28.
Hawley Street, **68,** 70.
Hawthorne, Nathaniel, 201, 213, 266.
Haymarket Theatre, 101.
Haynes, Tilly, 80, **82.**
Heath, 26.
Herald, the Boston, *52*, 125, **126, 127.**
Hemenway Building, **12, 116,** 83.
Higginson, Thos. W., 14.
High School for Boys, 178, **179,** *186.*
Hill, Estate of Wm. H., **34,** *32*, **228, 221, 205.**
Hingham, 263, "Old Ship," 265, 260, **257.**
Historical, 7-10.
Hobby, Sir Charles, 26.

Hodgman & Worth, 54.
Hollander (L. P.) & Co., 133, *186.*
Hollis-St. Theatre, 176, 180, *186.*
Holmes, Oliver Wendell, 17, 94, 97, 123, 132, 138, 140, 150, 162, 196, 202, **213,** 216, 259 ; house, **178.**
Homeopathic Hospital, Mass., 183.
Hoosac Tunnel Route, 195.
Horse Cars, **7.**
Horticultural Hall, *10*, *91*.
Horticultural Society, the Mass., 90, *91*
Houghton, Mifflin & Co., 94, 250.
Houston & Henderson, *91*.
Hovey (C. F.) & Co., 125.
Howard Athenæum, 14.
Howard Nat'l Bank, **33,** *34*, 48, **52,** *74*.
Howard Street, 14, *10.*
Howe, Gen., 26.
Howells, Wm. D , 83, 97, 130, **134, 140,** 150, 167, 172, 184, 202, 205, **213,** 246, **252.**
Hub of the Solar System, **7.**
Huguenot Merchant, 22.
Hull, 260, 262.
Hull Yacht Club, 262, **257.**
Huntington Avenue, 153, **154, 155.**
Huntington Hotel, **154,** *157*.
Hutchinson's (Anne) dwelling, **123.**
Hutchinson, Gov., 19.
Ideal City of America, **7.**
Immaculate Conception Church, **183, 214.**
Incorporation of Boston, **9.**
Independence Park, 76.
Indians, 9.
India Street, 40, **43,** 47.
India Wharf, *2*, *74*, 202.
Institute of Technology, *157*, 140, **139, 142, 166,** *186.*
Internal Revenue Offices, 48.
International Steamship Co., 197, **198,** 199.
International Trust Co., 60, **65,** *91*, *52*.
Irish Immigrants, 76, 187, 205.
Italians, 187, 188, 189.
Jail, Suffolk-County, 167.
Jamaica Plain and West Roxbury, 232, *230*, 238.
Jamaica Plain, 76, 228; Monument, **242.**
Jesuits, 183.
Jews, 188.
Johnson, Andrew, 101, 168.
Jones, McDuffee & Stratton, 5, 70, *74*, **75.**
Jordan, Marsh & Co., 108, **111,** *91*, *106.*
Journal, Morning and Evening, *52*, 125.
Keith's New Theatre, 104, **109,** *106.*
Kelley (Stillman F.) & Co., **4,** *21*, 40, **46.**
Kidd, Capt., 14.
Kidder, Peabody & Co., *52*, *91*.
Kilby Street, *34*, **35, 38,** 40, **46,** 48, 49.
Kindergarten for the Blind, 232.
King's Chapel, *10*, 11, 83, **190,** 86, *91*.

King's Chapel Burial-Ground, 83, 10.
King George's tyranny, 24.
King (Geo. F.) & Merrill, 52, 68, 70, 74, 91.
King, Moses, 1, 3, 52.
King Philip's War, 17; Samp bowl, 83.
King Street, 40.
King William III, 9.
Kneeland Street, 11.
La Farge, John, 142, 146.
Lafayette, 14, 22, 94.
Lake, James H., 54.
Lamb Tavern, 108.
Lamkin, G., 11, 12.
Langham Hotel, 184.
Lasell Seminary, 242.
Latin School for Boys, 86, 178, **179**, *186*.
Law Library, 14.
Lee & Shepard, *52*, 120.
Leeson (J. R.) & Co., 70, **73**, 74.
Leverett, Gov. John, 17, 26.
Lewis (J. B.) Co., 208, **209**.
Lewis Wharf, 197.
Lexington, 269, 3, 184.
Liberty Square, 48, **66**.
Liberty Tree, 104, *106*.
Libraries, 14, 83, 104, 130, 159, 160, 162, **215**.
Lighthouse Offices, 48.
Lincoln, Abraham, 24; Statue, 131, **160**, *139*, 162.
Lincoln, Gen., 32.
Lincolnshire Seaport, 7.
Lincoln Wharf, 196.
Lind, Jenny, 90, 168, **195**.
Lion Theatre, 104.
Literary World, 159.
Little, Brown & Co., *52*, 128, **127**.
Liverpool Wharf, 24, 208.
Longfellow, Henry, W., 123, 97, 259.
  house at Cambridge, 258, **252**.
Long Island, 260.
Long Lane, 80.
Long Wharf, 40, 197, 199, 202.
Longwood, 239.
Lorimer, Rev. Dr. Geo. C., 90.
Louisburg Square, 164, 165.
Lovell (John P.) & Sons, *10*.
Lowell, James R., 123, 97, 140, 167, 213, 259.
Lowell's house at Cambridge, 259, **254**.
Lowell Railroad, 192.
Lower Mills, Dorchester, 225.
Lunatic Hospital, 221.
Lyman, Theo., 14.
McClellan's Reception, 22.
McKim, Mead & White, 146, **254**.
McLean Asylum, 167.
Mackerel Lane, 40.
Macullar, Parker & Co., **6**, 5, 8, **7**, 66, 113, 114, *91*, 112, 267-278.
Macullar, Williams & Parker, 6.
Mann, Horace, 17; Statue, **192**, 162, 266.

Mann (Horace) School for the Deaf, **173**.
Maps, *2*, 10, *21*, *52*, 74, 91, *106*, 157, **158**, *186*, *240*, *253*.
  The City of Boston, folded inside the back cover.
  Main Portion, or Boston Proper, 2.
  Court House and City Hall District, 10.
  Faneuil Hall, Stock Exchange and Custom House, 21.
  City Hall and Post Office District, 52.
  Wholesale District, 74.
  Retail District, Northern Portion, 91.
  Retail District, Southern Portion, 106.
  Back-Bay District, 157.
  Boston's Park System, 158.
  South End, 186.
  Boston and its surroundings, 240.
  Harvard University and vicinity, 253.
Marblehead, Tucker's Landing, **261**.
Marcella-Street Home, 232.
Marine insurance, 48.
Marine Park, 223, **236**, **235**, 156, *158*.
Marion, Joseph, 48.
Markets, **24**, **25**, 26.
Marston (Russell) & Co., *10*, 19, **20**.
Marston's Dining Rooms, *10*, 19, **20**, 187.
Marter, Fred'k B. K., 54.
Mason Building, 48, **66**.
Masonic Temple, 101, **102**, *186*, **103**, *106*.
Masonic Temple, the Old, 99.
Massachusetts, 9; origin of name, 7.
Massachusetts Ave., 156, 176, 184, 243.
Mass. Charitable Mechanic Assn., **157**, **155**, 153.
Mass. General Hospital, 167.
Mass. Historical Society, *10*, 83, **116**.
Massachusetts Hospital Life Ins. Co., *32*, **39**.
Massachusetts National Bank, 34.
Massachusetts Title Ins. Co., *52*, **91**.
Massacre, 9, 19, 28, 92, 94, 101.
Mather Tomb, 192, **216**.
Mattapan, 225.
Mechanics Fair B'ld'g, *157*, **155**, 153, *180*.
Mechanics' National Bank, **118**.
Medical Schools, 183.
Medical Society, the Mass., 130.
Meeting-House Hill, 225.
Memorial Hall, Cambridge, 256, 253.
Mercantile Fire and M. Ins. Co., **39**.
Merchants' National Bank, 28, **29**, *52*.
Merchants' Row, 40, *21*.
Metcalf (Theo.) Co., *10*, 86, **87**, **112**.
Methodist Bookstore, *10*, *91*.
Methodists, 90, 159, 165, 189.
Metropolitan Parks, 229, *158*.
Middlesex Fells, 230.
Military, 26.
Milk Street, **120**, 80, 47, **51**, 54, **55**, **57**, **59**, 60, 61, 62, 63, 64, 65, 67.

Mill Dam, 156.
Mill Dam Road, 243.
Millerite Tabernacle, 14.
Milmore, Martin, 90, 97, **148**.
Milton, 170, 229.
Ministers' Theatre, 83.
Modern Athens, 7, 11.
Moody & Sankey Tabernacle, **176**.
Morse, S. B., 215.
Motley, John L., 151, 213.
Mount Auburn Cemetery, 259; Sphinx, 259, **256**.
Mount Desert Steamers,
Mount Hope Cemetery, 236; Soldiers' Monument, **242**.
Mount-Vernon Church, 156, **190**, 160.
Mount-Vernon, St., 165.
Murdock Parlor Grate Co., *186*, 131, **132**.
Museum, the Boston, **10**, **11**, **12**, **112**, **116**, 83, 86, 87.
Music Hall, 92, 99, *91*, 165.
Mutual Life Insurance Co. of N. Y., 54, **55**, *74*.
Mutual Life Tower Views, **56**, **57**, **58**.
Mystic River, 266, *240*.
Nantasket Beach, 262, 260, **258**, **259**.
Narragansett Indians, 32.
Nash, Spaulding & Co., *21*.
Nat'l Bank of the Commonwealth, *52*.
National Revere Bank, 7, **72**, **71**, *74*.
National Security Bank, **10**, 19.
Natural History Museum, *157*, 138, **139**, *186*.
Naval Brigade, 142.
Naval Hospital, U. S., **266**.
Naval Pay offices, 48.
Navy Yard, U. S., 196, 215.
Neal (John R.) & Co., 199, **200**.
Neck, Boston, 9, 160, 170
New England Conservatory of Music, 92, **213**, 183, 226.
New England Historic Genealogical Soc., 160
New-England Hospital for Women, 228, 232.
New England Mutual Life Ins. Co., 54, **55**, **59**, *74*.
New-Jerusalem Church, 160.
News-Letter, the Boston, 128.
Newspaper Row, **11**, 17, 83, 125, 128, **127**, **126**.
Newton, 239, 148.
New Washington Street, **19**.
New York & New England R. R., 208.
New York, New Haven & Hartford R. R., **171**, *157*, *74*.
Niver, James B., 54.
Niles Building, *10*, *52*, *91*.
Ninth Regiment, 183.
Noddle's Island, 218.
Non-importation League, 9.

Norcross, Otis, 70.
Norfolk House, 226.
Normal School, 174.
North End Park, 190, 195.
Northern Depot, 192, **193**; Entrance, **224**, 130.
North Square, 188, 189.
North Street, 188.
Norumbega Tower, **266**.
Notre-Dame School, 138, *157*, **189**, **228**, *232*.
Noyes Brothers, **7**, **85**.
Oak Square, 245.
Ober's French Restaurant, 99.
Odd-Fellows Hall, 176, *186*.
Ohabei Shalom Congregation, 178.
Old Brick Church, 140.
Old Colony Railroad, 80, 208.
Old Corner Bookstore, **10**, *52*, 123, **124**, 90, *91*.
Old North Church, 189.
Old North End, 187–191.
Old South, 7, *52*, 66, 84, **120**, **119**, **121**, *91*.
Old South Congregational Church, *157*, 146, **147**, **139**.
Old State House, **11**, 14, **15**, 26, **27**, 28, 32, **41**, *52*, *202*.
Old State House, view from balcony, **16**.
Oldest bank, 34.
Oldest church, 190.
Oldest hotel, 17.
Oldest savings bank, 99.
Oldest theatre, 83.
Oldest Y. M. C. A., 138.
Olmsted, Fredk. L., 230.
Original Area, 9.
Orkney Islands, 11.
Otis, Harrison Gray, 12, 22, 26, **164**.
Otis, James, 22.
Otway's, "The Orphan," 48.
Page (Geo. G.) Box Co., 250, **251**.
Paige, John C., *21*, 48, **49**, *52*.
Paine Memorial Hall, 178.
Parker, Harvey D., 86, **89**.
Parker House, *10*, 11, 86, **89**, 90, **12**, *91*.
Parker, Theo., 14, 22, 92, 104, 178; Memorial Hall, 78.
Parkman, Francis, 86, 148, 165, 168, **178**, 259.
Parks, *158*, 218, 221, 230, 234, 229.
Park Square, 131, **159**, **171**, *186*.
Park Street, 92, 93, 95.
Park St. Church, *10*, 92, **128**, **130**.
Park System Map, *158*.
Park Theatre, 104, *106*
Parsons, Theophilus, 17.
Peabody & Stearns, 34, 54.
Pearl Street, 45.
Pearmain & Brooks, 34, **37**.

Pelham, the, 101, 130, *106*, *180*.
Pemberton Square, *10*, *12*, **13, 14.**
Pension Office, 48.
People's Church, 172, *157*, *180*.
Percival (D. G.) & Co., 113.
Perkins' Institute for the Blind, 221, 234.
Pharmacy, Mass., College of, 153.
Phillips, Wendell, 14, 22, 104, 164, 181.
Pianofortes, 5, **177.**
Piano Row, 101.
Pierce (S. S.) Co., *10*, **12.**
Pierce House in Dorchester, 224, **238.**
Pillory, 32, 99.
Pilot, the, 104.
Plymouth, 263.
Plymouth Rock, 263.
Poe, Edgar A., 76.
Pope, Col. Albert A., 172, 173.
Pope Mnfg. Co., *157*, 172, **173,** *180*.
"Pops," 92.
Population, 9.
Portland Steam Packet Co., 202, **204.**
Porter, Alex. S., 28, **30,** 34.
Post, the, 125, **126**
Post-office, 48, *52*. **50, 51, 53,** 54, **56**.
Post-office Square, **32, 33,** 48, **59, 50, 51,** *52*, 54, **55, 56.**
Prang (L.) & Co., 104, 226, **227,** 107, 232.
Prang Educational Co., 104, **107.**
Pray (John H.) Sons & Co., *106*, 104, **107, 6.**
Press Club, 92.
Prescott, 76.
Presco t, Col., 83 ; Sword, 83 ; Statue, **230,** 216.
Prince School, 150.
Prince of Wales, 108.
Prison Lane, 14.
Probate Office, **116, 12,** 86, 83.
Providence Line, 131
Providence Station, *186*, 131, **150, 171.**
Provident Institution for Savings, 99, *91*.
Province House, 116.
Provincial Council, 28.
Provincial Navy, 14.
Public Garden, *2*, 133, *158*, *161*.
Public Garden Views, **136, 137, 161.**
Public Library, 157, 130, **145,** 142, *186*.
Pudding Lane, 80.
Puritan Club, 164.
Puritan Costume, **11, 12.**
Puritans, 9.
Quaker Lane, 48.
Quakers, 9.
Quarantine station, 261.
Queen Street, 14.
Quincy House, *10*, 17, **20.**
Quincy, Josiah, 26.
Quincy Mansion, 94.
Quincy Market, *21*, **25,** 26.

Quincy Mutual Ins. Co., **30.**
Quincy Statue, *10*, 90, **123.**
Radcliffe College, 256.
Record, the, 125, **127,** 128.
Red Coat Regiments, 9.
Redding, Baird & Co., **69,** 70, *74*, *91*.
Retail District, 83-129 ; Map of Northern portion, *91*, Southern portion, *106*.
Revere-Beach Railroad, 205.
Revere House, 168.
Revere, Paul, 62, 191, 195 ; 189, **215;**
Revere Sugar Refinery, 250, **248.**
Reynolds Hotel, 104, *106*.
Rhodes, J. B., **30.**
Rialto Building, *52*, **57,** 60, *91*.
Rice, Alex. H., 97, 174.
Rice Training School, 174.
Richards Building, **42.**
Richardson, H. H., 140, 148.
Richardson, Hill & Co., *52*, **53,** 54, **50, 51,** 208.
Rich, Isaac, 70.
Ridge Path, 94.
Riding Academy, 153.
Rindge Public Buildings, 250. **245, 246.**
Risteen (F. R.) & Co., 157, 153, **154.**
Riverside (Newton), 242.
Riverside Press, 250, 244.
Robinson (C. H.) & Co., **19, 22.**
Roberts Brothers, 159.
Rogers Building, *10*, *52*.
Roxbury, 226-231.
Roxbury, 9, 170, 213.
Roxbury High Fort, 226.
Roxbury High School, 228, **241.**
Roxbury Latin School, 228.
Rowe's Wharf, 74, 205, **228,** 260, **221.**
Royal Exchange of London, 26.
Royal Exchange Tavern, 32.
Royal Province, 9.
St. Andrew's Mission, 167.
St. Augustine's Church, 167.
St. Boat-Helps Town, 7.
St. Botolph, 7, 140.
St. Botolph Club, 138, **157.**
St. Gaudens, Aug., 97, 138.
St. James Catholic Church, 180.
St. James Episcopal Church, 228.
St. John's Ecclesiastical Seminary, 245.
St. John the Baptist Portuguese Church, 189.
St. John the Evangelist Church, 160.
St. Mary's Catholic Church, 191.
St. Paul's Episcopal Church, 99, **134.**
St. Stephen's Catholic Church, 189.
Sage's Trunk Store, *106*.
Sailors' Snug Harbor.
Salem, 9.
Salem Street, 188, 100.
Sargent (Wm. P.) & Co., **192, 194, 195.**
School Board, *100*.

School Street, 86, *10*.
Schwarz, Richard, *91*, 1c8, **111**, *106*.
Scollay's Building, 11.
Scollay Square, *10*, **11**, **12**, **16**, 17, 83.
Scollay, William, 11.
Scots' Charitable Society, 180.
Sears Building, *10*, **15**, 17, *52*, 164.
Second Church, Cong'l, 224.
Second Church, Unitarian, 148, *157*, 189.
Second Universalist Church, 174, *186*.
Security Safe Deposit Co., *52*, 54, **62**.
Sentry Hill, 164.
Shaw, Col. Robt. G., 97.
Shawmut, 7.
Shawmut Congregational Church, 180.
Shawmut National Bank, *52*, **53**.
Shepard Church, Cambridge, 257, **250**.
Shepard, Norwell & Co., *91*, 97, **98**, 99.
Shepley, Rutan & Coolidge, 17, 40.
Ship building, 9.
Shoe & Leather Exchange, 66.
Shreve, Crump & Low Co., *106*.
Signal Service, 48.
Simmons Building, **50**, **51**, **53**, *52*.
Slavery meetings, 24, 14.
Sleeper (Jacob) Hall, 14.
Smibert, the painter, 22.
Smith & Porter, 74, 76, **77**.
Smith, Rev. Dr. Samuel F., 242.
Snow's Arch Wharf, 208.
Social Law Library, 14.
Soldiers' Home (Mass.), 266.
Somerset Club, 159, 164.
Somerset Street, **13**.
Somerville, — ; Powder House, **263**.
Sons of Liberty, 104.
Sons of the Revolution, 187.
Soule Photograph Co., *52*, 116, **119**, *91*.
Southack, Capt. Cyprian, 14.
South Armory, 142.
South Bay, 169.
South Boston, 219-223, 66, 76.
South-Boston Iron Co., 219.
South Burying Ground, 183.
South Congregational Church, *157*, **150**, 178, **180**.
South End, 169-186, map, *186*.
Springer Brothers, *106*.
Spring Lane, 125.
Spiritual Temple, *157*, 50, **182**.
Spurzheim, 76.
Squire (John P.) & Co., 5, *21*, 250, **249**.
Stamp Act Riots, 9, 26.
Standard, the Daily, *91*, 112, 125, **115**.
State Constitution, 26.
State House, 162, **163**, **190**, **192**.
State Library, 162.
State Mutual Life Assurance Co., 48, **52**.
"State of Maine," Steamship, 197, 198, 199.

State Prison, Mass., 216.
State Street, 19, 26, **27**, **29**, **30**, **31**, **32**, *32*, 34, **35**, **36**, **37**, **38**, 40, **39**, **41**, **42**, **43**, **44**, **45**, **48**.
State Street Block, 42.
State-Street Exchange Building, 34, **35**, **36**, **37**.
Stearns (R. H.) & Co., 99.
Stevens, Benj. F., 54.
Stickney & Poor Spice Co., *21*, 40, 216, **217**.
Stock Exchange, *21*, *52*, 28, **32**, 34, **35**, **36**, **37**, 40, **49**, **56**.
Stock Exchange, view west from, **15**.
Strandway, 156.
Strangers' Sabbath Home, 90.
Stuart, Gilbert, 76.
Studio Building, 90.
Sturtevant (B. F.) Co., 76, 238, **237**.
Suburbs, 213-214.
Sub-Treasury, the U. S., 48, **51**.
Subway, the, 22, **130**, **131**.
Suffolk County Court House, **13**, **12**.
Suffolk National Bank, *21*, **39**.
Suffolk Savings Bank, *10*, **112**.
Suggestions to Visitors, 5.
Summer Street, 66, 80.
Sumner, Charles, 22, 94, 97, 162, 167, 259; Statue, **137**, 134.
Sun Fire office, 48.
Swedenborgians, 160, 228.
Sweetser, M. F., 3.
Symphony Orchestra, 92, **166**.
Talleyrand, 32.
Tariff Meetings, 24.
Tavern Club, 130.
Tavern, the Boston, *10*, 52, 116.
Tavern, the first, 32.
Taylor, Bayard, 213.
Tea Party, 9, 120, 208.
Telephone Building, 48, **66**.
Temple Church, 90.
Temple Place, 98, 99, **100**.
Thanksgiving Day Fire of 1889, **80**.
Theatre District, 104, **109**.
Thompson's Island, 260.
Thompson's Spa, *52*, 128, **129**.
Thorndike Hotel, 133, *186*.
Ticknor, George, 94, 146.
Ticknor & Fields, 123.
Tiffany Glass & Decorating Co., 138, 142.
Torrey & Bentley Co., *21*, 40, **45**.
Town Dock and House, 26.
Town Pound, 92.
"Transcript," *52*, **119**, **120**, 125, *91*.
Traveler, the Boston, *10*, 28, *52*, 123, **122**, 125, *91*.
Treasury, U. S., offices, 48, **51**.
Tremont House, *10*, 90.
Tremont National Bank, **32**.
Tremont Row, **11**, 14.

Tremont Street, 12, 83, 90, 112, 169, 176.
Tremont-Street Mall, 130.
Tremont-Street Methodist Church, 180.
Tremont St., south from Park St., 133; south from Eliot St., 205.
Tremont Temple, 10, 90, 91.
Tremont Theatre, 90, 101, 106, 186.
Tri Montaine, 7, 164.
Trinity Episcopal Church, 157, 140, 143, 167, 156, 161, 186.
Tudor Boston, 11.
T Wharf, 2, 199.
Turner's headquarters, 176.
Union Boat Club, 165.
Union Church, 174, 180.
Union Club, 94.
Union Park, 178, 158.
Union Railroad Station, 192, 193; entrance, 224, 130.
Union Wharf, 196.
Unitarian Building, 160, 189, 188.
Unitarian Church, Jamaica Plain, 242.
United States Bank, 28.
United States Courts, 48.
United States Naval Hospital, 266.
United States Hotel, 74, 82, 80.
United States Sub-Treasury, 48, 51.
Universalists, 99, 174, 180.
University Club, 150.
Upham's Corner, 225.
Valuation, 9.
Vane, Gov. Sir Harry, 32, 86.
Vassall Mansion, 258.
Vendome Hotel, 157, 150, 152, 151, 169, 170.
Venus Statue, 134.
Veterinary School, Harvard, 176.
Vercellis, 133.
Victoria Hotel, 148, 157.
Wakefield Rattan Co., 19.
Walden Pond, 266.
Wales, Prince of, 90, 168.
Walker, Admiral Sir Hovenden, 14.
Walker, Francis.
Walker-Stetson-Sawyer Co., 74, 80, 81.
Waltham, 112.
Waltham Watch Co., 5, 112.
Walworth Mnfg. Co., 74, 76, 219, 222.
Wanderers, Home for little, 174.
Ward, J. Q. A., 134.
Warren-Ave. Baptist Church, 174, 180.
Warren, Gen., 26, 187, 216.
Warren, M. R., 119.
Warren, Nathan, 54.
Warren, William, 83, 168.
Washington Elm at Cambridge, 257, 250.
Washington Equestrian Statue, 137.
Washington, George, 12, 24, 28, 40, 86, 90, 165, 162, 190, 258.
Washington Market, 170.
Washington Street in horse car days, 7.

Washington Street, 8, 17, 18, 19, 27, 41, 169, 180, 158.
Washington Street, from Macullar, Parker & Co., North 84, South 85.
Washington Headquarters at Cambridge, 258, 252.
Water Street, 48, 50, 51, 53.
Webster, Daniel, 3, 12, 22, 24, 76, 99; Statue, 192, 162, 165, 187, 215.
Webster-Parkman Tragedy, 14, 167, 168.
Wellesley College, 266, 265.
Wells' Memorial Institute, 181.
Welsh Fusileers, 76.
Wesleyan Building, 90, 91.
West Boston Bridge, 243, 246.
West-Chester Park, 156.
West Church, Unitarian, 167, 197.
West End, 165.
West Roxbury, 232, 9, 234.
West Street, 99.
Western Union Telegraph Co., 21.
Whipping Post, 32, 99.
Whipple (J. R.) & Co., 89.
White (R. H.) & Co., 108, 106, 109.
Whiting (John L.) & Son Co., 74, 76, 79.
Whitney, Anne, 19, 148, 165.
Whitney (T. D.) & Co., 99, 100, 91, 106.
Whittier, John G., 172.
Whittier Machine Co., 219, 220.
Wholesale Business District, 11-82, 74.
Williams Court, 128.
Williams & Everett, 186, 133, 135.
Winter-Place Hotel, 99.
Winter Street, 97, 98.
Winthrop, Gov. John, 11, 26, 123.
Winthrop, Robert C., 164.
Winthrop Square, 70, 73, 74, 76.
Winthrop Sq. in Charlestown, 216.
Winthrop Statue, 10, 11.
Winthrop, Robert C., 146.
Witches, 9, 120.
Woman's Club, New England, 94.
Woman's Journal, 94.
Woodland-Park Hotel, 239.
Worcester Square, 154, 184, 185.
Worthington B'ld'g, 28, 31, 32, 52, 56.
Worthington, Roland, 28, 31.
Woodlawn Cemetery.
Yachting, 138, 223, 225.
Yale College, 11.
Yale, David, 11.
Young, George, 14.
Young Men's Christian Ass'n, 138, 157, 181.
Young Men's Christian Union, 101, 103, 106, 105, 181.
Young's Hotel, 10, 14, 52, 128.
Young Women's Christian Ass'n, 176, 178, 181.
Youth's Companion, 157, 172, 173, 186.
Zion's Herald, 92.

www.ingramcontent.com/pod-product-compliance
Lightning Source LLC
Chambersburg PA
CBHW031332230426
43670CB00006B/319